THEORY AND APPLICATIONS OF OPERATIONS RESEARCH

THEORY AND APPLICATIONS OF OPERATIONS RESEARCH

By

Dr Dilip Kumar Adhwarjee

BE (REC-Durgapur), M-Tech (REC-Durgapur)
PhD (NIT-Durgapur)
Diploma (TQM & ISO9000)
Principal, MIET, Bandel, West Bengal

UNIVERSITY SCIENCE PRESS
(An Imprint of Laxmi Publications Pvt. Ltd.)
An ISO 9001:2015 Company

BENGALURU • CHENNAI • GUWAHATI • HYDERABAD • JALANDHAR
KOCHI • KOLKATA • LUCKNOW • MUMBAI • RANCHI
NEW DELHI

THEORY AND APPLICATIONS OF OPERATIONS RESEARCH

Printed and bound in India
Typeset at : Goswami Associates, Delhi
First Edition : 2009, 2021, *Edition* : 2022
ISBN : 978-81-318-0511-4

Branches

Bengaluru	080-26 75 69 30
Chennai	044-24 34 47 26
Guwahati	0361-254 36 69
Hyderabad	040-27 55 53 83
Jalandhar	0181-222 12 72
Kochi	0484-405 13 03
Kolkata	033-40 04 77 79
Lucknow	0522-430 36 13
Ranchi	0651-224 24 64

PUBLISHED IN INDIA BY

UNIVERSITY SCIENCE PRESS
(An Imprint of Laxmi Publications Pvt. Ltd.)

An ISO 9001:2015 Company
113, GOLDEN HOUSE, GURUDWARA ROAD, DARYAGANJ,
NEW DELHI - 110002, INDIA
Telephone : 91-11-4353 2500, 4353 2501
www.laxmipublications.com
info@laxmipublications.com

C—R/021/11
Printed at : Sanjeev Offset Printers, Delhi.

Dedicated to

SADHANA, RATNA, SANTANA, SOMA,
GUDLU, JINNE AND RIMA

Contents

DIRECTOR
Office : 0342-2546397
www. NITDGP.AC.IN

NATIONAL INSTITUTE OF TECHNOLOGY: DURGAPUR
(DEEMED UNIVERSITY)
MAHATAMA GANDHI AVENUE, DURGAPUR—713209

Dr. (Mrs.) K. Basu
Asst. Professor & HOD
Department of Mathematics
NIT, Durgapur
Durgapur: 713209

Date: 10.12.2007

To
Prof. Dilip Kumar Adhwarjee
Dr. B.C. Roy Engineering College
Durgapure: 713206

Foreword

The book "Theory and Applications of Operations Research", written by Prof. Dilip Kumar Adhwarjee, is a good addition to the existing list of books on similar topics. With his long years of industrial and academic experience, Prof. Dilip Kumar Adhwarjee has produced concepts in a more lucid manner. He has used his class notes during his study at REC Durgapur (NIT) and updated those for the students of the Indian Universities. I wish the concise treatment of the topics of Operations Research will prove beneficial to the under graduate students of Indian Universities.

With best Wishes

Kajla Basu
Dr. (Mrs.) K. Basu

Kajla Basu
Dr. (Mrs.) K. Basu
Asst. Professor & HOD
Department of Mathematics
NIT,Durgapur: 9

Preface

I am delighted to present the book titled, "Theory and Applications of Operations Research" to the students of B.Tech/B.E./MBA/MCA. Keeping in view of general requirements of the students, the course contents of the book are sufficient for Indian Universities. The students will be able to understand by self study. Each and every topic has been explained in a simple and easy language. Some salient features of this book are:

- Solved examples have been given in each chapter.
- Tables, diagrams and figures are neatly drawn so that students can understand the text easily.
- The language is simple and easy to understand.

All possible attempts have been made to make this book useful for B.Tech.B.E. students. Any suggestion regarding the improvement of this book will be appreciated and incorporated in the next edition. The author will welcome any value-added criticism.

—Author

Acknowledgement

I express my gratitude to Dr. D.K. Pal, ex-professor of NIT, Durgapur. I have used class notes given by him at M.Tech (1989–1992) level. I am also thankful to the other professors of NIT, Durgapur who taught me O.R. during 1975–1980 at B.E. level.

Finally, I also thank to Mr. Dulal Mitra, secretary of BCREC, Durgapur, for encouraging me constantly to write this book

—Author

Chapter 1

INTRODUCTION TO OPERATION RESEARCH

1.1 DEFINITION

It is the use of scientific methods by interdisciplinary teams to problems involving the control of organised system so as to derive solution which best serves the interest of the company as a whole.

1.2 ROLE OF OPERATIONS RESEARCH IN DECISION MAKING

The tools of operations research may be applied in almost all fields where decision making is involved. It is the management science of problem solving. It helps the managers to take decisions. It gives better solutions of the problems. Every day we take many minor decisions such as choosing alternative shop for purchasing, choosing to be doctors or engineers. The decision making requires identifying three components:

(*i*) what are the decision **alternatives** ?

(*ii*) under what **restrictions** is the decision made

(*iii*) what is the appropriate **objective criterion** for evaluating the alternatives ?

Once the above three components are known, we can think of improving the characteristics so as to improve upon the decision itself.

Let us take a decision making problem of simple type. We are two friends, we have to catch the train within 10 minutes time. We are three kilometers away from the station. There are three alternatives of conveyance local bus, autorickshaw and man driven ordinary rickshaw.

In the first level of decision, by intuition we choose autorickshaw *i.e.*, it is decided at random. It is highly emotional and qualitative way of decision making.

In the second level of decision, the three conveyances are compared. The autorickshaw is chosen because it takes less time (< 10 minutes), it is comfortable though a little costly.

In the third level of decision, the three alternatives compared, the bus will take more time it can not reach station in time. The autorickshaw will take $\frac{1}{3}$ rd time than the ordinary rickshaw. The cost is only 5% more than ordinary rickshaw, but comfortable. The decision making can be categorised as bad, good, best respectively for 1st, 2nd and 3rd level of decision making. The 3rd one is best because it is scientific and quantitative.

The scientific quantification used in OR helps management for making better decisions. The mathematical modeling of the problems has solutions in scientific quantification. The most prominent OR technique is linear programming which is designed for models with strict linear objective and constraint functions. Other techniques include integer programming (in which the variables are having integer values), dynamic programming (in which the original model can be decomposed into smaller sub problems), network programming (in which the problems are expressed through network), and non-linear programming (in which the functions of the model are non-linear). These OR tools can be used in different situations for better decision making.

1.3 APPLICATIONS OF O.R. IN INDUSTRY

Sr. no.	*Area*	*Application in*
1.	Manufacturing	• inventory control, production scheduling, production smoothing, projection marketing balance.
2.	*R* and *D*	• product introduction, planning, controlling, *R* and *D* projects.
3.	Marketing and distribution	allocation of sales efforts and advertising budget, sales compensation plan, transportation to warehouses.
4.	Finance and investment	• long-term corporate planning, portfolio selection, replacement and renewal of equipments, forecasting, risk and sensitivity analysis, capital budgeting, investment problems.
5.	Purchasing	• optimal reordering, materials transfer, optimal buying.
6.	Organizational behaviour	• personnel justification/planning, training programmes schedule, skills balancing, recruitment of employees.
7.	Accounting	• cash flow planning, credit policy analysis.
8.	Construction	• determination of proper work force, deployment of work forçe, allocation of resources to projects. Project scheduling, monitoring and control.

OR were initiated in England during World War II. When British scientists set out to make decisions regarding the best utilization of war material.

1.4 CONCEPT OF 'OR' MODEL BUILDING—TYPES AND METHODS

Model is an idealized representation of the real-life situation. The purpose of modelling is to provide a means for analysing the behaviour of the system for improving its performance.

1.4.1 Models by Degree of Abstraction

Predetermined data/information is used in this model.

(*a*) **Mathematical models:** The mathematical representation of problems is called the mathematical modelling. This requires the knowledge of mathematics—Linear programming, transportation, assignments problems are of this type of modelling.

(*b*) **Language models:** This is expressed through languages. Example—a cricket or football match commentary, writing a book.

1.4.2 Models by Function

(*a*) **Descriptive models:** The real-life situation is expressed in non-mathematical language defining the functional relationship and interaction between various operations. Example—organization chart, Man-Machine chart, pie-diagram.

(*b*) **Predictive models:** Forecasting the future behaviours of real-life. Example—exponential smoothing forecast model (future demand prediction).

(*c*) **Normative or optimization models:** It is optimizing the objective function subject to constraints involving non-negative variables.

1.4.3 Models of Structure

(*a*) **Iconic or physical models:** It is the representation of the real-life system by scaling it down. *Example:* a big river bridge is analysed by its iconic model in the laboratory, a city map.

(*b*) **Analog or schematic models:** These models are made by analogous properties for convenience of analysis. Example—a graphical inventory model.

(*c*) **Symbolic or mathematical models:** This model uses mathematical symbols to represent decision variables of the system. Then the objective function is expressed in terms of these variables. These are mostly used in OR.

1.4.4 Models by Nature of Environment

(*a*) **Deterministic models:** All the related parameters are known with certainty at the time of decision.

Example: EOQ model, B.E.A. (Break even analysis), CPM (Critical path method)

(*b*) **Probabilistic Models:** When risk and uncertainty are involved, probabilistic models are used.

Example: PERT (Program evaluation and review technique).

1.4.5 Models by the Extent of Generality

(*a*) **General models:** The models which are used in almost all the situations are called general models. Linear programming and simulation are general models.

(*b*) **Specific models:** Sales response curve or equation as a function of advertising is applicable in the marketing function alone. Gantt chart is used in production schedule. These are of two types:

(*i*) **Static models:** Here time factor is not considered.
Example: EOQ for next phase considering demand in planning period constant.

(*ii*) **Dynamic models:** Here time factor is considered.
Example: All dynamic programming.

1.5 GENERAL SOLUTION METHODS FOR O.R. MODELS

There are three methods:

1. Analytical or Deductive Methods

Here calculus, finite differences etc. are used for solving an O.R. model.

2. Numerical Methods

Applied numerical methods are widely used for approximate solution of the problem when direct method fails to solve the problems. These are hit and trial methods that end at a certain step after which no further improvement is possible.

3. Monte Carlo Methods

It is a simulation technique. Probability and sampling concepts are used here.

Chapter 2 LINEAR PROGRAMMING (L.P.)

2.1 DEFINITION

Linear programming (L.P.) is a technique to take decisions of an optimum, subject to restrictions of available resources.

2.2 FORMULATION OF LINEAR PROGRAMMING

Generalised mathematical formulation for linear programming uses the values of decision variables $x_1, x_2, x_3 \ldots x_n$.

The objective function: optimize Z where

$$Z = c_1x_1 + c_2x_2 + c_3x_3 + \ldots + c_jx_j + \ldots + c_nx_n$$

Subject to constraints

$$\begin{array}{l}
a_{11}x_1 + a_{12}x_2 + \ldots + a_{1j}x_j + \ldots + a_{1n}x_n = b_1 \\
a_{21}x_1 + a_{22}x_2 + \ldots + a_{2j}x_j + \ldots + a_{2n}x_n = b_2 \\
\ldots \quad \ldots \quad \ldots \quad \ldots \quad \ldots \quad \ldots \quad \ldots \\
\ldots \quad \ldots \quad \ldots \quad \ldots \quad \ldots \quad \ldots \quad \ldots \\
a_{i1}x_1 + a_{i2}x_2 + \ldots + a_{ij}x_j + \ldots + a_{in}x_n = b_i \\
\ldots \quad \ldots \quad \ldots \quad \ldots \quad \ldots \quad \ldots \quad \ldots \\
\ldots \quad \ldots \quad \ldots \quad \ldots \quad \ldots \quad \ldots \quad \ldots \\
a_{m1}x_1 + a_{m2}x_2 + \ldots + a_{mj}x_j + \ldots + a_{mn}x_n = b_m
\end{array}$$

and $x_1, x_2, \ldots, x_j \ldots, x_n \geq 0$ where $m < n$

$$i = 1, 2, 3, \ldots, m$$
$$j = 1, 2, 3, \ldots, n$$

Standard Form

1. All the constraints are expressed in the form of equations, except the non-negativity constraints which remain inequalities (≥ 0).
2. The right hand side of each constraint equation is non-negative.
3. All the decision variables are non-negative.
4. The objective function is of the maximization or minimization type.

The inequality constraints are changed to equality constraints by adding or subtracting a non-negative variable from the left hand side of such constraints. These new variables are called slack variables. They are added if the constraints are ($\leq$); and subtracted if the constraints are ($\geq$). Since in the case of ($\geq$) constraints the subtracted variables represent the surplus of left hand side over right hand side, it is commonly known as **surplus variables** and the surplus variable is, in fact, a **negative slack variable**.

Example 1

A small carpentry shop produces tables and chairs which involve mainly manual job of roughing, furnishing and painting operation in sections A, B and C respectively. The man hour availability of these three sections, unit manufacturing time and unit profit of manufacturing these products in the market are shown in the table 2.1.

Table 2.1

Sections → / ↓Product	A (hrs/unit)	B (hrs/unit)	C (hrs/unit)	Profit/unit
Tables	10	7	2	Rs. 12.00
Chairs	2	3	4	Rs. 3.00
Total hrs available per week	100	77	80	

The objective is to (1) maximize weekly profit (2) achieve maximum weekly production (3) Utilize man power resources to the fullest extent.

Solution:

Decision variables: Number of tables and chairs produced in a week, say, x_1 and x_2 respectively.

Objective function

(1) Maximize profit, $Z = 12x_1 + 3x_2$

(2) Maximize $(x_1 + x_2)$

(3) Maximize $(10x_1 + 7x_1 + 2x_1) + (2x_2 + 3x_2 + 4x_2)$ *i.e.*, maximize $= 19x_1 + 9x_2$.

Subject to

$$10x_1 + 2x_2 \leq 100$$
$$7x_1 + 3x_2 \leq 77$$

$$2x_1 + 4x_2 \leq 80 \quad \text{and} \quad x_1, x_2 \geq 0$$

The inequations constraints can be expressed into equations.

So,
$$10x_1 + 2x_2 + x_3 = 100$$
$$7x_1 + 3x_2 + x_4 = 77$$
$$2x_1 + 4x_2 + x_5 = 80$$
$$x_1, \ldots\ldots, x_5 \geq 0$$

Here x_1, x_2 are legitimate variables and x_3, x_4, x_5 are slack variables.

2.2.1 Canonical Form

All linear programming problems can be presented in general form

Maximize $\quad Z = \sum_{j=1}^{n} c_j x_j$

Subject to $\quad \sum_{j=1}^{n} a_{ij} x_j \leq b_i$

where $\quad x_j \geq 0 \quad$ and $\quad i = 1, 2, \ldots.. m$

$\quad j = 1, 2, \ldots.. n$

The above form of L.P. is called canonical form.

2.3 GRAPHICAL METHOD OF SOLUTION

Linear programming problems which involve only two decision variables can be solved graphically (convex method).

Example 2

A sheet metal company produces tea trays and ash trays in their press-shop. The following data relates to the plant capacity restrictions. Determine the optimum production schedule so as to maximize profit.

Operation ↓	*Ash tray* (x_1)	*Tea tray* (x_2)	*Available capacity per day*
Blanking	10 secs	20 secs	30,000 secs
Forming	15 secs	5 secs	30,000 secs
Painting	10 secs	8 secs	40,000 secs

The marginal profit is Rs. 0.20 and Rs. 0.30 for each ash tray and each tea tray respectively.

Solution:

We assume that the company should produce x_1 units of ash tray and x_2 units of tea tray. The formulation of the above problem is given below.

The objective function

maximize profit (Z) = $0.2\,x_1 + 0.3\,x_2$

Subject to constraints

$$10x_1 + 20x_2 \le 30{,}000 \quad (1)$$
$$15x_1 + 5x_2 \le 30{,}000 \quad (2)$$
$$10x_1 + 8x_2 \le 40{,}000 \quad (3)$$
$$x_1, x_2 \ge 0 \quad (4)$$

Procedure: We assume the constraints as equations and draw the four equations (actually there are five equations if we write $x_1 \ge 0$ and $x_2 \ge 0$) *i.e.*, five straight lines and then indicate their directions (arrow heads are towards the origin or away from the origin).

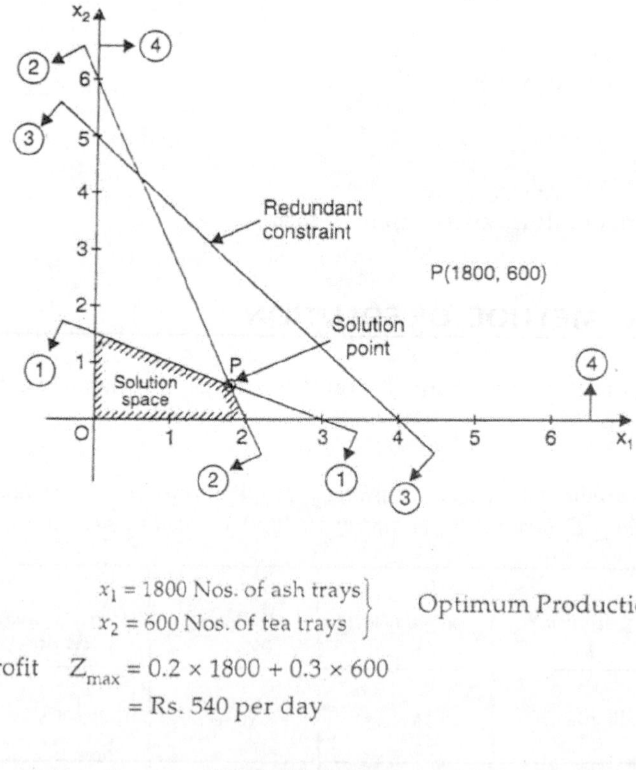

Answer:

$$\left.\begin{aligned} x_1 &= 1800 \text{ Nos. of ash trays} \\ x_2 &= 600 \text{ Nos. of tea trays} \end{aligned}\right\} \quad \text{Optimum Production Schedule} \quad \text{Ans.}$$

Maximum Profit $Z_{max} = 0.2 \times 1800 + 0.3 \times 600$

$= \text{Rs. } 540 \text{ per day}$

Example 3

A firm manufactures two types of screws, 'A' and 'B', 'A' screws earn a profit of Rs. 3.00 per thousand, and 'B', Rs. 1.50 per thousand. Type 'A' screws require a special chemical treatment. If all the available facilities in the firm are utilized; 40,000 of type 'A' screws can be produced per day against 60,000 of type 'B' per day. The chemicals required for type 'A' are restricted in supply and are sufficient for a maximum of 30,000 screws per day. The total packing capacity in the firm is restricted to 50,000 screws per day. How many of type 'A' and 'B' in thousands should the firm manufacture to get the maximum profit ?

Solution:

Let x_1 and x_2 represent, in thousands, the number of type 'A' and the number of type 'B' respectively, produced per day.

Thus the objective function is to maximize $Z = 3x_1 + 1.5x_2$ (1)

Subject to constraints

$1000\, x_1 \leq 40{,}000$ (2)

$1000\, x_2 \leq 60{,}000$ (3)

Let us assume that the production department works for 8 hrs per day, thus we have

production of type $'A' = \dfrac{40000}{8} = 5000$ per hour

production of type $'B' = \dfrac{60000}{8} = 7500$ per hour

Thus $\dfrac{x_1}{5} + \dfrac{x_2}{7.5} \leq 8$

or $3x_1 + 2x_2 \leq 120$ (4)

The other constraints are

$x_1 + x_2 \leq 50$ (5)

$x_1 \leq 30$ (6)

$x_1, x_2 \geq 0$ (7)

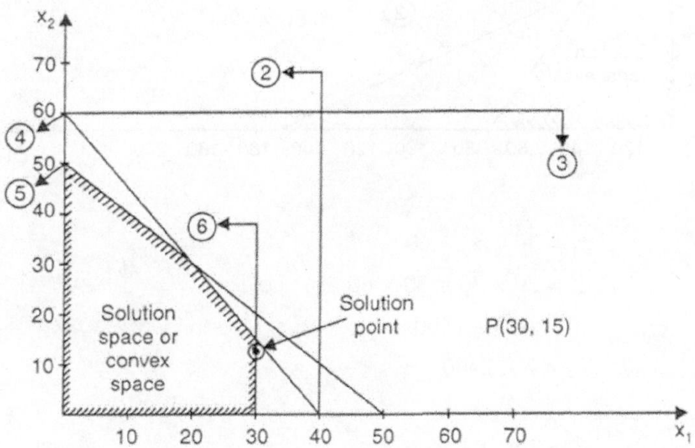

Answer:

$x_1 = 30 \quad \therefore$ No. of type 'A' screws = 30,000,

$x_2 = 15 \quad \therefore$ No. of type 'B' screws = 15,000.

$Z_{max} = 3 \times 30 + 1.5 \times 15$

$= 90 + 22.5 =$ Rs. 112.5.

Example 4

A firm manufacturing two types of electrical items, A and B, can make a profit of Rs. 20 per unit of A and Rs. 30 per unit of B. Both A and B make use of two essential components, a motor and a transformer. Each unit of A requires 3 motors and 2 transformers, and each unit of B requires 2 motors and 4 transformers. The total supply of components per month is restricted to 210 motors and 300 transformers. Type B is an export model requiring a voltage stabilizer, which has a supply of maximum 65 units per month. How many each of A and B should the firm manufacture per month to maximize its profit ? How much is this profit ?

Solution:

Let x_1 and x_2 be the number of units of type *A* and type '*B*' respectively produced per month.

Objective function is to maximize profit $Z_{max} = 20\,x_1 + 30\,x_2$

Subject to the constraints

$$3x_1 + 2x_2 \le 210 \quad (1)$$
$$2x_1 + 4x_2 \le 300 \quad (2)$$
$$x_2 \le 65 \quad (3)$$
$$x_1, x_2 \ge 0 \quad (4)$$

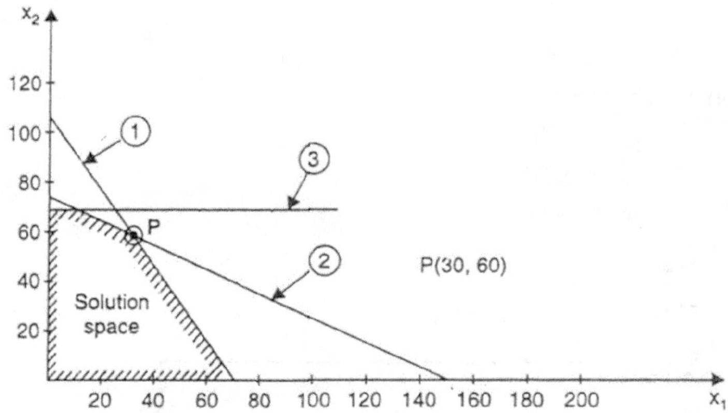

Answer:

$$x_1 = 30 \quad x_2 = 60$$
$$Z_{max} = 20 \times 30 + 30 \times 60$$
$$= 600 + 1800$$
$$= \text{Rs. } 2400.$$

Example 5

Maximize $Z = 2\,x_1 + 3\,x_2$

Subject to the constraints

$$x_1 + x_2 \le 30 \quad (1)$$
$$x_2 \ge 3 \quad (2)$$
$$x_2 \le 12 \quad (3)$$

$$x_1 - x_2 \geq 0 \quad (4)$$
$$x_1 \leq 20 \quad (5)$$
$$x_1, x_2 \geq 0 \quad (6)$$

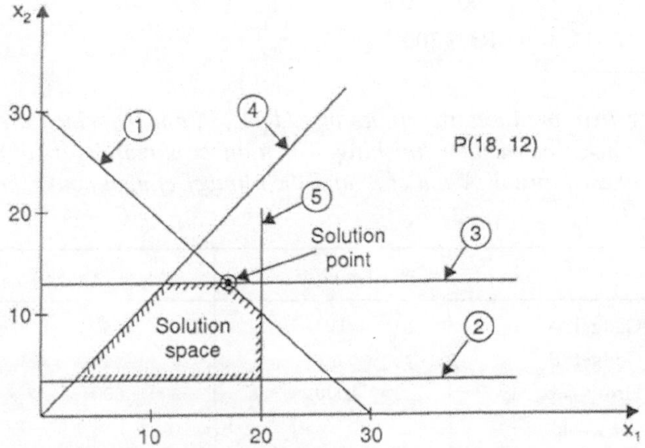

Answer:

$$x_1 = 18$$
$$x_2 = 12$$
$$Z_{max} = 2 \times 18 + 3 \times 12 = 36 + 36 = \text{Rs. } 72.00$$

Example 6

Maximize $\qquad Z = 6x_1 + 5x_2$

Subject to the constraints

$$x_1 \leq 100 \quad (1)$$
$$x_2 \leq 200 \quad (2)$$
$$4x_1 + 2x_2 \leq 600 \quad (3)$$
$$x_1, x_2 \geq 0 \quad (4)$$

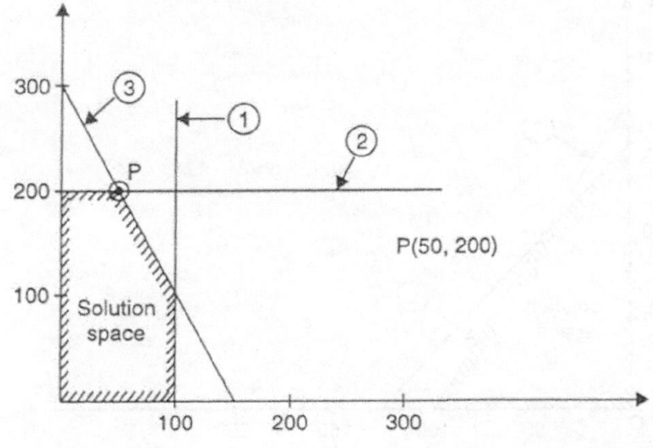

Answer:

$$x_1 = 50$$
$$x_2 = 200$$
$$Z_{max} = 6 \times 50 + 5 \times 200$$
$$= 300 + 1000$$
$$= \text{Rs. } 1300.$$

Example 7

A small manufacturing firm produces two types of gadgets, A and B, which are first processed in the foundry, then sent to the machine shop for finishing. The number of man hours of labour required in each shop for the production of each unit of A and of B, and the number of man hours the firm has available per week are as follows.

	Foundry	*Machine shop*
Gadget 'A'	10	5
Gadget 'B'	6	4
Firm's capacity per week	1000	600

The profit on the sale of A is Rs. 30 per unit as compared to Rs. 20 per unit of B. How many units of A and of B should be produced per week in order to maximize the profit ? What is the amount of profit in such case ?

Solution:

Let x_1 units of A and x_2 units of B be produced per week.

The objective function is to maximize profit

$$Z_{max} = 30\,x_1 + 20\,x_2$$

Subject to the constraints.

$$10x_1 + 6x_2 \leq 1000 \quad (1)$$
$$5x_1 + 4\,x_2 \leq 600 \quad (2)$$
$$x_1, x_2 \geq 0 \quad (3)$$

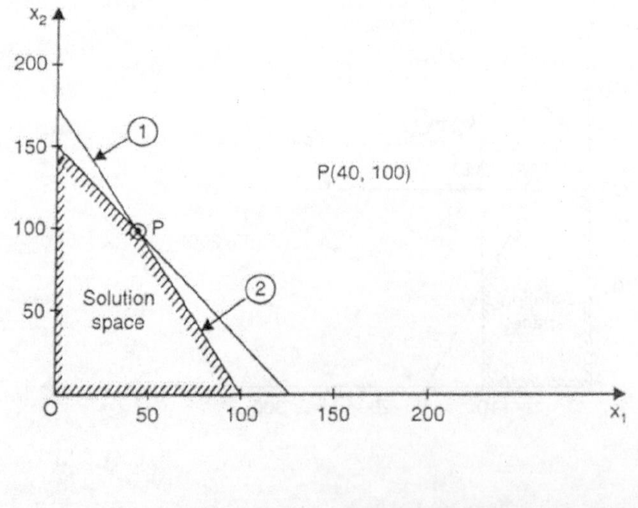

Answers:

$$x_1 = 40$$
$$x_2 = 100$$
$$Z_{max} = 30x_1 + 20x_2 = 30 \times 40 + 20 \times 100.$$
$$= 1200 + 2000 = \text{Rs. } 3200.$$

Example 8

A firm manufactures headache pills in two sizes, A and B. Size A contains 2 grains of aspirin, 5 grains of bicarbonate and 1 grain of codeine; size B contains 1 grain of aspirin, 8 grains of bicarbonate and 6 grains of codeine. It has been found by users that it requires at least 12 grains of aspirin, 74 grains of bicarbonate, and 24 grains of codeine for providing immediate effect.

Determine the least number of pills a patient should take to get immediate relief. Determine also the quantity of codeine consumed by the patient.

Solution:

Let x_1 number of pills of size A and x_2 number of pills of size B, be taken by the patient to get immediate relief.

The objective function is to minimize $Z = x_1 + x_2$

Subject to the constraints.

$2x_1 + x_2 \geq 12$ (1) (aspirin constraints)

$5x_1 + 8x_2 \geq 74$ (2) (bicarbonate constraints)

$x_1 + 6x_2 \geq 24$ (3) (codeine constraints)

$x_1, x_2 \geq 0$ (4)

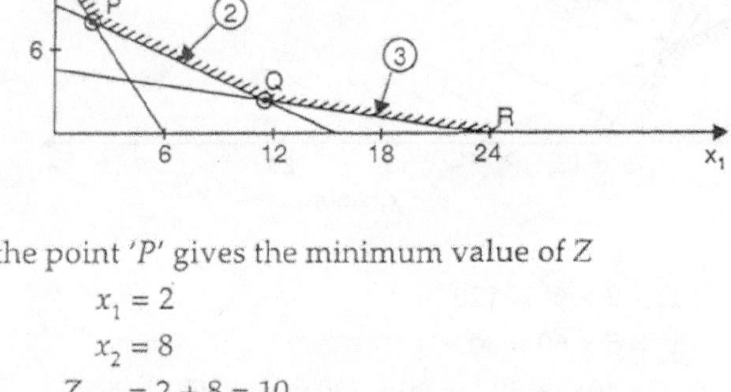

Answer:

Among P, Q, R and S the point 'P' gives the minimum value of Z

$$x_1 = 2$$
$$x_2 = 8$$
$$Z_{min} = 2 + 8 = 10$$

The quantity of codeine consumed by the patient

$$= x_1 + 6\,x_2 = 2 + 6 \times 8 = 2 + 48 = 50 \text{ grains.}$$

Example 9

A confectioner manufactures two types of biscuits, A and B. The type biscuits A is sold at a profit of Rs. 40 per box, whereas type B brings a profit of Rs. 50 per box. The biscuits are processed in three main operations: blending, cooking and packaging. The average time taken in minutes for each box, for each processing operations, is as follows:

	Blending	*Cooking*	*Packaging*
Type *A*	1 min	5 mins	3 mins
Type *B*	2 mins	4 mins	1 min

The blending equipment is available for a maximum of 12 machine hours, the cooking facilities for almost 30 hours, and packaging equipment for more than 15 hours.

Determine how many boxes of each type the confectioner should manufacture in order to maximize his profit. How much is this profit ?

Solution:

Let type *A* boxes are manufactured in x_1 quantity and type *B* boxes are manufactured in x_2 quantity.

Our objective function is to maximize profit $Z = 40x_1 + 50x_2$

Subject to the constraints

$$x_1 + 2x_2 \leq 12 \times 60 \quad (1)$$

$$5x_1 + 4x_2 \leq 30 \times 60 \quad (2)$$

$$3x_1 + x_2 \leq 15 \times 60 \quad (3)$$

$$x_1, x_2 \geq 0 \quad (4)$$

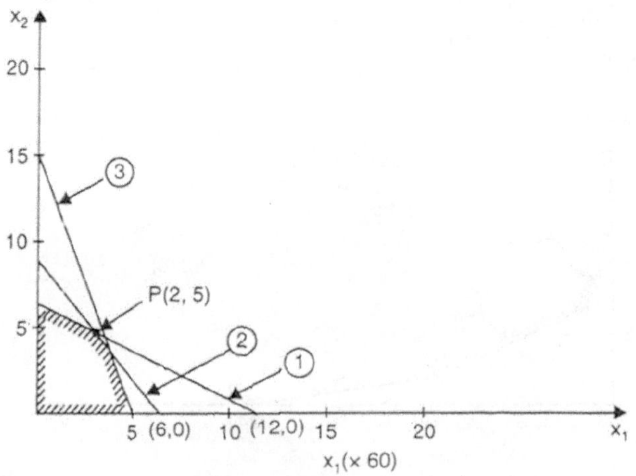

Answer:

$$x_1 = 2 \times 60 = 120$$

$$x_2 = 5 \times 60 = 300$$

$$Z_{max} = 40x_1 + 50x_2 = 40 \times 120 + 50 \times 300$$

$$= 4800 + 15000 = \text{Rs. } 19{,}800$$

Example 10

International Instruments manufactures two types of automobile speedometers, A and B, which they sell to car dealers at a profit Rs. 20 per unit of A and Rs. 10 per unit of B. The number of man-hours of labour required, on an average, in each department of international instruments for the production of each unit of A and of B, and the number of man-hours the firm has available for each production run are as follows:

	Assembly	*Plating and finishing*	*Testing and packing*
Speedometer *A*	15	5	1
Speedometer *B*	6	4	2
Firm's capacity	3000	1300	500

How many speedometers each of *A* and of *B* should international instruments produce in order to realize the maximum profit from each production run, and how much is this profit ?

Solution:

Let the firm produce x_1 units of *A* and x_2 units of *B*.

Our objective function is to maximize profit $Z = 20\,x_1 + 10\,x_2$

Subject to constraints

$$15x_1 + 6x_2 \le 3000 \qquad (1)$$

$$5x_1 + 4x_2 \le 1300 \qquad (2)$$

$$x_1 + 2x_2 \le 500 \qquad (3)$$

$$x_1, x_2 \ge 0 \qquad (4)$$

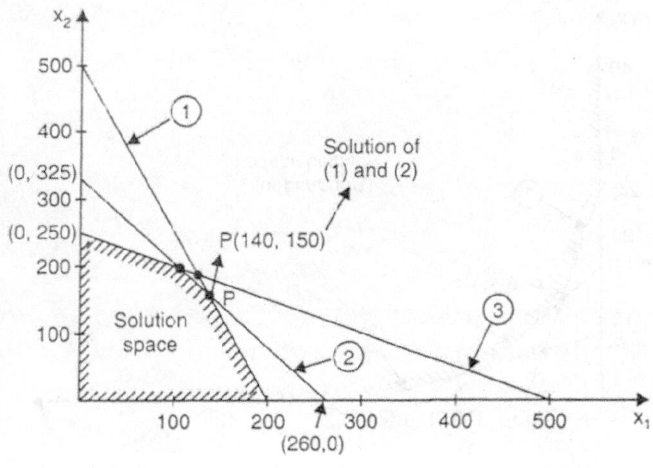

Answer:

$$x_1 = 140$$

$$x_2 = 150$$

$$Z_{max} = 20 \times 140 + 10 \times 150 = \text{Rs. } 4300.$$

Example 11

A soft drinks firm has two bottling plants, one located at P and the other at Q. Each plant produces three different soft drinks, A, B and C. The capacities of the two plants, in number of bottles per day, are as follows:

Products	Plant P	Plant Q
A	3000	1000
B	1000	1000
C	2000	6000

A market survey indicates that during the month of April there will be a demand of 24,000 bottles of A, 16,000 bottles of B and 48,000 bottles of C. The operating costs, per day, of running plants P and Q are Rs. 600 and Rs. 400 respectively. How many days should the firm run each plant in April so that the production cost is minimized while still meeting the market demand ?

Solution:

Let, x_1 = No. of days for running plant P

x_2 = No. of days for running plant Q

Our objective is to minimize cost $Z = 600\, x_1 + 400\, x_2$

Subject to the constraints

$$3000\, x_1 + 1000\, x_2 \geq 24{,}000 \quad (1)$$
$$1000\, x_1 + 1000\, x_2 \geq 16{,}000 \quad (2)$$
$$2000\, x_1 + 6000\, x_2 \geq 48{,}000 \quad (3)$$
$$x_1, x_2 \geq 0 \quad (4)$$

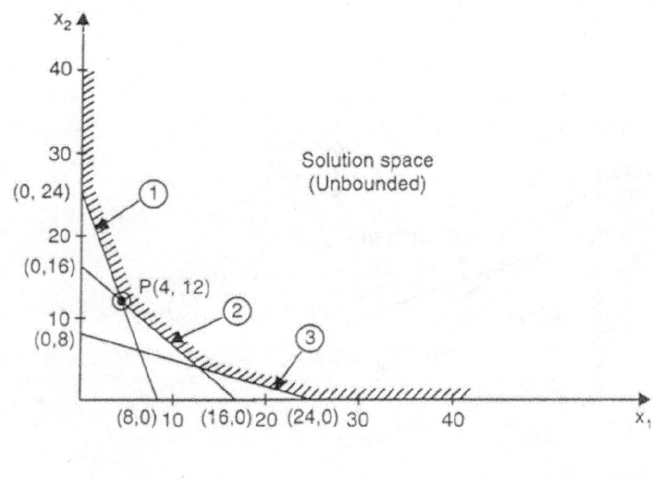

Answer:

$x_1 = 4$

$x_2 = 12$

$Z_{min} = 600 \times 4 + 400 \times 12 = 2400 + 4800 =$ Rs. 7200.

Chapter 3

SIMPLEX METHOD (DEVELOPED BY G.B. DANTZIG)

3.1 THEORY OF SIMPLEX METHOD

Let us take the objective function: Minimize CX (1)

where C is a row vector given by

$$C = (c_1, c_2, \ldots, c_n)$$

and X is a column vector given by

$$X = \begin{pmatrix} x_1 \\ x_2 \\ \vdots \\ x_n \end{pmatrix}$$

Subject to

$$x_1 P_1 + x_2 P_2 + \ldots + x_n P_n = P_0 \tag{2}$$

i.e.,

$$\begin{aligned} a_{11} x_1 + a_{12} x_2 + \ldots + a_{1n} x_n &= b_1 \\ \vdots \qquad \vdots \qquad \quad \vdots \quad & \vdots \\ a_{m1} x_1 + a_{m2} x_2 + \ldots + a_{mn} x_n &= b_m \end{aligned}$$

Thus $$P_1 = \begin{pmatrix} a_{11} \\ a_{21} \\ \vdots \\ a_{m1} \end{pmatrix}, P_0 = \begin{pmatrix} b_1 \\ \vdots \\ \vdots \\ b_m \end{pmatrix}$$

$P_1, P_2 \ldots P_0$ are column vectors.

The Non-negativity constraints $X \geq 0$ (3)

Some related terms

(1) Basic feasible solution of Linear Programming problem: means the solution vector X, which satisfies conditions given in equations (2) and (3).

(2) Non-degenerate basic feasible solution (NDBFS) is a basic feasible solution which satisfies equations (2) and (3) but contain m number of decision variables.

(3) Minimum solution is feasible solution satisfying condition (equations) (1), (2) and (3).

Simplex method: It is iterative method where we start with an initial solution

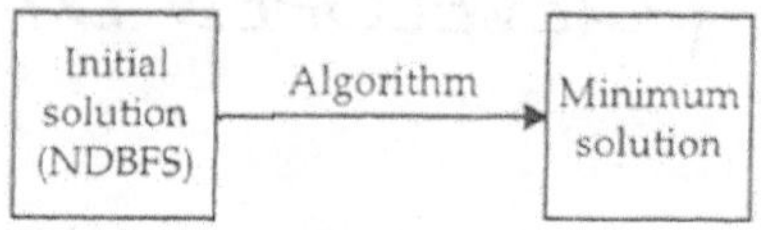

Let $X_0 = \begin{pmatrix} x_{10} \\ x_{20} \\ \vdots \\ x_{m0} \end{pmatrix}$, By condition (2) we get

$$x_{10} P_1 + x_{20} P_2 + \ldots.. + x_{m0} P_m = P_0 \quad (4)$$

By condition (3) we get $P_1, P_2 \ldots.. P_m$ is a set of linearly independent vectors and the value of the initial objective is

$$x_{10} C_1 + x_{20} C_2 + \ldots.. + x_{m0} C_m = Z_0 \quad (5)$$

Any vector P_j ($j = 1, 2, \ldots.. n$) can be expressed as

$$x_{1j} P_1 + x_{2j} P_2 + \ldots.. + x_{mj} P_m = P_j \quad (6)$$

and let us define

$$x_{1j} C_1 + x_{2j} C_2 + \ldots.. + x_{mj} C_m = Z_j \quad (7)$$

Theorem:

If for any fixed j, the condition $Z_j - C_j > 0$ holds, then a new set of feasible solutions can be constructed such that the value of the objective function for a particular member of the set (Z) is less than Z_0, where the value of Z may be either bounded or unbounded.

Case 1 (Bounded): If the lower bound of Z is finite, a new feasible solution consisting of exactly m positive variables can be constructed whose value of the objective function is less than the value of the preceding solution.

Case 2 (Unbounded): If the lower bound is infinite, a new feasible solution consisting of exactly (m + 1) positive variables can be constructed whose value of the objective function can be made arbitrarily small.

Proof: Multiplying equation (6) by a small number θ and subtracting from (4), we get

$$(x_{10} - \theta x_{1j}) P_1 + (x_{20} - \theta x_{2j}) P_2 + \ldots.. + (x_{mo} - \theta x_{mj}) P_m + \theta P_j = P_0 \quad \ldots(8)$$

Again multiplying equation (7) by the same θ and subtracting from (5) and adding θC_j to both sides, we get

$$(x_{10} - \theta x_{1j}) C_1 + (x_{20} - \theta x_{2j}) C_2 + \ldots.. + (x_{m0} - \theta x_{mj}) C_m + \theta C_j = Z_0 - \theta (Z_j - C_j) \quad \ldots(9)$$

The solution $X_0' = \begin{pmatrix} x_{10} - \theta x_{1j} \\ x_{20} - \theta x_{2j} \\ \vdots \\ x_{m0} - \theta x_{mj} \\ \theta \end{pmatrix}$ $\rightarrow$ to be basic feasible solution to satisfy equation (3)

$\theta \geq 0$, for non-degenerate θ is positive.

The left hand side of the equation (9) implies

$$Z_0' < Z_0$$

All $x_{10} - \theta\, x_{1j}$ is positive

$$\theta_{max} = \min_j = \left| \frac{x_{i0}}{x_{ij}} \right|_{min} \quad \text{for } x_{ij} > 0\text{, where it occurs it vanishes.}$$

Case 2. θ becomes infinitely high.

For maximizing problem

$$Z_0' > Z_0 \quad \text{and} \quad Z_j - C_j < 0.$$

3.2 BASIC PRINCIPLES AND FLOW DIAGRAM OF SIMPLEX METHOD

Based on the two theorems simplex method works as under:

(1) Obtain a non-degenerate initial solution which satisfies the restrictions including the non-negativity one and determine the corresponding value of the objective.

(2) For all the variables of the problem, evaluate $Z_j - C_j$ using equation (7).

(3) A positive value of $Z_j - C_j$ indicates that inclusion of that variable into the solution would decrease the objective (for minimization problem). Choose the variable with highest positive $(Z_j - C_j)$ because that decreases the objective by the highest amount.

Note: If there are more than one column where highest $Z_j - C_j$ values occur, any column amongst them may be choosen as key column. However, in most of the computations, among the tied columns, the column with lower index number is choosen as key column.

	i	*Basis vectors*	*Cost coefficient of basic variables*	*Solution vector* (P_0)	C_1 / P_1	C_2 / P_2	...	C_j / P_j	...	C_n / P_n
Key row →	1	P_1	C_1	x_{10}	a_{11}	(a_{12})	...	a_{1j}	...	a_{1n}
	2	P_2	C_2	x_{20}	a_{21}	a_{22}	...	a_{2j}	...	a_{2n}
	⋮	⋮	⋮	⋮	⋮	⋮		⋮		⋮
	m	P_m	C_m	x_{m0}	a_{m1}	a_{m2}	...	a_{mj}	...	a_{mn}
				Z_0	Z_1-C_1	Z_2-C_2	...	Z_j-C_j	...	Z_n-C_n

(a_{12}) → Key Number   ↑ Key Column (column Z_2-C_2)

For minimization $Z_j - C_j > 0$

Several $Z_j - C_j > 0$ we choose highest $Z_j - C_j$ say $Z_2 - C_2$ is the maximum positive, we call it the key column.

$$\theta = \left| \frac{x_{i0}}{x_{ij}} \right|_{min}$$

$$\text{1st ratio} = \frac{x_{10}}{a_{12}}, \text{ 2nd ratio} = \frac{x_{20}}{a_{22}}, \text{ take only positive ratios,}$$

Let $\theta = \frac{x_{10}}{a_{12}}$ be the minimum therefore a_{12} is the key number and that row which contains a_{12}, is the key row.

For going to next table we use the following two rules:

Rule 1. New element in key row $= \dfrac{\text{Old element}}{\text{Key number}}$

Rule 2. Other new elements = Old element $- \dfrac{\text{Product of corresponding numbers in key column and key row}}{\text{Key number}}$.

Example 1

Minimize $Z = x_2 - 3x_3 - 2x_5$

Subject to constraints

$$x_1 + 3x_2 - x_3 + 2x_5 = 7 \quad (1)$$

$$-2x_2 + 4x_3 + x_4 = 12 \quad (2)$$

$$-4x_2 + 3x_3 + 8x_5 + x_6 = 10 \quad (3)$$

$$x_j \geq 0, j = 1, 2, 3 ..... 6 \quad (4)$$

Solution:

$$AX = b$$

$$A = \begin{pmatrix} 1 & 3 & -1 & 0 & 2 & 0 \\ 0 & -2 & 4 & 1 & 0 & 0 \\ 0 & -4 & 3 & 0 & 8 & 1 \end{pmatrix}$$

$$X = \begin{pmatrix} x_1 \\ x_2 \\ \vdots \\ x_6 \end{pmatrix}, b = \begin{pmatrix} 7 \\ 12 \\ 10 \end{pmatrix}$$

Let us try to locate a unit matrix of dimension (3 × 3).

$$I_{3\times 3} = \begin{pmatrix} 1 & 0 & 0 \\ 0 & 1 & 0 \\ 0 & 0 & 1 \end{pmatrix}$$

The unit matrix is available at x_1, x_4 and x_6 and others *i.e.*, $x_2 = 0, x_3 = 0, x_5 = 0$. By putting the values of x_2, x_3, x_5 in the constraints equations, we get $x_1 = 7$, $x_4 = 12$ and $x_6 = 10$.

Thus

$$\left.\begin{array}{ll} x_1 = 7 & x_2 = 0 \\ x_4 = 12 & x_3 = 0 \\ x_6 = 10 & x_5 = 0 \end{array}\right\}$$ These are the initial solution.

We write down the initial table.

Initial Table

i	Basis	C	P_0	0	1	–3	0	2	0		
				P_1	P_2	P_3	P_4	P_5	P_6		
1	P_1	0	7	1	3	–1	0	2	0		
2	P_4	0	12	0	–2	(4)	1	0	0	$\frac{12}{4} = 3$	Minimum ← Key row
3	P_6	0	10	0	–4	3	0	8	1	$\frac{10}{3} = 3.3$	
4			0	0	–1	3	0	–2	0		

Value of objective function (↑ P_0 in row 4)

Key column (maximum positive number 3) (↑ P_3)

(4) → Key number

Table 2

i	Basis	C	P_0	0	1	–3	0	2	0		
				P_1	P_2	P_3	P_4	P_5	P_6		
1	P_1	0	10	1	($\frac{5}{2}$)	0	$\frac{1}{4}$	2	0	$10 \div \frac{5}{2} = 4$	← Key row
2	P_3	–3	3	0	$-\frac{1}{2}$	1	$\frac{1}{4}$	0	0		
3	P_6	0	1	0	$-\frac{5}{2}$	0	$-\frac{3}{4}$	8	1		
4			–9	0	$\frac{1}{2}$	0	$-\frac{3}{4}$	–2	0		

Key Column (↑ P_2)

($\frac{5}{2}$) → Key Number

Table 3 (Final Table)

i	Basis	C	P_0	0	1	-3	0	2	0		
				P_1	P_2	P_3	P_4	P_5	P_6		
1	P_2	1	4	$\frac{2}{5}$	1	0	$\frac{1}{10}$	$\frac{4}{5}$	0		
2	P_3	-3	5	$\frac{1}{5}$	0	1	$\frac{3}{10}$	$\frac{2}{5}$	0		
3	P_6	0	11	1	0	0	$-\frac{1}{2}$	10	1		
4			-11	$-\frac{1}{5}$	0	0	$-\frac{4}{5}$	$-\frac{12}{5}$	0	←	$Z_j - C_j$

Table (3) is the final table because $Z_j - C_j \not> 0$. (*i.e.*, there is no positive non zero number in this $Z_j - C_j$ row).

Answer:

$$x_2 = 4$$
$$x_3 = 5$$
$$x_6 = 11 \quad \text{and} \quad Z_{min} = -11.$$

Example 2

Solve the following Linear Programming problem by simplex method.

Maximize $\qquad Z = 2x_1 + 3x_2$

Subject to constraints

$$-x_1 + 2x_2 \leq 4$$
$$x_1 + x_2 \leq 6$$
$$x_1 + 3x_2 \leq 9$$
$$x_1, x_2 \geq 0$$

The constraints in equations are changed to equations keeping right hand side positive.

$$-x_1 + 2x_2 + x_3 = 4$$
$$x_1 + x_2 + x_4 = 6$$
$$x_1 + 3x_2 + x_5 = 9$$
$$x_1, x_2, x_3, x_4, x_5 \geq 0$$

Here x_1 and x_2 are legitimate variables and x_3, x_4 and x_5 are slack variables.

The objective function can be changed to minimization problem as explained below

$$Z_{min} = -2x_1 - 3x_2 + 0x_3 + 0x_4 + 0x_5$$

Subject to constraints

$$-x_1 + 2x_2 + x_3 = 4$$
$$x_1 + x_2 + x_4 = 6$$

$$x_1 + 3x_2 + x_5 = 9$$
$$x_j \geq 0,\ j = 1 \text{ to } 5$$

Matrix A is given by

$$A = \begin{pmatrix} -1 & 2 & 1 & 0 & 0 \\ 1 & 1 & 0 & 1 & 0 \\ 1 & 3 & 0 & 0 & 1 \end{pmatrix}$$

Thus $I_{3\times 3} = \begin{pmatrix} 1 & 0 & 0 \\ 0 & 1 & 0 \\ 0 & 0 & 1 \end{pmatrix}$ is available with variables x_3, x_4 and x_5, so others $x_2 = x_1 = 0$.

Thus the initial solution is

$$x_3 = 4 \qquad x_2 = 0$$
$$x_4 = 6 \qquad x_1 = 0$$
$$x_5 = 9$$

Initial Table

i	*Basis*	C	P_0	–2	–3	0	0	0	
				P_1	P_2	P_3	P_4	P_5	
1	P_3	0	4	–1	(2)	1	0	0	$\frac{4}{2} = 2$ ← Min ← Key row
2	P_4	0	6	1	1	0	1	0	$\frac{6}{1} = 6$
3	P_5	0	9	1	3	0	0	1	$\frac{9}{3} = 3$
4			[0]	2	3	0	0	0	← 3 is the maximum $Z_j - C_j$ value i.e., key column criteria

↑ Key column

Table 2

i	*Basis*	C	P_0	–2	–3	0	0	0	
				P_1	P_2	P_3	P_4	P_5	
1	P_2	–3	2	$-\frac{1}{2}$	1	$\frac{1}{2}$	0	0	
2	P_4	0	4	$\frac{3}{2}$	0	$-\frac{1}{2}$	1	0	$4 \div \frac{3}{2} = 2.66$
3	P_5	0	3	($\frac{5}{2}$)	0	$-\frac{3}{2}$	0	1	$3 \div \frac{5}{2} = 1.2$ (Min) ← Key row
4			[–6]	$\frac{7}{2}$	0	$-\frac{3}{2}$	0	0	

↑ Key Column

Table 3

i	Basis	C	P_0	-2	-3	0	0	0	
				P_1	P_2	P_3	P_4	P_5	
1	P_2	-3	$\frac{13}{5}$	0	1	$\frac{1}{5}$	0	$\frac{1}{5}$	$\frac{13}{5} \div \frac{1}{5} = 13$
2	P_4	0	$\frac{11}{5}$	0	0	$\boxed{\frac{2}{5}}$	1	$-\frac{3}{5}$	$\frac{11}{5} \div \frac{2}{5} = \frac{11}{2}$ ← Min ← Key row
3	P_1	-2	$\frac{6}{5}$	1	0	$-\frac{3}{5}$	0	$\frac{2}{5}$	
4			$\boxed{-\frac{51}{5}}$	0	0	$\frac{3}{5}$	0	$-\frac{7}{5}$	

↑ Key Column

Table 4 (Final Table)

i	Basis	C	P_0	-2	-3	0	0	0	
				P_1	P_2	P_3	P_4	P_5	
1	P_2	-3	$\frac{3}{2}$	0	1	0	$-\frac{1}{2}$	$\frac{1}{2}$	
2	P_3	0	$\frac{11}{2}$	0	0	1	$\frac{5}{2}$	$-\frac{3}{2}$	
3	P_1	-2	$\frac{9}{2}$	1	0	0	$\frac{3}{2}$	$-\frac{1}{2}$	
4			$\boxed{-\frac{27}{2}}$	0	0	0	$-\frac{3}{2}$	$-\frac{1}{2}$	← $Z_j - C_j$

As all $Z_j - C_j$ values in the 4th table is ≤ 0, the solution can not be further improved. Therefore the optimal solution is

$$x_1 = \frac{9}{2}$$

$$x_2 = \frac{3}{2} \quad x_4 = 0$$

$$x_3 = \frac{11}{2} \quad x_5 = 0 \quad Z_{min} = -\frac{27}{2}$$

$$\therefore \quad Z_{max} = \frac{27}{2} \quad \textbf{Ans.}$$

Here $x_3 = \frac{11}{2}$ → slack capacity of resources corresponding to the first restriction.

Example 3

To maximize $Z = 6\,x_1 + 5\,x_2$

Subject to the constraints

$$4x_1 + 2x_2 \leq 600$$
$$x_1 \leq 100$$
$$x_2 \leq 200$$
$$x_1, x_2 \geq 0$$

Solution:

To minimize $Z = -\,6x_1 - 5x_2 + 0x_3 + 0x_4 + 0x_5$

Subject to the constraints

$$4x_1 + 2x_2 + x_3 = 600$$
$$x_1 + x_4 = 100$$
$$x_2 + x_5 = 200$$
$$x_1, x_2, x_3, x_4, x_5 \geq 0$$

where x_3, x_4 and x_5 are slack variables.

$$A = \begin{pmatrix} 4 & 2 & 1 & 0 & 0 \\ 1 & 0 & 0 & 1 & 0 \\ 0 & 1 & 0 & 0 & 1 \end{pmatrix}$$

$$I_{3\times 3} = \begin{pmatrix} 1 & 0 & 0 \\ 0 & 1 & 0 \\ 0 & 0 & 1 \end{pmatrix}$$

is available with x_3, x_4 and x_5, others $x_1 = 0, x_2 = 0$ putting the values of $x_1 = x_2 = 0$ in the constraints equations

we get $x_3 = 600,\ x_4 = 100$ and $x_5 = 200$

Initial Table

i	Basis	C	P_0	P_1 (−6)	P_2 (−5)	P_3 (0)	P_4 (0)	P_5 (0)	← Coefficient of objective
1	P_3	0	600	4	2	1	0	0	$\frac{600}{4} = 150$
2	P_4	0	100	(1)	0	0	1	0	$\frac{100}{1} = 100$ ← Min ← Key row
3	P_5	0	200	0	1	0	0	1	$\frac{200}{0} = \infty$
4			[0]	6	5	0	0	0	

↑ Key Column (P_1)

Table 2

i	*Basis*	*C*	P_0	-6	-5	0	0	0	
				P_1	P_2	P_3	P_4	P_5	
1	P_3	0	200	0	(2)	1	-4	0	$\frac{200}{2} = 100$ ← Min ← Key row
2	P_1	-6	100	1	0	0	1	0	$\frac{100}{0} = \infty$
3	P_5	0	200	0	1	0	0	1	$\frac{200}{1} = 200$
4			-600	0	5	0	-6	0	

↑ Key Column (P_2)

Table 3

i	*Basis*	*C*	P_0	-6	-5	0	0	0	
				P_1	P_2	P_3	P_4	P_5	
1	P_2	-5	100	0	1	$\frac{1}{2}$	-2	0	
2	P_1	-6	100	1	0	0	1	0	$\frac{100}{1} = 100$
3	P_5	0	100	0	0	$-\frac{1}{2}$	(2)	1	$\frac{100}{2} = 50$ ← Min ← Key row
4			-1100	0	0	-2.5	4	0	

↑ Key Column (P_4)

Table 4 (Final Table)

i	*Basis*	*C*	P_0	-6	-5	0	0	0	
				P_1	P_2	P_3	P_4	P_5	
1	P_2	-5	200	0	1	0	0	1	
2	P_1	-6	50	1	0	$\frac{1}{4}$	0	$-\frac{1}{2}$	
3	P_4	0	50	0	0	$-\frac{1}{4}$	1	$\frac{1}{2}$	
4			-1300	0	0	$-\frac{6}{4}$	0	-2	

Answer:

$x_1 = 50,$

$x_2 = 200, \quad Z_{min} = -1300$

$x_4 = 50,$

$x_3 = x_5 = 0, \quad \therefore \quad Z_{max} = 1300(\text{Rs}).$

3.3 SIMPLEX METHOD INVOLVING ARTIFICIAL BASIS

So far the L.P. problems that we have considered were feasible and contained an unit matrix that could be used for the initial basis. Many problems do not contain an identity matrix of the required dimensions. An initial solution is not easily available for such problems. We then use artificial basis.

Example 4

To maximize $$Z = x_1 + 2x_2 + 3x_3 - x_4$$

Subject to

$$x_1 + 2x_2 + 3x_3 = 15$$
$$2x_1 + x_2 + 5x_3 = 20$$
$$x_1 + 2x_2 + x_3 + x_4 = 10$$
$$x_1, x_2, x_3, x_4 \geq 0$$

Though the constraints are equations, there is no unit matrix available. We use artificial variables in the constraints.

$$x_1 + 2x_2 + 3x_3 + x_5 = 15$$
$$2x_1 + x_2 + 5x_3 + x_6 = 20$$
$$x_1 + 2x_2 + x_3 + x_4 = 10$$
$$x_1, x_2, x_3, x_4, x_5, x_6 \text{ all} \geq 0$$

Here x_5 and x_6 are called artificial variables.

Now $I_{3\times 3} = \begin{pmatrix} 1 & 0 & 0 \\ 0 & 1 & 0 \\ 0 & 0 & 1 \end{pmatrix}$ is available in the above equations involving artificial variables.

$$A = \begin{pmatrix} 1 & 2 & 3 & 0 & 1 & 0 \\ 2 & 1 & 5 & 0 & 0 & 1 \\ 1 & 2 & 1 & 1 & 0 & 0 \end{pmatrix}$$

3.3.1 Charne's 'Big M' Method is Used to Solve above Problem

Objective function is to minimize $Z = -x_1 - 2x_2 - 3x_3 + x_4 + Mx_5 + Mx_6$ where M is a large positive number.

The initial solution is given by

$$x_5 = 15, x_6 = 20 \text{ and } x_4 = 10, \text{ others } x_1 = x_2 = x_3 = 0.$$

Table 1

i	Basis	C	P_0	-1	-2	-3	1	M	M	
				P_1	P_2	P_3	P_4	P_5	P_6	
1	P_5	M	15	1	2	3	0	1	0	$\frac{15}{3} = 5$
2	P_6	M	20	2	1	(5)	0	0	1	$\frac{20}{5} = 4$ ← Min ← Key row
3	P_4	1	10	1	2	1	1	0	0	
4			35 M + 10	3 M + 2	3 M + 4	8 M + 4	0	0	0	

↑ Key column

In table 1

As the leaving vector P_6 is an artificial vector, column P_6 is subsequently dropped.

Table 2

i	Basis	C	P_0	-1	-2	-3	1	M	
				P_1	P_2	P_3	P_4	P_5	
1	P_5	M	3	$-\frac{1}{5}$	($\frac{7}{5}$)	0	0	1	$3 \div \frac{7}{5} = 2.1$ ← Min ← Key row
2	P_3	-3	4	$\frac{2}{5}$	$\frac{1}{5}$	1	0	0	$4 \div \frac{1}{5} = 20$
3	P_4	1	6	$\frac{3}{5}$	$\frac{9}{5}$	0	1	0	$6 \div \frac{9}{5} = 3.3$
4			3M −6	−M/5 +2/5	7M/5 +16/5	0	0	0	

↑ Key column

In table 2

As the leaving vector P_5 is an artificial vector, column P_5 is subsequently dropped.

Table 3

i	Basis	C	P_0	-1	-2	-3	1	
				P_1	P_2	P_3	P_4	
1	P_2	-2	$\frac{15}{7}$	$-\frac{1}{7}$	1	0	0	
2	P_3	-3	$\frac{25}{7}$	$\frac{3}{7}$	0	1	0	$\frac{25}{7} \div \frac{3}{7} = 8.33$
3	P_4	1	$\frac{15}{7}$	($\frac{6}{7}$)	0	0	1	$\frac{15}{7} \div \frac{6}{7} = 2.5$ ← Min ← Key row
4			$-\frac{90}{7}$	$\frac{6}{7}$	0	0	0	

↑ Key Column

Table 4

i	Basis	C	P_0	−1	−2	−3	1	
				P_1	P_2	P_3	P_4	
1	P_2	−2	$\frac{5}{2}$	0	1	0	$\frac{1}{6}$	
2	• P_3	−3	$\frac{5}{2}$	0	0	1	$-\frac{1}{2}$	
3	P_1	−1	$\frac{15}{6}$	1	0	0	$\frac{7}{6}$	
4			−15	0	0	0	−1	

There is no $Z_j - C_j > 0$. Thus table 4 is the final table.

Answer:

$$x_2 = x_3 = \frac{5}{2}$$

$$x_1 = \frac{15}{6} \quad \text{others are zero}$$

$$Z_{min} = -15$$

$$\boxed{Z_{max} = 15}$$

Determination of alternative optimal solution: The final simplex table is the starting point for finding these alternative optimum solutions. If $Z_j - C_j = 0$ for one or more non-basis vectors, any such vector can be inserted into the basis to yield an alternative optimum solution; if $a_{ij} > 0$ for atleast one i and minimum of (b/a) ratios is positive.

Example 5

Suppose that we are given the following final table. We have to find alternative optimal solution.

Final Table (To Start with)

i	Basis	C	P_0	1	4	2	5	19	1	5	3		
				P_1	P_2	P_3	P_4	P_5	P_6	P_7	P_8		
1	P_1	1	2	1	0	0	0	1	0	(1)	2	$\frac{2}{1} = 2$	$\frac{2}{1} = 2$ ←
2	P_2	4	3	0	1	0	0	2	−3	1	0	$\frac{3}{2} = 1.5$	$\frac{3}{1} = 3$
3	P_3	2	0	0	0	1	0	0	2	0	0		
4	P_4	5	1	0	0	0	1	(2)	2	0	2	$\frac{1}{2} = 0.5$ ← Min ← Key row	
5			[19]	0	0	0	0	0	1	0	9		

↑ Key Column ↑ (under P_5 and P_7)

Solution:

The vectors P_5 and P_7 (which are not in the basis) have their $Z_j - C_j = 0$. Therefore, they can each be brought into the basis to develop a set of alternative optimum solutions.

The alternative solutions are as follows

Alternative Solution Table 1

i	*Basis*	C	P_0	1	4	2	5	19	1	5	3
				P_1	P_2	P_3	P_4	P_5	P_6	P_7	P_8
1	P_1	1	$\frac{3}{2}$	1	0	0	$-\frac{1}{2}$	0	–1	1	1
2	P_2	4	2	0	1	0	–1	0	–5	1	–2
3	P_3	2	0	0	0	1	0	0	2	0	0
4	P_5	19	$\frac{1}{2}$	0	0	0	$\frac{1}{2}$	1	1	0	1
5			19	0	0	0	–5	0	–9	0	–1

P_5 has been brought in the basis. Alternative solution is

$$x_1 = \frac{3}{2}, \quad x_5 = \frac{1}{2}$$
$$x_2 = 2, \quad x_4 = x_6 = x_7 = x_8 = 0$$
$$x_3 = 0,$$

Alternative Solution Table 2

i	*Basis*	C	P_0	1	4	2	5	19	1	5	3
				P_1	P_2	P_3	P_4	P_5	P_6	P_7	P_8
1	P_7	5	2	1	0	0	0	1	0	1	2
2	P_2	4	1	–1	1	0	0	1	0	0	–2
3	P_3	2	0	0	0	1	0	0	–3	0	0
4	P_4	5	1	0	0	0	1	2	2	0	2
5	$Z_j - C_j$		19	–3	0	0	0	10	1	0	9

P_7 has been brought in the basis. Alternative solution is

$$x_2 = 1, \quad x_7 = 2$$
$$x_3 = 0, \quad x_1 = x_5 = x_6 = x_8 = 0$$
$$x_4 = 1,$$

Unique optimum: If all the non-basis variables have a negative value for their relative profits, then there does not exist alternate solutions.

Ties in key column: For ties in the selection of key column, we can select any one of them arbitrarily, since selecting the non-basis variable that gives the largest per unit improvement in Z need not necessarily give the largest total improvement in Z and minimize the number of simplex iterations.

Ties in key row: We can try with any one as arbitrarily.

Degenerate: A basic feasible solution in which one or more basic variables are zero is called degenerate basic feasible solution.

Non-degenerate: A basic feasible solution in which all the basic variables are positive is said to be non-degenerate.

Degenerate in basic does not improve the objective function.

3.3.2 Two-Phase Method for Artificial Variables

Phase 1: This phase consists of finding an initial basic feasible solution to the original problem. In other words, the removal of the artificial variables is taken up first. For this an artificial objective function is created which is the sum of all the artificial variables. The artificial objective is then minimized using the simplex method. If the minimum value of the artificial problem is zero, then all the artificial variables have been reduced to zero and we have a basic feasible solution to the original problem. We then go to phase 2.

Phase 2: In this phase, the basic feasible solution found at the end of phase 1 is optimized with respect to the original objective function. In other words, the final tableau of phase 1 becomes the initial tableau for phase 2 after changing the objective function. The simplex method is once again applied to determine the optimal solution.

SOLVE BY BIG-M & 2 PHASE METHODS

Example 6

Minimize $Z = -3x_1 + x_2 + x_3$

Subject to $x_1 - 2x_2 + x_3 \le 11$

$-4x_1 + x_2 + 2x_3 \ge 3$

$2x_1 - x_3 = -1$

$x_1, x_2, x_3 \ge 0$

Solution:

First the problem is converted to the standard form as follows.

Minimize $Z = -3x_1 + x_2 + x_3$

Subject to $x_1 - 2x_2 + x_3 + x_4 = 11$

$-4x_1 + x_2 + 2x_3 - x_5 = 3$

$-2x_1 + x_3 = 1$

$x_1, x_2, x_3, x_4, x_5 \ge 0$

$$A = \begin{pmatrix} 1 & -2 & 1 & 1 & 0 \\ -4 & 1 & 2 & 0 & -1 \\ -2 & 0 & 1 & 0 & 0 \end{pmatrix}$$

There is no unit matrix, we introduce artificial variables as follows.

$$x_1 - 2x_2 + x_3 + x_4 = 11$$
$$-4x_1 + x_2 + 2x_3 - x_5 + x_6 = 3$$
$$-2x_1 + x_3 + x_7 = 1$$
$$x_{1 \text{ to } 7} \text{ all} \geq 0$$

Here x_6 and x_7 are artificial variables, x_1, x_2, x_3 are legitimate variables and x_4 is slack variable, x_5 is surplus variable.

Now

new $$A = \begin{pmatrix} 1 & -2 & 1 & 1 & 0 & 0 & 0 \\ -4 & 1 & 2 & 0 & -1 & 1 & 0 \\ -2 & 0 & 1 & 0 & 0 & 0 & 1 \\ & & & \downarrow & & \downarrow & \downarrow \\ & & & x_4 & & x_6 & x_7 \end{pmatrix}$$

The initial solutions are

$$x_4 = 11,\ x_6 = 3,\ x_7 = 1$$
$$x_1 = x_2 = x_3 = x_5 = 0$$

Solution by big M method

Minimize $Z = -3x_1 + x_2 + x_3 + Mx_6 + Mx_7$ here M is a very large positive number.

Table 1

i	Basis	C	P_0	-3	1	1	0	0	M	M	
				P_1	P_2	P_3	P_4	P_5	P_6	P_7	
1	P_4	0	11	1	-2	1	1	0	0	0	$\frac{11}{1} = 11$
2	P_6	M	3	-4	1	2	0	-1	1	0	$\frac{3}{2} = 1.5$
3	P_7	M	1	-2	0	(1)	0	0	0	1	$\frac{1}{1} = 1$ ← Min ← Key row
4			+4M	-6M +3	M − 1	3M − 1	0	-M	0	0	

↑ Key Column (maximum positive number)

For Table: 1

As the leaving vector P_7 is an artificial vector; column P_7 is subsequently dropped.

Table 2

i	Basis	C	P_0	−3	1	1	0	0	M	
				P_1	P_2	P_3	P_4	P_5	P_6	
1	P_4	0	10	3	−2	0	1	0	0	$\frac{10}{-2}$ not considered
2	P_6	M	1	0	(1)	0	0	−1	1	$\frac{1}{1}=1$ ← Min ← Key row
3	P_3	1	1	−2	0	1	0	0	0	$\frac{1}{0}=\infty$
4			[M + 1]	1	M − 1	0	0	−M	0	

↑ Key Column

As the leaving vector P_6 is an artificial vector, column P_6 is subsequently dropped.

Table 3

i	Basis	C	P_0	−3	1	1	0	0	
				P_1	P_2	P_3	P_4	P_5	
1	P_4	0	12	(3)	0	0	1	−2	$\frac{12}{3}=4$ ← Min ← Key row
2	P_2	1	1	0	1	0	0	−1	$\frac{1}{0}=\infty$
3	P_3	1	1	−2	0	1	0	0	
4			[2]	1	0	0	0	−1	

↑ Key Column

Now both the artificial variables are removed, so table 3 represents a basic feasible solution to the original problem. Of course, this is not an optimal solution since P_1 can reduce the objective function further by replacing P_4 in the basis.

Table 4

i	Basis	C	P_0	−3	1	1	0	0	
				P_1	P_2	P_3	P_4	P_5	
1	P_1	−3	4	1	0	0	$\frac{1}{3}$	$-\frac{2}{3}$	
2	P_2	1	1	0	1	0	0	−1	
3	P_3	1	9	0	0	1	$\frac{2}{3}$	$-\frac{4}{3}$	
4			[−2]	0	0	0	$-\frac{1}{3}$	$-\frac{1}{3}$	

Tableau 4 is optimal, and the unique optimal solution is given by

$$x_1 = 4 \quad x_4 = 0$$
$$x_2 = 1 \quad x_5 = 0 \qquad Z_{min} = -2$$
$$x_3 = 9 \quad x_6 = x_7 = 0$$

Solution by 2-phase method

Phase 1: Min $W = x_6 + x_7$ where W is the artificial objective function to get initial solution to the original objective function Z.

Subject to

$$x_1 - 2x_2 + x_3 + x_4 = 11$$
$$-4x_1 + x_2 + 2x_3 - x_5 + x_6 = 3$$
$$-2x_1 + x_3 + x_7 = 1$$
$$x_{1 \text{ to } 7} \geq 0$$

Tableau 1 (Phase 1)

i	Basis	C	P_0	0	0	0	0	0	1	1	
				P_1	P_2	P_3	P_4	P_5	P_6	P_7	
1	P_4	0	11	1	-2	1	1	0	0	0	$\frac{11}{1} = 11$
2	P_6	1	3	-4	1	2	0	-1	1	0	$\frac{3}{2} = 1.5$
3	P_7	1	1	-2	0	(1)	0	0	0	1	$\frac{1}{1} = 1$ ← Min ← Key row
4			W = 4	-6	1	3	0	-1	0	0	

↑ Key Column (P_3)

Tableau 2 (Phase 1)

i	Basis	C	P_0	0	0	0	0	0	1	1	
				P_1	P_2	P_3	P_4	P_5	P_6	P_7	
1	P_4	0	10	3	-2	0	1	0	0	-1	
2	P_6	1	1	0	(1)	0	0	-1	1	-2	$\frac{1}{1} = 1$ ← Key row
3	P_3	0	1	-2	0	1	0	0	0	1	
4			W = 1	0	1	0	0	-1	0	-3	

↑ Key Column (P_2)

Tableau 3 (Phase 1)

i	Basis	C	P_0	0	0	0	0	0	1	1	
				P_1	P_2	P_3	P_4	P_5	P_6	P_7	
1	P_4	0	12	3	0	0	1	-2	2	-5	
2	P_2	0	1	0	1	0	0	-1	1	-2	
3	P_3	0	1	-2	0	1	0	0	0	1	
4			W = 0	0	0	0	0	0	-1	-1	

We now have an optimal solution to phase 1 linear programme given by

$$x_1 = 0, x_2 = 1, x_3 = 1, x_4 = 12, x_5 = 0, x_6 = 0 \text{ and } x_7 = 0, W_{min} = 0.$$

Since the artificial variables x_6 and x_7 are zero, this tableau represents a basic feasible solution to the original problem. We now begin phase 2 of the simplex method to find the optimal solution to the original problem. The initial tableau for phase 2 is constructed by deleting the column corresponding to the artificial variables, and computing the new $Z_j - C_j$ row coefficients with respect to the original objective function as shown.

$$Z = -3x_1 + x_2 + x_3$$

Tableau 1 (phase 2)

i	Basis	C	P_0	-3	1	1	0	0	
				P_1	P_2	P_3	P_4	P_5	
1	P_4	0	12	(3)	0	0	1	-2	$\frac{12}{3} = 4$ ← Min ← Key row
2	P_2	1	1	0	1	0	0	-1	$\frac{1}{0} = \infty$
3	P_3	1	1	-2	0	1	0	0	
4			Z = 2	1	0	0	0	-1	

↑ Key Column

Tableau 2 (phase 2)

i	Basis	C	P_0	-3	1	1	0	0	
				P_1	P_2	P_3	P_4	P_5	
1	P_1	-3	4	1	0	0	$\frac{1}{3}$	$-\frac{2}{3}$	
2	P_2	1	1	0	1	0	0	-1	
3	P_3	1	9	0	0	1	$\frac{2}{3}$	$-\frac{4}{3}$	
4			-2	0	0	0	$-\frac{1}{3}$	$-\frac{1}{3}$	

An optimal solution has been reached, and it is given by

$$x_1 = 4 \quad x_4 = 0$$
$$x_2 = 1 \quad x_5 = 0 \quad Z_{min} = -2$$
$$x_3 = 9.$$

3.4 UNRESTRICTED VARIABLES

Example 7

Maximize $Z = 3x_1 + 2x_2 + x_3$

Subject to

$$2x_1 + 5x_2 + x_3 = 12$$
$$3x_1 + 4x_2 = 11$$
$$x_2, x_3 \geq 0$$

x_1 is unrestricted.

Method of handling unrestricted variables

Assume $x_1 = x_1' - x_1''$ where $x_1', x_1'' \geq 0$

The problem changes to

Maximize $\quad Z = 3(x_1' - x_1'') + 2x_2 + x_3 = 3x_1' - 3x_1'' + 2x_2 + x_3$

Subject to

$$2x_1' - 2x_1'' + 5x_2 + x_3 = 12$$
$$3x_1' - 3x_1'' + 4x_2 = 11$$
$$x_1', x_1'', x_2 \text{ and } x_3 \text{ each} \geq 0$$

Then solve the above problem by Big '*M*' method.

3.5 ABSOLUTE CONSTRAINT

$|a_{11}x_1 + a_{12}x_2| \leq b$ can be converted into

$$a_{11}x_1 + a_{12}x_2 \leq b$$

and $\quad -a_{11}x_1 - a_{12}x_2 \leq b.$

3.6 GAUSS- JORDAN METHOD

The solution of simultaneous linear equations can be easily obtained by Gauss-Jordan method.

Example 8.

Obtain the solution of the system of simultaneous equations

$$x_1 + 2x_2 = 8$$
$$3x_1 + x_2 = 9$$

Solution:

Step 1: The augmented matrix is obtained as follows:

$$[A : b] = \begin{bmatrix} 1 & 2 & : & 8 \\ 3 & 1 & : & 9 \end{bmatrix}$$

Step 2:

$$(i)\ R_2 - 3R_1 = \begin{bmatrix} 1 & 2 & : & 8 \\ 0 & -5 & : & -15 \end{bmatrix}$$

$$(ii)\ \frac{R_2}{-5} = \begin{bmatrix} 1 & 2 & : & 8 \\ 0 & 1 & : & 3 \end{bmatrix}$$

$$(iii)\ R_1 - 2R_2 = \begin{bmatrix} 1 & 0 & : & 2 \\ 0 & 1 & : & 3 \end{bmatrix}$$

Step 3: Rewriting the set of equations, we have

$$\left.\begin{matrix} 1.x_1 + 0x_2 = 2 & \Rightarrow & x_1 = 2 \\ 0x_1 + 1x_2 = 3 & \Rightarrow & x_2 = 3 \end{matrix}\right\} \text{solution}$$

Example 9.

Solve the system of equations

$$x_1 + 2x_2 + x_4 = 7$$
$$x_2 + x_3 + x_4 + x_5 = 24$$
$$x_1 - 3x_3 + 2x_5 = 8$$

for x_1, x_3 and x_5 in terms of the remaining variables x_2 and x_4.

Solution:

$$\begin{matrix} & C_1 & C_2 & C_3 & C_4 & C_5 & & C_6 \\ & \downarrow & \downarrow & \downarrow & \downarrow & \downarrow & & \downarrow \\ R_1 \rightarrow & 1 & 2 & 0 & 1 & 0 & : & 7 \\ R_2 \rightarrow & 0 & 1 & 1 & 1 & 1 & : & 24 \\ R_3 \rightarrow & 1 & 0 & -3 & 0 & 2 & : & 8 \end{matrix}$$

Since the columns corresponding to variables x_1, x_3 and x_5 are indicated by C_1, C_3 and C_5 respectively, we operate rows R_1, R_2 and R_3 till the columns C_1, C_3 and C_5 becomes

$\begin{bmatrix} 1 \\ 0 \\ 0 \end{bmatrix}$, $\begin{bmatrix} 0 \\ 1 \\ 0 \end{bmatrix}$ and $\begin{bmatrix} 0 \\ 0 \\ 1 \end{bmatrix}$ respectively.

Thus

$$(i)\ R_3 - R_1 \Rightarrow \begin{bmatrix} 1 & 2 & 0 & 1 & 0 & : & 7 \\ 0 & 1 & 1 & 1 & 1 & : & 24 \\ 0 & -2 & -3 & -1 & 2 & : & 1 \end{bmatrix}$$

$$(ii)\ 3R_2 + R_3 \Rightarrow \begin{bmatrix} 1 & 2 & 0 & 1 & 0 & : & 7 \\ 0 & 1 & 1 & 1 & 1 & : & 24 \\ 0 & 1 & 0 & 2 & 5 & : & 73 \end{bmatrix}$$

$$(iii)\ \frac{R_3}{5} \Rightarrow \begin{bmatrix} 1 & 2 & 0 & 1 & 0 & : & 7 \\ 0 & 1 & 1 & 1 & 1 & : & 24 \\ 0 & 1/5 & 0 & 2/5 & 1 & : & 73/5 \end{bmatrix}$$

$$(iv)\ R_2 - R_3 \Rightarrow \begin{bmatrix} 1 & 2 & 0 & 1 & 0 & : & 7 \\ 0 & 4/5 & 1 & 3/5 & 0 & : & 47/5 \\ 0 & 1/5 & 0 & 2/5 & 1 & : & 73/5 \end{bmatrix}$$

Rewriting as a set of equation, we have

$$\left.\begin{aligned} x_1 + 2x_2 + x_4 &= 7 \\ \frac{4}{5}x_2 + x_3 + \frac{3}{5}x_4 &= 47/5 \\ \frac{1}{5}x_2 + \frac{2}{5}x_4 + x_5 &= 73/5 \end{aligned}\right\}.$$

Thus

$$x_1 = 7 - 2x_2 - x_4$$

$$x_3 = \frac{47}{5} - \frac{4}{5}x_2 - \frac{3}{5}x_4$$

$$x_5 = 73/5 - \frac{1}{5}x_2 - \frac{2}{5}x_4.$$

Chapter 4

TRANSPORTATION MODEL

4.1 INTRODUCTION

Transportation is a special class of Linear Programming problem. It is used to assign quantities of a single commodity from various origins to certain destinations. The objective in a transportation problem is to identify the transportation routes which result in either minimum cost or maximum profit. To achieve this objective, we must know the amount and location of the available supplies and the quantities demanded. In addition, we must know the cost or return that results from transporting one unit of resource from its origin to destination. Cost or return may be either independent or interdependent. We shall, however, consider in this problems as independent cost.

Let us express the above in a tabular form as given below:

i \ j	1	2	. . .	j	. . .	n	*Supply or availability*	
1	C_{11} X_{11}	C_{12} X_{12}	. . .	C_{1j} X_{1j}	. . .	C_{1n} X_{1n}	a_1	
2	C_{21} X_{21}	C_{22} X_{22}	. . .	C_{2j} X_{2j}	. . .	C_{2n} X_{2n}	a_2	
⋮							⋮	
i	. . .	. . .	. . .	C_{ij} X_{ij}	. . .	. . .	a_i	
⋮								
m	C_{m1} X_{m1}	. . .	. . .	C_{mj} X_{mj}		C_{mn} X_{mn}	a_m	
Demand	b_1	b_2		b_j		b_n		

Here C_{ij} = the cost of shipping one unit from i th origin to the j th destination.

and X_{ij} = the corresponding optimal amount that is to be transported.

Objective function:

Minimize $$Z = \sum_{i=1}^{m} \sum_{j=1}^{n} C_{ij} X_{ij} \quad (1)$$

Subject to $$\sum_{j=1}^{n} X_{ij} = a_i, \; i = 1, 2, \ldots m \quad (2)$$

$$\sum_{i=1}^{m} X_{ij} = b_j, \; j = 1, 2, \ldots n \quad (3)$$

and $$X_{ij} \geq 0 \quad (4)$$

In order that equations (2) and (3) are consistant, we must have

$$\sum_{i=1}^{m} \sum_{j=1}^{n} X_{ij} = \sum_{i=1}^{m} a_i \quad \text{and} \quad \sum_{j=1}^{n} \sum_{i=1}^{m} X_{ij} = \sum_{j=1}^{n} b_j$$

Thus $$\sum_{i=1}^{m} a_i = \sum_{j=1}^{n} b_j \quad (5)$$

The equation (5) shows that the sum of available supply is equal to the sum of the required demand and the transportation problem is said to be **balanced** transportation problem.

However if $\Sigma a_i > \Sigma b_i$ then we use dummy destination.

Example 1

(2 × 3) problem

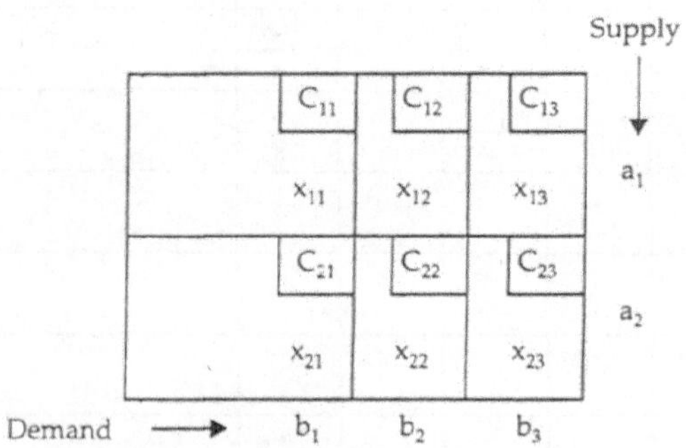

Let us assume this is a balanced transportation problem. So

$$a_1 + a_2 = b_1 + b_2 + b_3 \quad (1)$$

In the problem $m = 2$, $n = 3$, decision variables

$$m \times n = 2 \times 3 = 6$$

Objective function

Minimize $\quad Z = c_{11}x_{11} + c_{12}x_{12} + \ldots.. + c_{23}x_{23}$

Subject to $\quad x_{11} + x_{12} + x_{13} = a_1$

$$x_{21} + x_{22} + x_{23} = a_2$$
$$x_{11} + x_{21} = b_1$$
$$x_{12} + x_{22} = b_2$$
$$x_{13} + x_{23} = b_3$$

Summing the last three equations, we get

$$(x_{11} + x_{12} + x_{13}) + (x_{21} + x_{22} + x_{23}) = b_1 + b_2 + b_3$$

or
$$a_1 + (x_{21} + x_{22} + x_{23}) = a_1 + a_2$$

or
$$x_{21} + x_{22} + x_{23} = a_2$$

thus we get back the 2nd equation which is redundant. Thus we have $(m + n - 1)$ constraint equations in the system *i.e.*, here $(2 + 3 - 1) = 4$ constraint equations.

4.2 MODI METHOD (MODIFIED DISTRIBUTED METHOD)

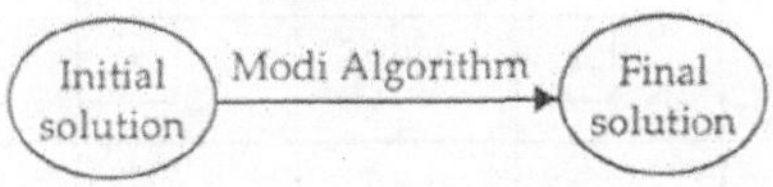

Initial solution by

North-West corner rule (N-W corner rule)

Vogel's approximation method (VAM)

4.2.1 N-W corner rule

In applying this rule, transportation costs are not taken into account.

Table 1

i \ j	1	2	3	4	5	6	Supply ↓
1	x_{11} 8	x_{12} 6	x_{13} 4	x_{14}	x_{15}	x_{16}	~~18~~ ~~10~~ ~~4~~
2	x_{21}	x_{22}	x_{23} 2	x_{24} 10	x_{25} 7	x_{26} 4	~~23~~ ~~21~~ ~~11~~ ~~4~~
3	x_{31}	x_{32}	x_{33}	x_{34}	x_{35}	x_{36} 6	~~6~~
Demand →	~~8~~	~~6~~	~~6~~ ~~2~~	~~10~~	~~7~~	~~10~~ ~~6~~	47 / 47

As total demand = total supply this is a balanced transportation problem.

We start by considering the north-west cell of transportation matrix and locate as much as possible by comparing the supply and demand (minimum of supply and demand) we continue in this manner by satisfying the rim condition till we reach the south-east corner. We next check whether there are $(m + n - 1)$ allocations in independent positions.

Solution of Table 1: The N-W corner variable is x_{11}, value of which is set at 8 (8 being smaller of 8 and 18). It implies that the demand of the first destination is satisfied and thus x_{21} and x_{31} are zero. The next N-W corner available is x_{12} and the maximum value that can be assigned to this variable is 6 (6 being smaller of the demand of second destination 6 and the remaining supply with 1st origin 10) we proceed in this manner to reach the south-east corner variable x_{36} which has been assigned a value of 6. The variables of the cells where nothing has been allocated have zero values. We now check for number of allocated cells and their positions. We find that required number $(3 + 6 - 1) = 8$ of allocations have been made in independent positions and thus the above allocation may serve as a feasible initial solution.

4.2.2 VAM

This method is more powerful. Vogel's approximation method gives a better initial solution. It takes into account not only the least cost (C_{ij}) but also the costs that just exceed C_{ij}. The steps of this method are as follows:

Table 1

					Supply
1	2	3	11	7	6 [1] ↓
2	1	0	6	1 1	1 [1]
3	5	8	15	9	10 [3]
Requirement →	7	5	3	~~2~~, 1	
	[1]	[3]	[5]	[6] ↑	

Sub step 1: Write down the cost matrix as shown in table (1). Enter the difference between the smallest and second smallest elements in each column below the corresponding column; and the difference between the smallest and second smallest elements in each row to the right of the row. Put these numbers in parenthesis. For example, In column 1 of table (1), the two lowest elements are 1 and 2 and their difference is 1 which is written as [1] below column 1. Similarly, the two smallest elements in row 2 are 0 and 1 and their difference 1 is entered as [1] to the right of row 2. A row or column "difference" indicates the unit penalty incurred by failing to make an allocation to the smallest cost cell in that row or column.

Sub step 2: Select the row or column with the greatest difference and allocate as much as possible within the restrictions of the rim conditions (supply and requirement conditions) to the lowest cost cell in the row or column selected. Thus in table (1), [6] is the greatest number in parenthesis, we choose column 4 and allocate as much as possible to the cell (2, 4) since supply is 1 while demand is 2, the maximum possible allocation is 1.

Sub step 3: Cross out the row or column (here row 2) completely satisfied by the allocation just made. In table (1) row 2 is crossed out and shrunken matrix is written in table (2).

Table 2

(2)	(3) 5	(11)	(7)	~~6~~, 1 [1]
(5)	(8)	(15)	(9)	10 [3]
7 [3]	5 [5] ↑	3 [4]	1 [2]	

In table (2), the matrix consists of rows and columns where allocations have not yet been made, including revised row and column totals which take the already made allocation into account.

Sub step 4: Repeat steps 1 to 3 until all assignments have been made.

Table 3

(2) 1	(11)	(7)	1 [5] ←
(5)	(15)	(9)	10 [4]
~~7~~, 6 [3]	3 [4]	1 [2]	

Table 4

(5) 6	(15) 3	(9) 1	10
6	3	1	

Thus all allocations made during the above procedure are shown below in the allocation matrix.

Table 5

(2) 1	(3) 5	(11)	(7)	6
(1)	(0)	(6)	(1) 1	1
(5) 6	(8)	(15) 3	(9) 1	10
7	5	3	2	

The above repetitions can be made in a single matrix as shown below:

					Supply / Penalties
	2 / 1	3 / 5	11	7	6 [1] [1] [5] ←
	1	0	6	1 / 1	1 [1]
	5 / 6	8	15 / 3	9 / 1	10 [3] [3] [4]
Demand	~~7~~, ~~6~~	5	5	~~2~~, ~~1~~	
Penalties	[1] [3] [3]	[3] [5] ↑	[5] [4] [4]	[6] ↑ [2] [2]	

Transportation cost Z for initial solution is given by

$$= \text{Rs. } \{(2 \times 1) + (3 \times 5) + (1 \times 1) + (5 \times 6) + (3 \times 15) + (9 \times 1)\}$$

$$= \text{Rs. } 102$$

4.2.3 Modified Distribution Method (MODI Method)

For any basic feasible solutions numbers u_i and v_j can be found such that for those x_{ij} in the basic solution; we have

$$u_i + v_j = C_{ij}$$

If $u_i + v_j = \overline{C}_{ij}$ for those variables not in the basic solution (unoccupied cells) and if all $\overline{C}_{ij} - C_{ij} = 0$ then the basic feasible solution is also a minimum solution.

For illustration, we consider the table below

u_i \ v_j	$v_1 = 10$	$v_2 = 0$	$v_3 = -5$	$v_4 = 8$
$u_1 = 0$	10 / (12) + θ	10	30	8 / (8) − θ
$u_2 = 10$	16 / 4	9 / 1	5 / (14)	26
$u_3 = 12$	22 / (4) − θ	12 / (16)	7 / (10)	15 / 5 + θ ↑ Maximum positive

We first put v_j's and u_i's in the head row and column. In order to determine u_i and v_j, we have the following:

$$
\begin{array}{ll}
\text{Let} & u_1 = 0 \\
u_1 + v_1 = 10 \quad \therefore & v_1 = 10 \\
u_1 + v_4 = 8 & v_4 = 8 \\
u_2 + v_3 = 5 & u_3 = 12 \\
u_3 + v_1 = 22 & v_2 = 0 \\
u_3 + v_2 = 12 & v_3 = -5 \\
u_3 + v_3 = 7 & u_2 = 10
\end{array}
$$

We next find $\overline{C}_{ij} = u_i + v_j$ for all cells obviously for alloted cells $\overline{C}_{ij} = C_{ij}$, for empty cells, it may have a different value. We next compute $(\overline{C}_{ij} - C_{ij})$. For alloted cells, this is zero and for empty cells, they may be either positive, zero or negative. A positive value of $(\overline{C}_{ij} - C_{ij})$ in an empty cell indicates that if a revised solution is prepared by making an allocation in that cell, transportation cost will go down. For one unit of allocation, cost will go down by $(\overline{C}_{ij} - C_{ij})$. A zero value of $(\overline{C}_{ij} - C_{ij})$ implies that the present solution is optimum but alternate optimum solution is available. A negative value shows that the current solution is optimum and no further improvement is possible.

For obvious reasons, only the positive values of $(\overline{C}_{ij} - C_{ij})$ are written at the top left hand corner of empty cells and we take maximum $(\overline{C}_{ij} - C_{ij}) > 0$ variable to be entering into solution at maximum possible value. $(\overline{C}_{ij} - C_{ij})$ values are indicated in the table below with the cell marked asterisk or (θ) or to be entering into the next revised solution.

Example 2

(3 × 4) type problem. Find out the minimum total cost of transportation. Use VAM for initial solution.

					Supply ↓
	10	10	30	8	20
	16	9	5	26	14
	22	12	7	15	30
Demand →	16	16	24	8	64 / 64

Balanced problem

VAM

Table 1

				Supply
[10] 12	[10]	[30]	[8] 8	20 [2] [0]
[16] 4	[9] 10	[5]	[26]	14 [4] [4] [4] [4]
[22]	[12] 6	[7] 24	[15]	30 [5] [5] [5] [5] ←
16	16	24	8	
[6]	[1]	[2]	[7]	
[6]	[1]	[2]	↑	
↑				
[6]	[3]	[2]		
↑	[3]	[2]		

Modi Algorithm

Table 2

u_i \ v_j	$v_1 = 10$	$v_2 = 3$	$v_3 = -2$	$v_4 = 8$
$u_1 = 0$	[10] $12 + \theta$	[10]	[30]	[8] $8 - \theta$
$u_2 = 6$	[16] $4 - \theta$	[9] $10 + \theta$	[5]	[26]
$u_3 = 9$	[22]	[12] $6 - \theta$	[7] 24	2 [15] θ

$\overline{C}_{ij} - C_{ij} = 2$ Maximum positive put θ here.

See that the loop corners are in θ, $u_i + v_j = C_{ij}$. Where cost coefficient is 15 *i.e.*, at (3, 4) cell, we find $\overline{C}_{ij} - C_{ij} = 2$ which is maximum positive number, we put here θ.

In table 2 we find that as θ should be as high as possible ($\theta \geq 0$), the value of θ is 4 (four). By putting $\theta = 4$, we form table 3.

Table 3

u_i \ v_j	$v_1 = 10$	$v_2 = 5$	$v_3 = 0$	$v_4 = 8$
$u_1 = 0$	[10] 16	[10]	[30]	[8] 4
$u_2 = 4$	[16]	[9] 14	[5]	[26]
$u_3 = 7$	[22]	[12] 2	[7] 24	[15] 4

In table 3 we find that $\overline{C}_{ij} - C_{ij} < 0$. Thus this is the optimum solution.

Total cost = Z_{min} = (16 × 10) + (4 × 8) + (14 × 9) + (2 × 12) + (24 × 7) + (4 × 15)

= 160 + 32 + 126 + 24 + 168 + 60 = Rs. 570. **Ans.**

Example 3

Three refineries with maximum daily capacity of 6, 5 and 8 millions gallons of gasoline supply to three distribution areas with daily demand of 4, 8 and 7 millions gallons. Gasoline is transported to the distribution areas through a network of pipe lines. The mileage table summarised below shows the length of different pipe lines.

Refinery \ Distribution area	1	2	3
1	120	180	—
2	300	100	80
3	200	250	120

The transportation cost is estimated based on the length of the pipe line at about Re. 1.0 per 100 gallons per kilometer. Determine the optimal transportation schedule.

Solution:

This is a balanced problem. Let us find out the initial solution by VAM.

Table 1

	1	2	3	Supply
1	[120] 4	[180] 2	[∝]	61 [60] [60] [60]
2	[300]	[100] 5	[80]	5 [20]
3	[200]	[250] 1	[120] 7	8 [80] [80] [50]
Demand →	4 [80] [80] [80] ↑	8 [80] ↑ [80] [70]	7 [40] [120] ↑	

Table 2

u_i \ v_j	$v_1 = 120$	$v_2 = 180$	$v_3 = 50$
$u_1 = 0$	[120] 4	[180] 2	[∝]
$u_2 = -80$	[300]	[100] 5	[80]
$u_3 = 70$	[200]	[250] 1	[120] 7

In table 2 we find that $\overline{C}_{ij} - C_{ij} < 0$. Thus VAM sometimes gives optimum solution.

Table 2 is the optimum table.

Total cost = 10^4 (4 × 120 + 2 × 180 + 5 × 100 + 1 × 250 + 7 × 120)

= Rs. 2430 × 10^4 Ans.

Example 4

A farmer has three firms A, B, and C which need respectively 100, 300 and 50 units of water annually. There are two methods of irrigation namely canel and tube well apart from rain. The canel can supply 150 units and tube well 200 units while the balance is left at the mercy of nature. The following table shows cost per unit of water in a dry season when the rains totally fail. Find how the canel and tube well water should be utilized to minimize the total cost of irrigation.

	A	B	C
Canel	3	5	7
Tube well	6	4	10
Failure of rain	8	10	3

Solution:

We apply VAM to table 1 for initial solution.

Table 1

	[3] 100	[5] 50	[7]	150 [2] [2]
	[6]	[4] 200	[10]	200 [2] [2]
	[8]	[10] 50	[3] 50	100 [5] ← [2]
	100 [3] [3] ↑	300 [1] [1]	50 [4]	

Table 2 (also final table)

u_i \ v_j	$v_1 = 3$	$v_2 = 5$	$v_3 = -2$
$u_1 = 0$	[3] 100	[5] 50	[7]
$u_2 = -1$	[6]	[4] 200	[19]
$u_3 = 5$	[8]	[10] 50	[3] 50

Total cost = 100 × 3 + 50 × 5 + 200 × 4 + 50 × 10 + 50 × 3

(Minimum) = 300 + 250 + 800 + 500 + 150

= Rs. 2000 **Ans.**

Example 5

(*a*) *Solve the problem given in 4.2.2 by N-W corner rule and then apply MODI to reach optimum solution.*

(*b*) *Apply MODI to VAM initial solution to reach optimum solution.*

Solution:

(*a*) N-W rule: Start in the North-West corner of whole table.

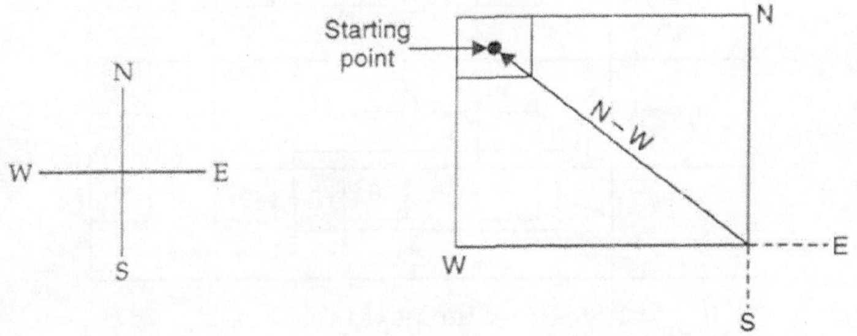

Procedure:

(*i*) In starting square fulfil the demand (D) or supply (S) which is minimum. In our case it is 6.

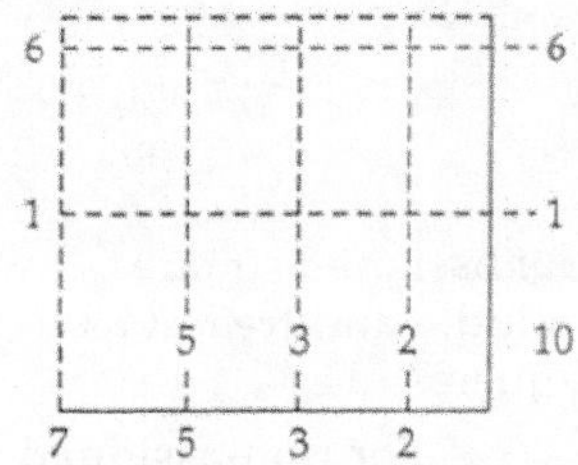

(*ii*) If $D > S$ proceed vertically downward and fulfil the next square. In our case 1 is put here.

(*iii*) If $D < S$ proceed horizontally right. In our case 5, 3, 2 are put to satisfy demand and supply.

(*iv*) If $D = S$ proceed diagonally.

(*v*) The number thus obtained should be put in the original matrix spaces (within the centre of the small square accordingly).

Please note that we have not taken into account the cost coefficient in N-W corner rule.

The initial table 1 thus obtained by N-W corner rule is given below:

Table 1

				Supply
2 / 6	3	11	7	6
1 / 1	0	6	1	1
5	8 / 5	15 / 3	9 / 2	10
7	5	3	2	

$$\text{Total cost} = 6 \times 2 + 1 \times 1 + 5 \times 8 + 3 \times 15 + 2 \times 9$$
$$= 12 + 1 + 40 + 45 + 18 = \text{Rs. } 116.$$

(Note that we have already achieved Rs. 102 as total cost in VAM's initial solution. So VAM method is more powerful than N-W corner method)

Now we apply **MODI method** taking initial solution by N-W corner rule.

Table 2

u_i \ v_j	$v_1 = 2$	$v_2 = 5$	$v_3 = 12$	$v_4 = 6$
$u_1 = 0$	2 / 6	(2) 3	(1) 11	7
$u_2 = -1$	1 / $1-\theta$	(4) 0	(5) 6 / θ	(4) 1
$u_3 = 3$	5 / $\varepsilon + \theta$	8 / 5	15 / $3-\theta$	9 / 2

$\theta_{max} = 1$ we draw the next table.

For assigned squares:

C_{ij} = unit transportation cost from i to j

$\overline{C}_{ij} = u_i + v_j$

$C_{ij} = \overline{C}_{ij}$

for assigned squares. If we can not further proceed then we put ε for non-assigned squares at the middle and treat it as if assigned ε is a very very small number. Then proceed for non-assigned squares.

For non-assigned squares: ε is already put, then we calculate the square where θ is to be put. θ is any positive number. This θ is put in non-assigned square first. Proceed $u_i + v_j - C_{ij} > 0$. If

$u_i + v_j - C_{ij} < 0$, do not put anything. In our case θ is put first in the cell where cost coefficient is 6, here the $u_i + v_j - C_{ij}$ is maximum *i.e.*, 5. Then we put in other places satisfying the demand and supply requirements.

Then find the maximum value of θ. Here in our case for table 2; $\theta_{max} = 1$ and draw the table 3

Put $\varepsilon = 0$ and $\theta = 1$

Table 3

u_i \ v_j	$v_1 = 2$	$v_2 = 5$	$v_3 = 12$	$v_4 = 6$
$u_1 = 0$	2; 6 − θ	[2] 3; θ	[1] 11	7
$u_2 = -6$	1	0	6; 1	1
$u_3 = 3$	5; 1 + θ	8; 5 − θ	15; 2	9; 2

Total cost = Rs. 111

$\theta_{max} = 5$

Table 4

u_i \ v_j	$v_1 = 2$	$v_2 = 3$	$v_3 = 12$	$v_4 = 6$
$u_1 = 0$	2; 1 − θ	3; 5	[1] 11; θ	7
$u_2 = -6$	1	0	6; 1	1
$u_3 = 3$	5; 6 + θ	8	15; 2 − θ	9; 2

Total cost $= 1 \times 2 + 5 \times 3 + 1 \times 6 + 6 \times 5 + 2 \times 15 + 2 \times 9$

$= 2 + 15 + 6 + 30 + 30 + 18$

$=$ Rs. 101

$\theta_{max} = 1$ we go for table 5

Table 5

u_i \ v_j	$v_1 = 1$	$v_2 = 3$	$v_3 = 11$	$v_4 = 5$
$u_1 = 0$	[2]	[3] 5	[11] 1	[7]
$u_2 = -5$	[1]	[0]	[6] 1	[1]
$u_3 = 4$	[5] 7	[8]	[15] 1	[9] 2

Table 5 is the final table.

Total cost $= 5 \times 3 + 1 \times 11 + 1 \times 6 + 7 \times 5 + 1 \times 15 + 2 \times 9$

$= 15 + 11 + 6 + 35 + 15 + 18$

$=$ Rs. 100 **Ans.**

Solution:

(*b*) From table 5 of section 4.2.2, we get

Table 1

u_i \ v_j	$v_1 = 2$	$v_2 = 3$	$v_3 = 12$	$v_4 = 6$
$u_1 = 0$	[2] $1 - \theta$	[3] 5	1 ¦ [11] θ	[7]
$u_2 = -5$	[1]	[0]	1 ¦ [6]	[1] 1
$u_3 = 3$	[5] $6 + \theta$	[8]	[15] $3 - \theta$	[9] 1

$\theta_{max} = 1$

Table 2 is drawn by putting $\theta = 1$ in table 1

Table 2

u_i \ v_j	$v_1 = 1$	$v_2 = 3$	$v_3 = 11$	$v_4 = 5$
$u_1 = 0$	[2]	[3] 5	[11] 1	[7]
$u_2 = -4$	[1]	[0]	1 [6] θ	0 [1] 1 − θ
$u_3 = 4$	[5] 7	[8]	[15] 2 − θ	[9] 1 + θ

$\theta_{max} = 1$. The next table is as follows.

Table 3

u_i \ v_j	$v_1 = 1$	$v_2 = 3$	$v_3 = 11$	$v_4 = 5$	
$u_1 = 0$	[2]	[3] 5	[11] 1	[7]	6
$u_2 = -5$	[1]	[0]	[6] 1	[1]	1
$u_3 = 4$	[5] 7	[8]	[15] 1	[9] 2	10
	7	5	3	2	

Table 3 is the final table.

Total cost $= 5 \times 3 + 1 \times 11 + 1 \times 6 + 7 \times 5 + 1 \times 15 + 2 \times 19$

$= 15 + 11 + 6 + 35 + 15 + 18$

= Rs. 100.

4.3 UNBALANCED TRANSPORTATION PROBLEM

A transportation problem is said to be unbalanced when the total supply or capacity is greater or less than the total demand or requirement. We solve this type of problem by introducing dummy row or column. If the demand is more than supply a dummy row or source is added and the excess quantity is entered in the supply column (or supply side). And if the supply is more than the demand, a dummy column or destination is added; the excess quantity is entered in the demand row (or demand side). In both the cases unit cost of transportation in the dummy cells is taken as zero.

Example 6

Find out the minimum total cost of transportation

Factories \ Stores					Supply
	4	6	8	13	50
	13	11	10	8	70
	14	4	10	13	30
	9	11	13	8	50
Demand →	25	35	105	20	200 = Total supply / 185 = Total demand

In the matrix unit costs of transportation is given.

Here Total supply = 200

Total demand = 185

Surplus = 15

Here the total supply exceeds demand by 15 units. So this is unbalanced transportation problem. Thus one more store is added as dummy destination.

We use VAM

Table 1

					Dummy store	supply
	4 (25)	6 (5)	8 (20)	13	0	50 [4] [2] [2] [2] [5] ←
	13	11	10 (70)	8	0	70 [8] [2] [2] [2] [2] [2]
	14	4 (30)	10	13	0	30 [4] [6] ←
	9	11	13 (15)	8 (20)	0 (15)	50 [8] [1] [1] [3] [5] [5] ←
Demand →	25	35	105	20	15 ↑ Surplus added (8-8) in the column	200 / 200
	[5] [5] [5] ↑	[2] [2] [5] [5] ↑	[2] [2] [2] [2] [2] [3]	[0] [0] [0] [0] [0] [0]	[0]	

Table 1 shows the initial feasible solution.

From the above matrix we find that

(*i*) Number of allocations = 8 = $m + n - 1 = 4 + 5 - 1 = 8$

(*ii*) These 8 allocations are in the independent positions

Therefore optimality test can be performed.

Table 2

u_i \ v_j	$v_1 = 4$	$v_2 = 6$	$v_3 = 8$	$v_4 = 3$	$v_5 = -5$
$u_1 = 0$	[4] 25	[6] 5	[8] 20	[13]	[0]
$u_2 = 2$	[13]	[11]	[10] 70	[8]	[0]
$u_3 = -2$	[14]	[4] 30	[10]	[13]	[0]
$u_4 = 5$	[9]	[11]	[13] 15	[8] 20	[0] 15

The table 2 is the optimum table because $\overline{C}_{ij} - C_{ij} \leq 0$.

Total cost (minimum) of transportation is

$= 25 \times 4 + 5 \times 6 + 70 \times 10 + 20 \times 8 + 30 \times 4 + 15 \times 13 + 20 \times 8 + 15 \times 0$

$= 100 + 30 + 700 + 160 + 120 + 195 + 160 + 0$

= Rs. 1465.

4.4 LOWEST COST ENTRY METHOD FOR INITIAL FEASIBLE SOLUTION

The unit cost of each cell is taken into account. We allot to the cell with least cost of transportation by comparing its demand and supply amounts. Maximum possible *i.e.*, the minimum of demand and supply is entered to this least cost cell. Again we search for next lowest cost empty cell for which demand or supply is not fully exhausted. This process continues till total demand and supply is exhausted.

Example 7

The following table gives the factory to warehouse shipping costs in rupees, quantities available at each of the factories X, Y and Z and requirements at each of the warehouses A, B, C and D. Determine initial feasible solution by the lowest cost entry method.

Warehouse / Factory	A	B	C	D	Supply ↓
X	3	2	5	2 15	15
Y	2	1 12	4 12	4	~~24~~, ~~12~~, 0
Z	2 13	3	4 4	3 4	21
Demand →	~~13~~	~~12~~	~~16~~ ~~4~~	~~19~~ ~~4~~	60 60

Solution:

(1) The lowest cost of Re. 1 is in cell (2, 2) where demand (12) and supply 24. So we allot 12 units to cell (2, 2).

(2) The next lowest cost is Rs. 2 in cells (1, 2), (1, 4), (2, 1) and (3, 1). But we can not allocate to cell (1, 2) as the demand for B is exhausted. Now we see that demand of cell (2, 1) *i.e.*, 13 is more than available supply of 24 – 12 = 12 units. For cell (1, 4) demand 19 > supply 15 and for cell (3, 1) demand 13 < supply 21. Out of these maximum amount of 15 units can be alloted to cell (1, 4) only. So we choose cell (1, 4) and allocate 15 units to it and proceed this way.

Note: The unbalanced problem is converted into balanced problem by introducing a dummy plant or warehouse depending on the situation.

Case (*i*) An extra warehouse is added to table if supply is more than demand. In this case surplus supply is allocated to this dummy warehouse with transportation cost per unit from each plant to this warehouse is taken as zero.

Case (*ii*) An extra plant is added to the table if demand is more than supply. The extra demand is taken as the supply available at the dummy plant with cost of transportation from this plant to each warehouse is taken equal to zero.

Note: In a $(m \times n)$ transportation problem the solution is said to be feasible if $(m + n - 1)$ cells are occupied.

4.5 THE STEPPING-STONE METHOD (FOR OPTIMUM SOLUTION) AND INITIAL SOLUTION BY VAM

Table 1

Plant \ Warehouse	1	2	3	4	Supply
1	cost 2; (1 + 1)	cost 3; (5 − 1)	cost 11	cost 7	6
2	cost 1; 1(− 1)	cost 0; (+ 1)	cost 6	cost 1; 1	1 + 1 = 2
3	cost 5; 6	cost 8	cost 15; 3	cost 9; 1	10
Demand →	7 + 1 = 8	5	3	2	

The cost coefficients are in 100 i.e., (1, 1) = 200 etc.

Consider the matrix above giving the first feasible solution for the problem under consideration. Let us start with any arbitrary empty cell (a cell without allocation), say (2, 2) and allocate + 1 unit to this cell. As already discussed, in order to keep up the column 2 restriction, − 1 must be allocated to cell (1, 2) and to keep up the row 1 restriction, + 1 must be allocated to cell (1, 1) and subsequently − 1 must be allocated to cell (2, 1); this is shown in the matrix above. The net change in transportation cost as a result of this perturbation is called the evaluation of the empty cell in question.

$\therefore$ Evaluation of cell (2, 2) $= 100\{(0 \times 1) + 3 \times (-1) + 2\,(1) + 1\,(-1)\}$

$= 100\,(-3 + 2 - 1)$

$= -200$ (Rs.)

Naturally, as a result of perturbation, the transportation cost decreases by Rs. 200. Now the total number of cells will be $mn - (m + n - 1) = (m - 1)(n - 1)$. Therefore there are $(m - 1)(n - 1)$ such cell evaluations which must be calculated. If any cell evaluation is negative, the cost can be reduced so that the solution under consideration can be improved *i.e.*, it is not optimal. On the other hand, if all the cell evaluations are positive or zero, the solution in question must be optimal.

Example 8

"The Stepping-Stone Method"

"Stepping Stone" name is derived from comparing a transportation table to a pond. The basic or occupied cells are called stone square and unoccupied or non-basic cells are termed as water squares. Moving through occupied cells is visualized as stepping through stone squares. In this method, a path is sought from an occupied cell through the stepping stones and back.

An initial solution by N-W corner rule to a transportation problem is shown below. We are to find out whether further improvement in allocation is possible or not by stepping stone method.

From \ To	D	E	F	Capacity
A	80 [5]	20 [10]	[2]	100
B	[3]	10 [7]	15 [5]	25
C	[6]	[8]	75 [4]	75
Requirement	80	30	90	200

Balanced problem

Solution:

In the present position the transportation cost

$$T.C = (80 \times 5) + (20 \times 10) + (10 \times 7) + (15 \times 5) + (75 \times 4)$$
$$= \text{Rs. } 1045.$$

1st step: We start our investigation from the empty space *AF* (we can start conveniently from any empty space). Put + 1 in (*AF*), then to balance the row requirement we are putting (– 1) to (A, E), *i.e.*, make it 20 – 1 = 19. Again to balance column requirement, in (*B*, *E*) we put + 1 *i.e.*, 10 + 1 = 11 and again to make up for row requirement, in (*B*, *F*) we put (– 1) *i.e.*, 15 – 1 = 14.

The net result in this process = (+ 1 × 2) + (– 1) × 10 + (1) × 7 + (– 1) 5 = – 6

That is a saving of Rs. 6 in the loop (13 – 12 – 22 – 23). This is shown in Fig. 1.

Now we start from the other empty space and complete loop to calculate cost.

From \ To	D	E	F	Capacity
A	80 [5]	19 [10]	1 Start [2]	100
B	[3]	11 [7]	14 [5]	25
C	[6]	[8]	75 [4]	75
Requirement	80	30	90	200

Fig. 1 (*a*)

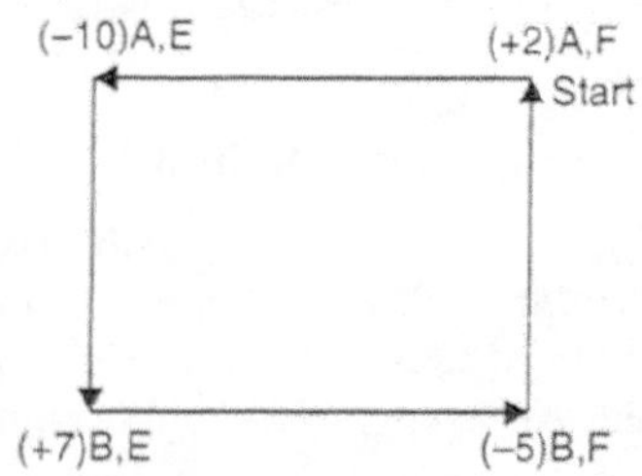

Fig. 1 (*b*)

2nd step (Fig. 2)

Result for Fig. 2 = + 3 − 5 + 10 − 7

= + 1 (adding cost)

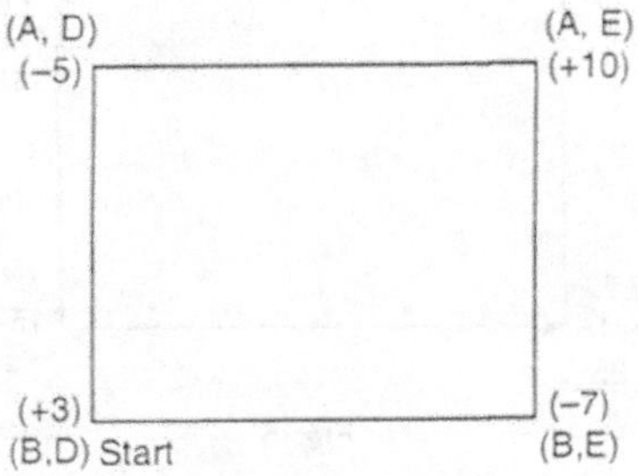

Fig. 2

3rd step (Fig. 3)

Result for Fig. 3 = + 6 − 4 + 5 − 7 + 10 − 5

= + 5 (adding cost)

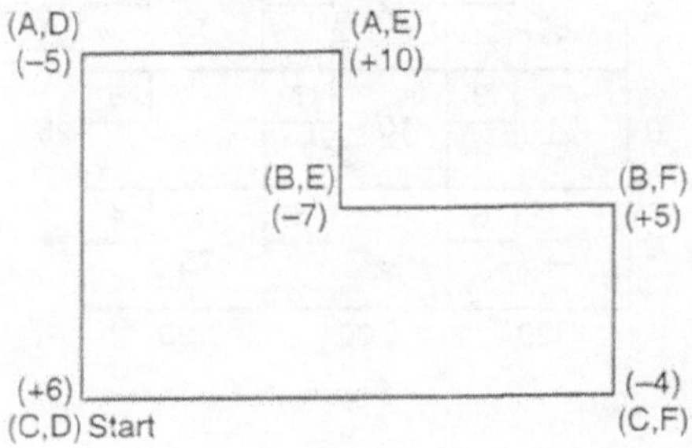

Fig. 3

4th step (Fig. 4)

Result = + 8 − 4 + 5 − 7

= + 2 (adding cost)

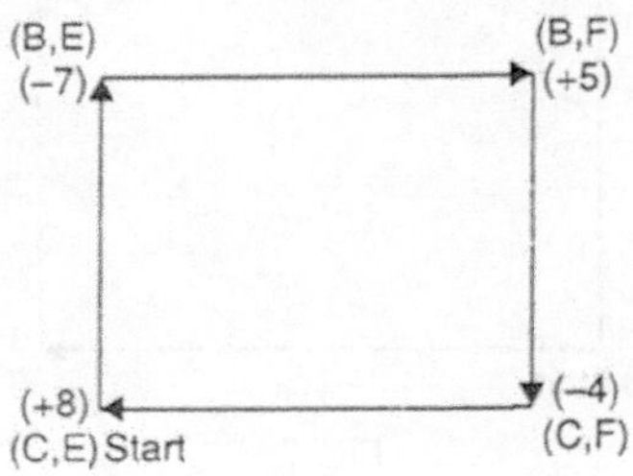

Fig. 4

With the above results we see that loop obtained in the first step is profitable. Hence we can transfer min {(*B*, *F*), (*A*, *E*)} = min (15, 20) = 15 to starting point (*A*, *F*) and adjust other squares accordingly. It is shown in Fig. 5 and 6 (Go clockwise or anticlockwise it is all the same)

$$T.C = (80 \times 5) + (5 \times 10) + (15 \times 2) + (25 \times 7) + (75 \times 4)$$
$$= \text{Rs. } 955.$$

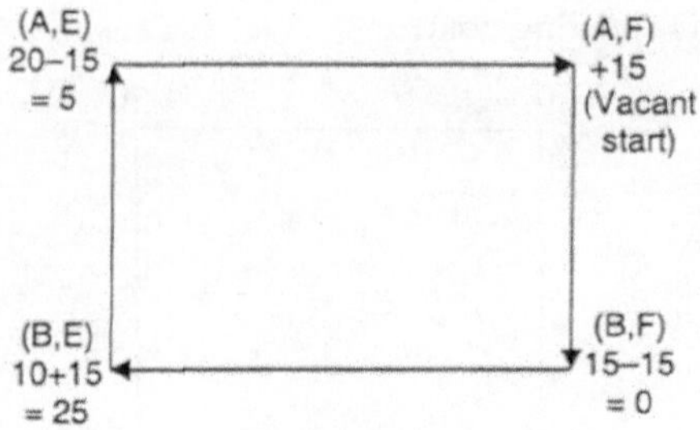

Fig. 5

Filled up values

Thus

A saving of Rs. 1045 – Rs. 955 = Rs. 90 is obtained from the above solution.

	D	E	F	
A	(5) 80	(10) ~~20~~ 5	(2) 15	100
B	(3) —	(7) ~~10~~ 25	(5)	25
C	(6) —	(8) —	(4) 75	75
	80	30	90	

Fig. 6

Now we investigate empty cells of Fig. 6.

5th Step (Fig. 7)

Result = + 6 – 4 + 2 – 5 = – 1

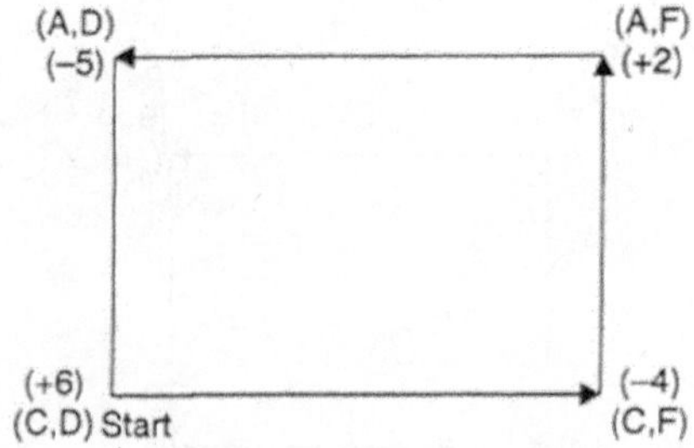

Fig. 7

6th Step (Fig. 8)

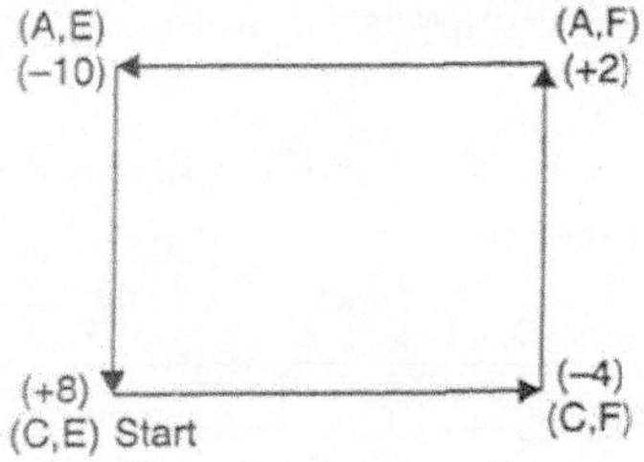

Fig. 8

Result = + 8 − 4 + 2 − 10 = − 4

For cell *BF* result = (5 + 10) − (7 + 2) = + 6 (no use)

For cell BD result = (3 + 10) − (7 + 5) = + 1 (no use)

The loop of Fig. 8 is preferred. Transfer 5 (min of 5, 75) to the empty cell (*C*, *E*) and adjust other squares accordingly. See Fig. 9 and 10.

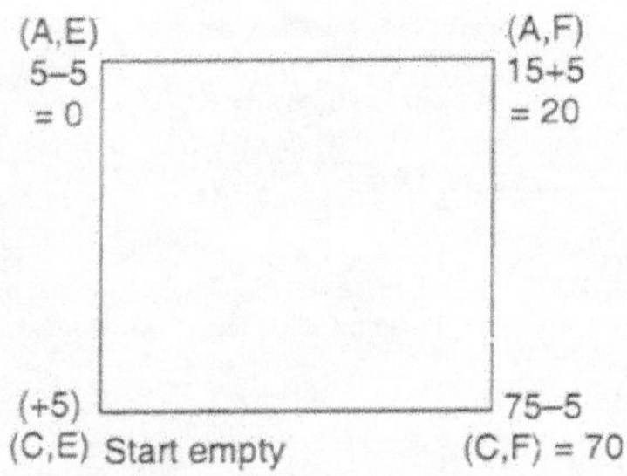

Fig. 9. Filled up values

	D	E	F	
A	80 [5]	~~5~~ [10]	~~15~~ 20 [2]	100
B	[3]	25 [7]	[5]	25
C	[6]	5 [8]	~~75~~ 70 [4]	75
	80	30	90	

Fig. 10

T.C. = (80 × 5) + (20 × 2) + (25 × 7) + (5 × 8) + (70 × 4) = Rs. 935 *i.e.*, further reduction.

Still we go for the other combination

For cell *BF* result = (5 + 8) − (7 + 4) = + 2 (no use)

For cell *AE* result = (10 + 4) − (8 + 2) = + 4 (no use)

7th step (Fig. 11)

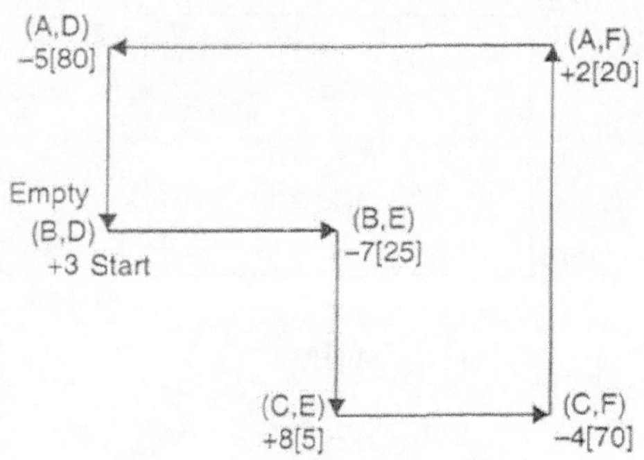

Filled up values are shown in [ ]

Fig. 11

Result = 3 − 7 + 8 − 4 + 2 − 5 = − 3

So loop of the 7th step is chosen. Shift 25 *i.e.*, min of (80, 25, 70) to the empty cell (*B*, *D*) and adjust the others accordingly (see Fig. 12).

T.C. = (55 × 5) + (45 × 2) + (25 × 3) + (30 × 8) + (45 × 4)

= 860 (further reduction)

	D	E	F
A	[5] 80–25 = 55	[10]	[2] 20+25 = 45
B	[3] +25	[7] 25–25 = 0	[5]
C	[6]	[8] 5+25 = 30	[4] 70–25 = 45

Fig. 12

9th step (Fig. 13): Again to choose empty square.

Result = 6 − 4 + 2 − 5 = − 1

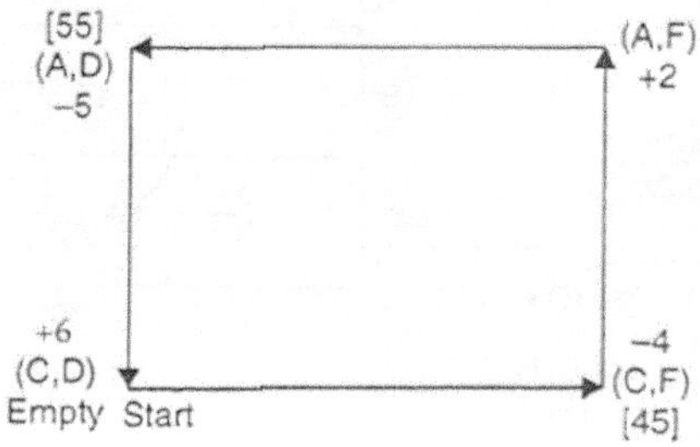

Fig. 13

10th step (Fig. 14)

Result = 10 − 2 + 4 − 8 = + 4

Fig. 14

11th step (Fig. 15)

Result = 5 – 2 + 5 – 3 = + 5

For cell *BE* result = (7 + 4 – 5) – (8 + 2 + 3) = + 3 (no use)

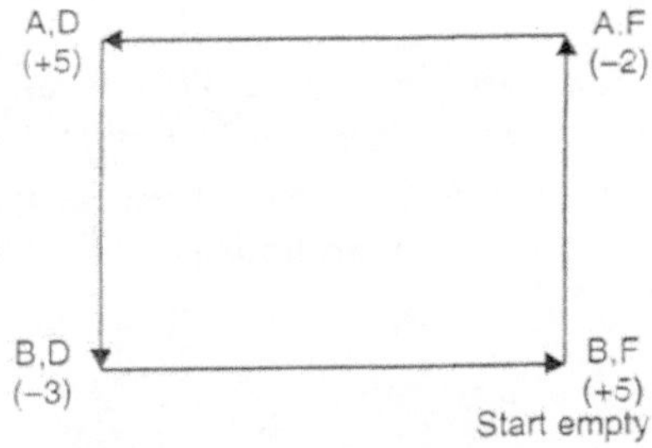

Fig. 15

It is evident that loop of the 9th step will be chosen. Shift 45 (min 45, 55) to (*CD*) and adjust squares suitably. See Fig. 16.

	D	E	F	
A	cost 5; 10	cost 10	cost 2; 90	100
B	cost 3; 25	cost 7	cost 5	25
C	cost 6; 45	cost 8; 30	cost 4	75
	80	30	90	

Fig. 16

T.C. = (10 × 5) + (90 × 2) + (25 × 3) + (45 × 6) + (30 × 8)

= Rs. 815 (Further reduction)

In order to see whether further improvement can be made, let us choose other unused squares cell *CF* = + 1, cell *AE* = + 3, cell *BF* = + 5, cell *BE* = + 2. Hence Fig. 16 is the optimal solution.

4.6 DEGENERACY IN TRANSPORTATION PROBLEM

Any solution of a transportation problem is said to be feasible if there are $(m + n - 1)$ occupied cells in the solution, m is the number of rows and n is the number of columns in the problem. Whenever the number of occupied cells at the initial solution or during the course of the improved solution is less than $(m + n - 1)$ then the problem is said to degenerate. The degeneracy during the process of improving the solution can occur when we have to vacate two or more occupied cells of the previous solution.

The problem is solved by allocating a very small quantity denoted by ε (epsilon) to some empty cells of the solution under consideration so that the number of occupied cells becomes $(m + n - 1)$. This infinitesimally small allocation 'ε' is placed in any independent cells with least cost.

The following rules may be observed for introducing 'ε' in the solution.

(*a*) In the initial solution ε should be introduced in least cost independent cells.

(*b*) During the process of improving the solution if degeneracy occurs at any iteration then 'ε' should be introduced in recently vacated cells with least cost.

Example 9

A company has three plants with capacities of 60, 70 and 80 units respectively to meet the demands of three warehouses with respective requirements of 50, 80 and 80 units. Given the following per unit costs of transportation, find the optimum transportation plan and cost.

		Warehouses		
		A	*B*	*C*
	X	8	7	3
Plants	*Y*	3	8	9
	Z	11	3	5

Solution:

Table 1

	A	B	C	
X	[8]	[7]	[3] 60	60 [4] [4]
Y	[3] 50	[8]	[9] 20	70 [5]←[1]
Z	[11]	[3] 80	[5]	80 [2] [2]
	50 [5]	80 [4] [4] ↑	80 [2] [2]	

Table 2

u_i \ v_j	$v_1 = -3$	$v_2 = 1$	$v_3 = 3$
$u_1 = 0$	[8]	[7]	[3] 60
$u_2 = 6$	[3] 50	[8]	[9] 20
$u_3 = 2$	[11]	[3] 80	[5] ε

If we observe the initial solution by VAM, we find that the number of occupied cells are 4 which is less than $(m + n - 1)$ *i.e.*, $(3 + 3 - 1) = 5$, hence the initial solution is not feasible and this is a problem of degeneracy. Thus to make the solution feasible we introduce a small number 'ε' in one of the independent empty cells of initial solution with least cost. Here we put ε in the cell (3, 3) because unit cost of transportation 5 is less than 11 among unoccupied cells.

Implicit cost $\overline{C}_{ij} = u_i + v_j$

$u_i + v_j - C_{ij} \leq 0$ for the above table 2.

Hence the solution obtained from table 2 is optimum.

Total cost (Min) $= 60 \times 3 + 50 \times 3 + 20 \times 9 + 80 \times 3$

$= 180 + 150 + 180 + 240 =$ Rs. 750.

Example 10

A company has three plants at locations A, B and C which supply to warehouses located at D, E, F, G and H. Monthly plant capacities are 800, 500 and 900 units respectively. Monthly warehouse requirements are 400, 400, 500, 400 and 800 units respectively. Unit costs (in rupees) of transportation are given below:

To

From	D	E	F	G	H
A	5	8	6	6	3
B	4	7	7	6	6
C	8	4	6	6	3

Determine an optimum distribution plan for the company in order to minimize the transportation cost.

Solution:

Here the total supply from the three plants is 800 + 500 + 900 = 2200 units and the total requirements at the five warehouses are 400 + 400 + 500 + 400 + 800 = 2500 units. Thus the requirements are more than supplies by 2500 – 2200 = 300 units. Hence it is an unbalanced problem. So we add a dummy plant '*d*' in the problem with a capacity of 300 units and all the cost of transportation from plant '*d*' to *D, E, F, G* and *H* are taken as zero. Thus the given problem is modified into the following balanced form.

Plant	D	E	F	G	H	
A	5	8	6	6	3	800
B	4	7	7	6	6	500
C	8	4	6	6	3	900
'd'	0	0	0	0	0	300
	400	400	500	400	800	2500 / 2500

Using VAM we get the solution as follows:

	u_i \ v_j	D $v_1 = 4$	E $v_2 = 4$	F $v_3 = 6$	G $v_4 = 6$	H $v_5 = 3$	
A	$u_1 = 0$	5	8	6 (500)	6	3 (300)	800
B	$u_2 = 0$	4 (400)	7	7	6 (100)	6	500
C	$u_3 = 0$	8	4 (400)	6	6	3 (500)	900
d	$u_4 = -6$	0	0	0 (ε)	0 (300)	0	300
		400	400	500	400	800	

No. of occupied cells = 7

Hence the solution is not feasible. So ε units are allocated to cell (d, F) which is independent with respect to the occupied cells and have minimum cost. Now the solution becomes feasible and the optimality test can be performed. The above table is OPTIMAL.

Example 11

For the following transportation problem, solve for initial solution by VAM. Find also the minimum transportation cost using MODI method. (Cost coefficients are in rupees).

Solution:

Warehouse (origins)	Stores 1	2	3	4	5	6	
1	9	12	9 (5)	6	9	10	5 [3] [3] [0] [0] [0] [0]
2	7	3 (4)	7	7	5	5 (2)	6 [2] [2] [2] [4]←
3	6 (1)	5	9 (1)	11	3	11	2 [2] [2] [2] [1] [3] [3]←
4	6 (3)	8	11	2 (2)	2 (4)	10	9 [0] [0] [4]←[2] [5]←
	4	4	6	2	4	2	
	[0] [0] [0] [0] [0] [3]	[2] [2] [2] [2]	[2] [2] [2] [2] [2] [0]	[4] [4] ↑	[1] [1] [1]	[5] ↑	

By VAM Total cost = T.C = Rs 112.

Degeneracy in transportation (at initial stage).

Table 1

						Supply
9	12	9 (5)	6	9	10	5
7	3 (4)	7	7	5	5 (2)	6
6 (1)	5	9 (1)	11	3 (ε)	11	2
6 (3)	8	11	2 (2)	2 (4)	10	9
4	4	6	2	4	2	22 / 22

By VAM, T.C = Rs. 112

Optimality test

(*a*) Number of allocations must be = $m + n - 1 = 4 + 6 - 1 = 9$. Actual number of allocations is only 8 which is less than 9. Hence optimality cannot be performed as such. Such a case is a case of degeneracy (Refer table 1).

(*b*) The second condition for non-degeneracy is that the $(m + n - 1)$ cells must be in independent position (*i.e.*, loaded cells must not form a closed Loop).

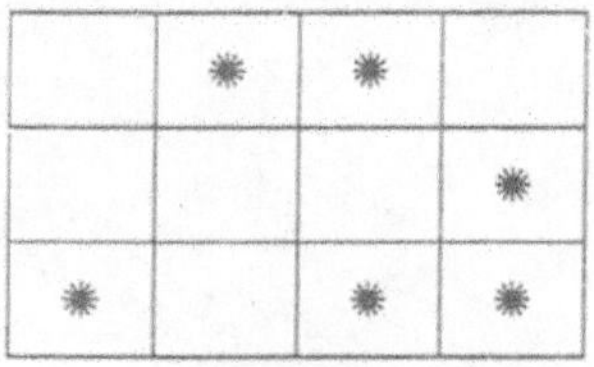
Loop not formed
(Table A)

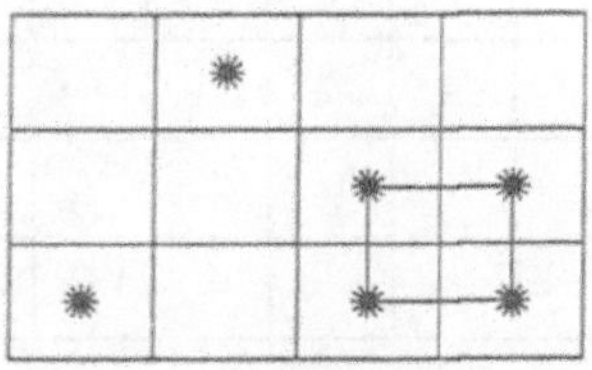
Closed loop formed
(Table B)

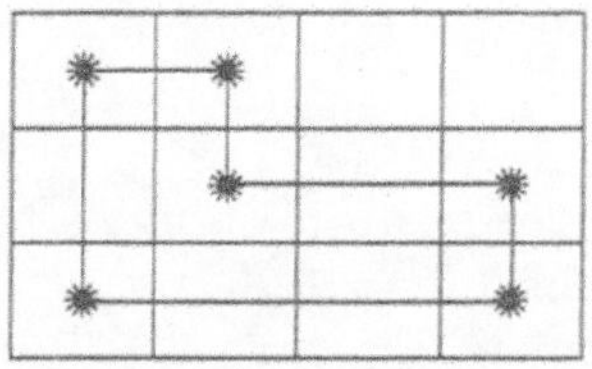
Closed loop formed
(Table C)

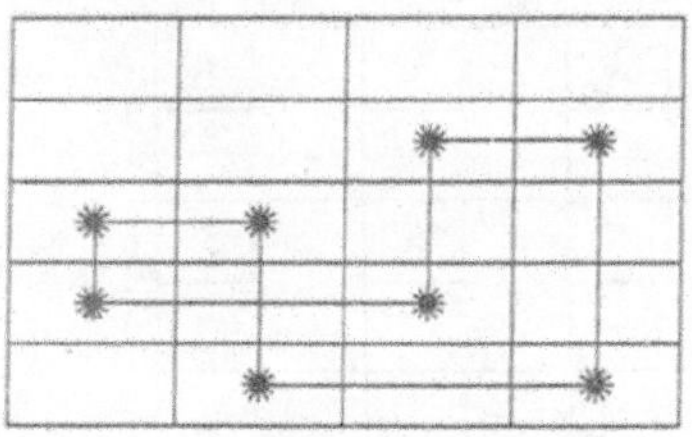
Closed loop formed
(Table D)

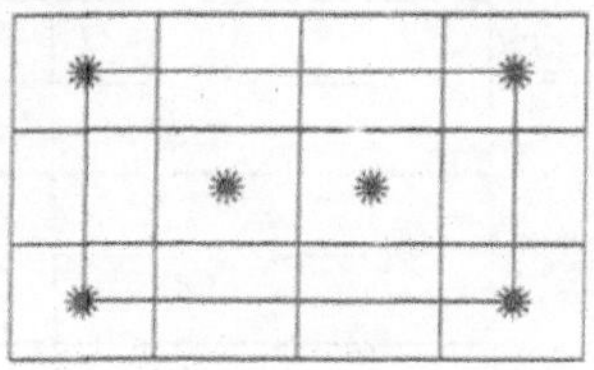
Closed loop formed
(Table E)

In table 1, condition of optimality test (*a*) is not satisfied. To fulfil this condition we allocate an infinitesimally small positive quantity ε (epsilon) to a least cost cell as a result of which the loop formation should not happen. So we can not put ε in cell (3, 5) because closed loop is formed by cells (3, 5), (3, 1), (4, 1) and (4, 5) so that allocations in these cells do not remain in independent position and condition (*b*) will be violated (see table 1). There are two next higher cost cells (2, 5) and (3, 2) with a cost of 5 units. Allocation in either of these cells does not result in a closed loop. Hence ε is put in cell (2, 5) (See table 2).

Table 2

	$v_1 = 6$	$v_2 = 0$	$v_3 = 9$	$v_4 = 2$	$v_5 = 2$	$v_6 = 2$
$u_1 = 0$	9	12	9 [5 *]	6	9	10
$u_2 = 3$	7 [2]	3 [4 *]	7 [5, θ]	7	5 [ε − θ *]	5 [2 *]
$u_3 = 0$	6 [1 + θ *]	5	9 [1 − θ]	11	3	11
$u_4 = 0$	6 [3 − θ *]	8	11	2 [2 *]	2 [4 + θ *]	10

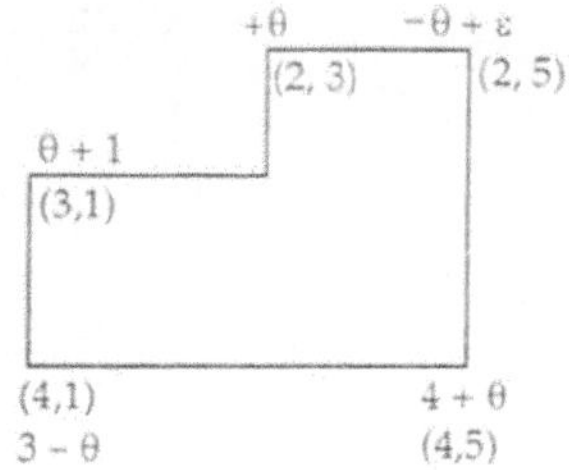

Mostly occupied row put $u_4 = 0$

Here two cells are positive $\bar{C}_{ij} - C_{ij}$. They are (2, 1) and (2, 3) in table 2. We choose the most positive value *i.e.*, 5 in cell (2, 3) for further treatment. We put θ in this cell (2, 3).

Thus θ = ε (where ε → 0).

		5			
	4	ε		ε − ε	2
1 + ε		1 − ε			
3 − ε			2	4 + ε	

Put ε = 0 (Keep ε = ε at 2, 3 cell)

	$v_1 = 6$	$v_2 = 5$	$v_3 = 9$	$v_4 = 2$	$v_5 = 2$	$v_6 = 7$	
$u_1 = 0$	9	12	9 [5]	6	9	10	5
$u_2 = -2$	7	3 [4]	7 [ε]	7	5	5 [2]	6
$u_3 = 0$	6 [1]	5	9 [1]	11	3	11	2
$u_4 = 0$	6 [3]	8	11	2 [2]	2 [4]	10	9
	4	4	6	2	4	2	

$$\text{T.C.} = 112 + 7\varepsilon = 112; \text{ (as } \varepsilon = 0)$$

Remarks: This transportation problem was a degenerate one in the initial stage itself. But sometimes the starting feasible solution in non-degenerate, it may become degenerate later at some iteration stage. This happens when the selection of the entering variable causes two or more current basic variables to become zero. We then allocate ε_1, ε_2 etc., to such cells so that there are exactly $(m + n - 1)$ cells in independent positions and the procedure is then carried on in the usual manner.

Example 12

Degeneracy During Solution Stages

Find the basic feasible solution of the following transportation problem by N-W corner method. Also find the optimal transportation plan.

	1	2	3	4	5	Available
A	4	3	1	2	6	80
B	5	2	3	4	5	60
C	3	5	6	3	2	40
D	2	4	4	5	3	20
Required	60	60	30	40	10	200 total / 200

Solution:

Table 1

	$v_1 = 4$	$v_2 = 3$	$v_3 = 4$	$v_4 = 1$	$v_5 = -1$	
$u_1 = 0$	[4] 60 − θ	[3] 20 + θ	3 ¦ [1]	[2]	[6]	80
$u_2 = -1$	[5]	[2] 40 − θ	[3] 20 + θ	[4]	[5]	60
$u_3 = 2$	3 ¦ [3]	[5]	[6] 10 − θ	[3] 30 + θ	[2]	40
$u_4 = 4$	6 ¦ [2] θ	3 ¦ [4]	4 ¦ [4]	[5] 10 − θ	[3] 10	20
TC = 670,	60	60	30	40	10	200 / 200

Test of optimality: As number of occupied cells = 8 (= $m + n - 1$= 4 + 5 − 1) and these are in independent position, optimality test can be performed.

$$\theta = 10$$

Table 2

50	30			
	30	30		
		⊙	40	
10			⊙	10

⊙ recently vacated cells

In table 2, we see that number of occupied cells are only 7 because cells (*C*, 3) and (*D*, 4) become empty simultaneously, these empty cells are marked ⊙. As number of occupied cells < $m + n - 1$, degeneracy occurs here. Degeneracy can be overcome by allocating ε to cell (*D*, 4) which has the lowest shipping cost of 5 out of two vacated cells {(*C*, 3) = 6)} and {(*D*, 4) = 5)}.

Table 3

	$v_1 = 2$	$v_2 = 1$	$v_3 = 2$	$v_4 = 5$	$v_5 = 3$
$u_1 = 2$	[4] 50 − θ	[3] 30	(3) [1]	(5) [2] θ	[6]
$u_2 = 1$	[5]	[2] 30	[3] 30	(2) [4]	[5]
$u_3 = -2$	[3]	[5]	[6]	[3] 40	[2]
$u_4 = 0$	[2] 10 + θ	[4]	[4]	[5] ε − θ	[3] 10

θ = ε

Table 4

	$v_1 = 4$	$v_2 = 3$	$v_3 = 4$	$v_4 = 2$	$v_5 = 5$	
$u_1 = 0$	[4] 50 − θ	[3] 30	(3) [1]	[2] ε + θ	[6]	80
$u_2 = -1$	[5]	[2] 30	[3] 30	[4]	[5]	60
$u_3 = 1$	(2) [3]	[5]	[6]	[3] 40 − θ	(4) [2] θ	40
$u_4 = -2$	[2] 10 + θ	[4]	[4]	[5]	[3] 10 − θ	20
	60	60	30	40	10	

θ = 10

Table 5

	$v_1 = 4$	$v_2 = 3$	$v_3 = 4$	$v_4 = 2$	$v_5 = 1$	
$u_1 = 0$	[4] 40	[3] $30 - \theta$	(3) [1] θ	[2] 10	[6]	80
$u_2 = -1$	[5]	[2] $30 + \theta$	[3] $30 - \theta$	[4]	[5]	60
$u_3 = 1$	(2) [3]	[5]	[6]	[3] 30	[2] 10	40
$u_4 = -2$	[2] 20	[4]	[4]	[5]	[3]	20
	60	60	30	40	10	

$\theta = 30$

Table 6

	$v_1 = 4$	$v_2 = 0$	$v_3 = 1$	$v_4 = 2$	$v_5 = 1$	
$u_1 = 0$	[4] $40 - \theta$	[3]	[1] 30	[2] $10 + \theta$	[6]	80
$u_2 = 2$	(1) [5]	[2] 60	[3] ε	[4]	[5]	60
$u_3 = 1$	(2) [3] θ	[5]	[6]	[3] $30 - \theta$	[2] 10	40
$u_4 = -2$	[2] 20	[4]	[4]	[5]	[3]	20
	60	60	30	40	10	

$\theta = 30$

Table 7

	$v_1 = 4$	$v_2 = 3$	$v_3 = 1$	$v_4 = 2$	$v_5 = 3$	
$u_1 = 0$	[4] 10	[3] ε	[1] 30	[2] 40	[6]	80
$u_2 = -1$	[5]	[2] 60	[3]	[4]	[5]	60
$u_3 = -1$	[3] 30	[5]	[6]	[3]	[2] 10	40
$u_4 = -2$	[2] 20	[4]	[4]	[5]	[3]	20
	60	60	30	40	10	

Put $\varepsilon = 0$ in the table.

There is no positive *i.e.*, here $(\bar{C}_{ij} - C_{ij}) \leq 0$

Table 7 is the final table where $\epsilon = 0$

Table 7 is rewritten after putting $\epsilon = 0$

Final Table

(4) 10	(3)	(1) 30	(2) 40	(6)	80
(5)	(2) 60	(3)	(4)	(5)	60
(3) 30	(5)	(6)	(3)	(2) 10	40
(2) 20	(4)	(4)	(5)	(3)	20
60	60	30	40	10	

T.C. = (10 × 4) + (30 × 1) + (40 × 2) + (60 × 2) + (30 × 3) + (10 × 2) + (20 × 2)

= 40 + 30 + 80 + 120 + 90 + 20 + 40

= 420 < 670 by NW - rule.

Example 13

Use MODI Method For the Following

(Initial solution by *N-W* corner rule) Balanced transportation problem

Table 1

T.C = 12200 (By N-W Corner)

u_i \ v_j	$v_1 = 11$	$v_2 = 13$	$v_3 = 9$	$v_4 = 6$	
$u_1 = 0$	(11) 200	(13) 50	(17)	(14)	250
$u_2 = 5$	(16)	(18) 175	(14) 125 − θ	1 (10) + θ	300
$u_3 = 4$	(21)	(24)	(13) 150 + θ	(10) 250 − θ	400
	200	225	275	250	950 / 950

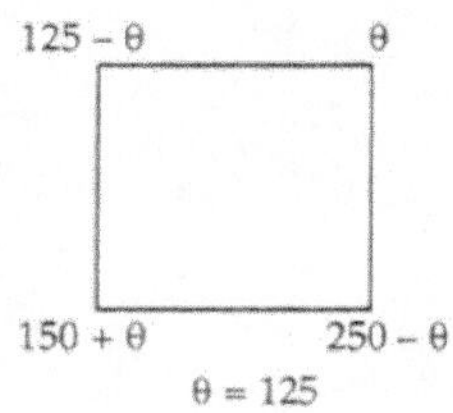

Number of occupied cell = $m + n - 1 = 3 + 4 - 1 = 6$.

This occupied cells are in independent position (*i.e.*, the occupied cells positions do not form closed loop).

The number of occupied cells (= 6) is equal to $(m + n - 1)$ so this is a non-degeneracy problem.

Next we identify a closed loop which starts and ends at the entering non-basic cell (empty cell). Connecting only the basic cells. Such closed path exists and is unique for any non-degenerate basic solution. Thus we put θ where $\overline{C}_{ij} - C_{ij} > 0$ and maximum. Here $(5 + 6 - 10) = 1$ and is put as [1] in the cell (2, 4). Rest we balance row and column restrictions.

θ = 125

T.C. = 12075

11 / 200	13 / 50	17	14
16	18 / 175	14	10 / 125
21	24	13 / 275	10 / 125

$\overline{C}_{ij} - C_{ij} = 0$ or negative So this is optimum solution

Exercise:

MODI

T.C = 779

	$v_1 = 19$	$v_2 = -2$	$v_3 = -10$	$v_4 = 10$	Capacity
$u_1 = 0$	19 / 5	30	50	10 / 2	7
$u_2 = 50$	70	30 (18) / $+\theta$	40 / 7	60 / $2 - \theta$	9
$u_3 = 10$	40	8 / $8 - \theta$	70	20 / $10 + \theta$	18
Requirement	5	8	7	14	34 / 34

u_i \ v_j	$v_1 = 19$	$v_2 = -2$	$v_3 = 8$	$v_4 = 10$	
$u_1 = 0$	19 / 5	30	50	10 / 2	7
$u_2 = 32$	70	30 / 2	40 / 7	60	9
$u_3 = 10$	40	8 / 6	70	20 / 12	18
	5	8	7	14	

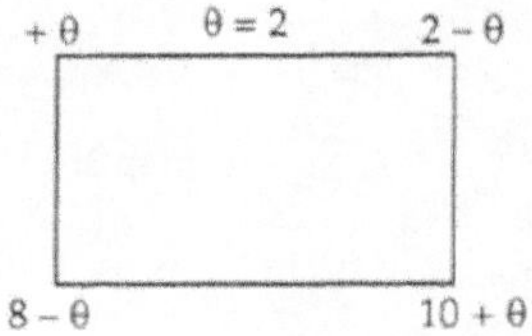

← Optimum table.

T.C. = (5 × 19) + (2 × 10) + (2 × 30) + (7 × 40) + (6 × 8) + (12 × 20)

= Rs. 743, A reduction of Rs. (779 − 743) = Rs. 36. **Ans.**

Chapter 5

ASSIGNMENT MODEL

5.1 INTRODUCTION

The assignment problem is a special kind of transportation problem. The assignment method is employed when a number of operations are to be assigned to an equal number of operators and each operator performs only one operation.

5.2 STEPS INVOLVED TO SOLVE ASSIGNMENT PROBLEMS OF MINIMIZATION TYPE

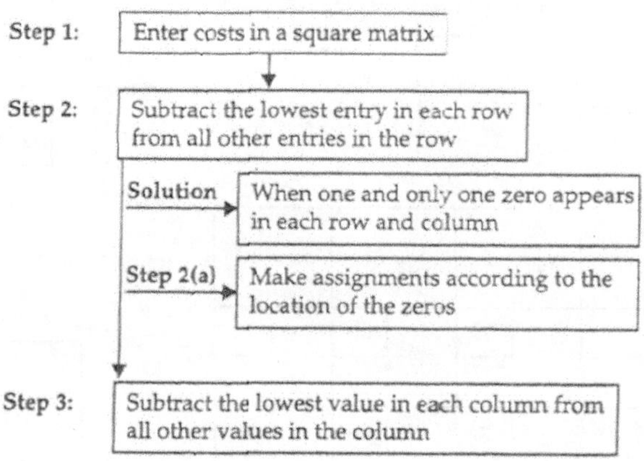

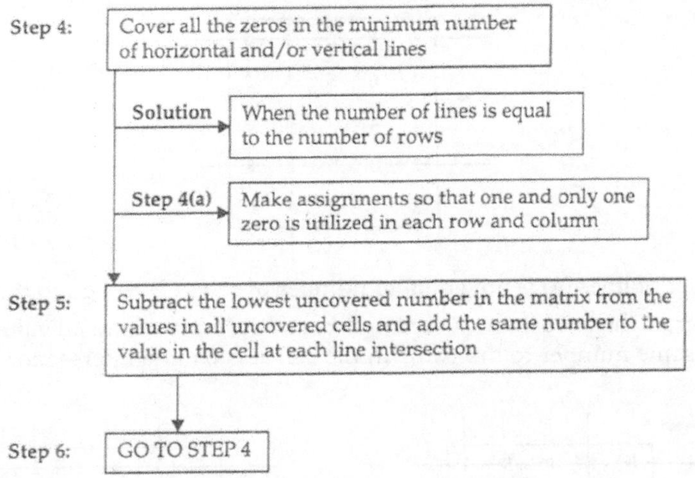

Example 1

Assign different jobs to different workers so that time required for completion of all the jobs is minimum. Times entered in the matrix below are in hours.

JOBS

	Step 1	1	2	3	4	5	Availability
	1	2	9	2	7	1	1
Workers	2	6	8	7	6	1	1
	3	4	6	5	3	1	1
	4	4	2	7	3	1	1
	5	5	3	9	5	1	1
Requirements		1	1	1	1	1	

Solution:

Step 2: Subtract the lowest entry in each row from all other entries (including the lowest entry) in that row.

	1	2	3	4	5
1	1	8	1	6	0
2	5	7	6	5	0
3	3	5	4	2	0
4	3	1	6	2	0
5	4	2	8	4	0

Step 3: Subtract the lowest value in each column from all other values in the column and

Step 4: Cover all the zeros in the minimum number of horizontal and/or vertical lines.

0	7	0	4	0
4	6	5	3	0
2	4	3	0	0
2	0	5	0	0
3	1	7	2	0

Here number of lines (4) is not equal to number of rows (5). We go to the next step.

Step 5: Subtract the lowest uncovered number in the matrix from all values in all uncovered cells and add the same number to the value in the cell at each line intersection. Then go to step 4 and repeat.

0	7	0	5	1
3	5	4	3	0
1	3	2	0	0
2	0	5	1	1
2	0	6	2	0

0	8	0	6	2
2	5	3	3	0
0	3	1	0	0
1	0	4	1	1
1	0	5	2	0

OPTIMAL ASSIGNMENT TABLE

					Lines
0	9	[0]	6	3	1
1	5	2	2	[0]	2
0	4	1	[0]	1	3
0	[0]	3	0	1	4
[0]	0	4	1	0	5

In the last table as the minimum number of lines to cover all zeros is five which is equal to number of rows, the optimal solution has been reached.

Let us make assignment so that one and only one zero is utilized in each row and column. Two solutions are available.

Assignment

			( )	
Job No.	*Man no.*	*Time (hrs.)*	*Man no.*	*Time (hrs.)*
1	5	5	3	4
2	4	2	5	3
3	1	2	1	2
4	3	3	4	3
5	2	1	2	1
	↑ Solution 1	13 hrs	↑ Solution 2	13 hrs.

0	9	(0)	6	3
1	5	2	2	(0)
(0)	4	1	0	1
0	0	3	(0)	1
0	(0)	4	1	0

Minimum time: 13 hrs.

Example 2

Travelling Salesman Problem of Maximization Type

A company has a team of 4 salesman and four districts where the company tries to expand its business. After taking into account the capabilities of salesman and the nature of districts, the company estimates the profit per day in rupees as follows

Salesman \ Districts	A	B	C	D
1	160	100	140	110
2	140	110	150	150
3	150	150	130	120
4	130	120	140	150

Find the assignments of salesman to various districts which will yield maximum profit.

Solution:

We calculate the problem by changing it to minimization. For this we put all the unit profit with negative sign.

Table 1

– 160	– 100	– 140	– 110	→ Lowest – 160
– 140	– 110	– 150	– 150	→ Lowest – 150
– 150	– 150	– 130	– 120	→ Lowest – 150
– 130	– 120	– 140	– 150	→ Lowest – 150

The lowest entry in Table 1 is – 160 in row 1.

We subtract – 160 *i.e.*, we add 160 to all other entries (including – 160 entry) in 1st row. The Table 2 is obtained.

Table 2

	A	B	C	D
1	[0]	60	20	50
2	10	40	[0]	0
3	0	[0]	20	30
4	20	30	10	[0]

← Optimum table

Table 2 is the optimum table because minimum number of lines to cover all zeros is four which is equal to row number.

Salesman	*District*	*Max. Profit/day*
1	A	160
2	C	150
3	B	150
4	D	150
		Rs. 610

Example 3

Four new machines M_1, M_2, M_3 and M_4 are to be installed in a machine shop. There are five vacant places A, B, C, D and E available. Because of limited space, machine M_2 cannot be placed at C and machine M_3 cannot be placed at A. C_{ij}, the assignment cost of machine i to place j in rupees is shown below. Find the optimal assignment schedule and minimum cost of installation.

	A	B	C	D	E
M_1	4	6	10	5	6
M_2	7	4	—	5	4
M_3	—	6	9	6	2
M_4	9	3	7	2	3

Solution:

We can assign infinity (α) cost in the restricted places (–). We also put dummy machine M_d and costs as zero.

Table 1

	A	B	C	D	E
M_1	4	6	10	5	6
M_2	7	4	∝	5	4
M_3	∝	6	9	6	2
M_4	9	3	7	2	3
M_d	0	0	0	0	0

We follow the steps already explained. We get the next table.

Table 2

	A	B	C	D	E
M_1	[0]	2	6	1	2
M_2	3	[0]	∝	1	0
M_3	∝	4	7	4	[0]
M_4	7	1	5	[0]	1
M_d	0	0	0	0	0

Table 2 is the optimal table because number of lines = 5 which is equal to number of rows (including dummy row).

Assignment

Machines	*Place*	*Cost*
M_1	A	4
M_2	B	4
M_3	E	2
M_4	D	2
		Rs. 12

Example 4

Assignment

Four different jobs can be done on four different machines. The set up and take down time costs are assumed to be prohibitively high for changeovers. The matrix below gives the cost in rupees of producing job i on machine j.

Step 1

	M_1	M_2	M_3	M_4	
J_1	5	7	11	6	← Min 5
J_2	8	5	9	6	← Min 5
J_3	4	7	10	7	← Min 4
J_4	10	4	8	3	← Min 3

How should the jobs be assigned to the various machines so that the total cost is minimised?

Solution:

Step 2:

0	2	6	1
3	0	4	1
0	3	6	3
7	1	5	0
↑ Min 0	↑ Min 0	↑ Min 4	↑ Min 0

Steps 3 and 4:

0	2	2	1
3	0	0	1
0	3	2	3
7	1	1	0

No. of lines 3 < 4 (No. of rows)

Min uncovered No. = 1

Step 5:

No. of lines 3 < 4 (No. of rows)

0	1	1	0
1	0	0	1
0	2	1	2
8	1	1	0

Min uncovered No. = 1

	M_1	M_2	M_3	M_4
J_1	[0]	0	0	0
J_2	5	[0]	0	2
J_3	0	1	[0]	2
J_4	8	0	0	[0]

Jobs	M/C	Cost	Alternative M/C	Alternative Cost
$J_1 \rightarrow$	M_1	5	M_4	6
$J_2 \rightarrow$	M_2	5	M_3	9
$J_3 \rightarrow$	M_3	10	M_1	4
$J_4 \rightarrow$	M_4	3	M_2	4
		Rs 23		Rs. 23

Example 5

Assignment

Step 1:

	E	F	G	H	
A	18	26	17	11	← Min 11
B	13	28	14	26	← Min 13
C	38	19	18	15	← Min 15
D	19	26	24	10	← Min 10

A departmental head has four subordinates, and four tasks to be performed. The subordinates differ in efficiency and the tasks differ in their intrinsic difficulty. His estimate of the time each man would take to perform each task is given in the matrix below. How should the tasks be allotted one to a man so as to minimise the total man hours?

Solution:

Step 2:

7	15	6	0
0	15	1	13
23	4	3	0
9	16	14	0
↑ Min 0	↑ Min 4	↑ Min 1	↑ Min 0

Steps 3 and 4:

No. of lines
3 < 4
No. of rows

7	11	5	0
0	11	0	13
23	0	2	0
9	12	13	0

Step 5

Min uncovered No. = 5

No. of lines
= 4
= No. of rows

	E	F	G	H
A	2	6	[0]	0
B	[0]	11	0	18
C	23	[0]	2	5
D	4	7	8	[0]

Assignments	*Time*
A → G	17
B → E	13
C → F	19
D → H	10
	59 hrs.

Example 6

Assign different jobs to different machines.

Step 1: Cost of assignments are given in the cells.

		Machines			
		M_1	M_2	M_3	
	J_1	5	7	9	← Min 5
Job	J_2	8	10	6	← Min 6
	J_3	8	7	5	← Min 5

Step 2: Subtract the lowest entry of each row from all entries of that row (including lowest entry cell).

	M_1	M_2	M_3
J_1	0	2	4
J_2	2	4	0
J_3	3	2	0

Step 3: Subtract the lowest value in each column from all entries in the column.

Step 4: Cover all the zeros in the minimum number of horizontal and/or vertical lines.

0	0	4
2	2	0
3	0	0

No. of rows = No. of lines

Total cost
$= 5 + 6 + 7$
$=$ Rs. 18

	M/C-1	M/C-2	M/C-3
Job 1	(0)	(0)	4
Job 2	2	2	[(0)]
Job 3	3	(0)	(0)

Job	To M/C
Job 1	M/C-1
Job 2	M/C-3
Job 3	M/C-2

Example 7

Step 1: Time (in Mins.) taken are shown in matrix.

		Assistants j					
		1	2	3	4	5	
	1	5	10	7	11	9	← Min 5
	2	4	9	8	5	7	← Min 4
Jobs, i	3	12	6	8	3	12	← Min 3
	4	6	4	8	3	12	← Min 3
	5	10	12	7	8	7	← Min 7

Step 2:

0	5	2	6	4
0	5	4	1	3
9	3	5	0	9
3	1	5	0	9
3	5	0	1	0
↑ Min 0	↑ Min 1	↑ Min 0	↑ Min 0	↑ Min 0

Steps 3 and 4:

No. of lines
< No. of rows
i.e., 4 < 5

0	4	2	6	4
0	4	4	1	3
9	2	5	0	9
3	0	5	0	9
3	4	0	1	0

Step 5: Subtract the lowest uncovered number in the matrix from the values in all the uncovered cells and add the same number to the value in the cell at each line intersection.

Here lowest entry (uncovered) = 2

No. of lines
= No. of rows in this case.
This is final table.

Assignments j

Jobs	1	2	3	4	5
1	0	2	(0)	6	2
2	(0)	2	2	1	1
3	9	0	3	(0)	7
4	5	(0)	5	2	9
5	5	4	0	3	(0)

Job	*Assignments*	*Time*
1	3	7
2	1	4
3	4	3
4	2	4
5	5	7
		25 Minutes

Chapter 6

ADVANCED TOPICS IN LINEAR PROGRAMMING

6.1 DUALITY IN LINEAR PROGRAMMING

The simplex problems, so far done, represent a class known as the "Primal problem", which results from those primary relationships normally observed when analysing the basic physical problem. Associated with every primal Linear Programming problem there is a corresponding optimization problem called the "Dual problem".

6.2 DUAL PROBLEM WHEN PRIMAL IS IN CANONICAL FORM

Maximize, $Z = c_1x_1 + c_2x_2 + c_3x_3 + \ldots\ldots + c_nx_n$

Subject to constraints

$$
\begin{aligned}
&a_{11}x_1 + a_{12}x_2 + a_{13}x_3 + \ldots\ldots + a_{1n}x_n \le b_1,\\
&a_{21}x_1 + a_{22}x_2 + a_{23}x_3 + \ldots\ldots + a_{2n}x_n \le b_2,\\
&\ldots\ldots \quad \ldots\ldots \quad \ldots\ldots \quad \ldots\ldots \quad \ldots\ldots \quad \ldots\ldots\\
&\ldots\ldots \quad \ldots\ldots \quad \ldots\ldots \quad \ldots\ldots \quad \ldots\ldots \quad \ldots\ldots\\
&a_{m1}x_1 + a_{m2}x_2 + a_{m3}x_3 + \ldots\ldots + a_{mn}\,x_n \le b_m
\end{aligned}
$$

where $x_1, x_2, x_3 \ldots\ldots, x_n$, all ≥ 0 (1)

If the above problem is considered as primal, then its associated dual will be

Minimize, $W = b_1y_1 + b_2y_2 + b_3y_3 + \ldots\ldots + b_my_m$ subject to constraints

$$
\begin{aligned}
&a_{11}y_1 + a_{21}y_2 + a_{31}y_3 + \ldots\ldots + a_{m1}y_m \ge c_1,\\
&a_{12}y_1 + a_{22}y_2 + a_{32}y_3 + \ldots\ldots + a_{m2}\,y_m \ge c_2,\\
&\ldots\ldots \quad \ldots\ldots \quad \ldots\ldots \quad \ldots\ldots \quad \ldots\ldots \quad \ldots\ldots\\
&\ldots\ldots \quad \ldots\ldots \quad \ldots\ldots \quad \ldots\ldots \quad \ldots\ldots \quad \ldots\ldots\\
&a_{1n}y_1 + a_{2n}y_2 + a_{3n}y_3 + \ldots\ldots + a_{mn}y_m \ge c_n
\end{aligned}
$$

where all the dual variables.

$$y_1, y_2, y_3, \ldots\ldots, y_m, \text{ all} \geq 0 \tag{2}$$

Equations (1) and (2) are called symmetric primal-dual pairs. The above pair of programmes can be written as follows:

Primal	Dual
maximize $Z = \sum_{j=1}^{m} c_j x_j$	minimize $W = \sum_{i=1}^{m} b_i y_i$
Subject to	Subject to
$\sum_{j=1}^{n} a_{ij} x_j \leq b_i ; i = 1, 2, 3, \ldots\ldots, m$	$\sum_{i=1}^{m} a_{ij} y_i \geq c_j,$
where $x_j \geq 0, j = 1, 2, 3, \ldots\ldots, n$	$j = 1, 2, 3, \ldots\ldots, n.$ where $y_i \geq 0, i = 1, 2, 3, \ldots\ldots, m.$

Example 1

Construct the dual to the primal problem, maximize $Z = 3x_1 + 5x_2$

Subject to

$$2x_1 + 6x_2 \leq 50$$
$$3x_1 + 2x_2 \leq 35$$
$$5x_1 - 3x_2 \leq 10$$
$$x_2 \leq 20$$

where $x_1 \geq 0, x_2 \geq 0.$

Solution:

Let y_1, y_2, y_3 and y_4 be the corresponding dual variables, then the dual programme can be written as

Minimize $W = 50\, y_1 + 35\, y_2 + 10\, y_3 + 20\, y_4$

Subject to

$$2y_1 + 3y_2 + 5y_3 \geq 3$$
$$6y_1 + 2y_2 - 3y_3 + y_4 \geq 5$$

where y_1, y_2, y_3, y_4 all $\geq 0.$

Here we have seen that there are two constraints of the dual problem. So the computation *i.e.*, number of tables in solving the dual will be lesser than the primal problem which involves four constraints.

Example 2

Construct the dual of the following primal problem.

Minimize $Z = 3x_1 - 2x_2 + 4x_3$

Subject to the constraints

$$3x_1 + 5x_2 + 4x_3 \geq 7$$
$$6x_1 + x_2 + 3x_3 \geq 4$$

$$7x_1 - 2x_2 - x_3 \le 10 \leftarrow$$
$$x_1 - 2x_2 + 5x_3 \ge 3$$
$$4x_1 + 7x_2 - 2x_3 \ge 2$$

where x_1, x_2, x_3 *all* ≥ 0.

Solution:

The given problem is of minimization type, all constraints should be of $\ge$ type.

i.e., multiplying third constraints by – 1 on both sides we get

$$-7x_1 + 2x_2 + x_3 \ge -10 \leftarrow$$

Now we can write the dual of the given primal.

Maximize $W = 7y_1 + 4y_2 - 10y_3 + 3y_4 + 2y_5$

subject to
$$3y_1 + 6y_2 - 7y_3 + y_4 + 4y_5 \le 3$$
$$5y_1 + y_2 + 2y_3 - 2y_4 + 7y_5 \le -2$$
$$4y_1 + 3y_2 + y_3 + 5y_4 - 2y_5 \le 4$$

where y_1, y_2, y_3, y_4 and y_5 all ≥ 0.

Example 3

Construct the dual of the following problem, maximize $Z = 3x_1 + 17x_2 + 9x_3$

Subject to
$$x_1 - x_2 + x_3 \ge 3 \leftarrow$$
$$-3x_1 + 2x_3 \le 1$$

where $x_1 \ge 0, x_2 \ge 0$ *and* $x_3 \ge 0$.

Solution:

First the $\ge$ constraint is converted into $\le$ constraint by multiplying 1st constraint by – 1.

i.e.,
$$-x_1 + x_2 - x_3 \le -3$$

Now the dual of the problem can be written as

Minimize $W = -3y_1 + y_2$

Subject to
$$-y_1 - 3y_2 \ge 3$$
$$y_1 \ge 17$$
$$-y_1 + 2y_2 \ge 9$$

where y_1, y_2 all ≥ 0.

6.3 DUAL PROBLEM WHEN PRIMAL IS IN THE STANDARD FORM

All constraints are expressed in equations (=) in standard form. Here we will find that an equality constraint in the primal corresponds to an unrestricted variable in the dual and vice-versa. For example we consider the following problem:

Maximize $Z = c_1x_1 + c_2x_2$

Subject to
$$a_{11}x_1 + a_{12}x_2 = b_1$$
$$a_{21}x_1 + a_{22}x_2 \le b_2 \quad (1)$$

where $x_1 \ge 0$ and $x_2 \ge 0$.

The first constraint is of equality form, when expressed in canonical form and is equivalent to $a_{11}x_1 + a_{12}x_2 \le b_1$ and $a_{11}x_1 + a_{12}x_2 \ge b_1$
or it can be expressed as

$$a_{11}x_1 + a_{12}x_2 \le b_1 \quad (2)$$

$$-a_{11}x_1 - a_{12}x_2 \le -b_1 \quad (3)$$

Let y_1', y_1'' and y_2 be the dual variables associated with the (1), (2) and (3) constraints. Then the dual problem can be written as

Minimize $W = b_1y_1' - b_1y_1'' + b_2y_2$
$= b_1(y_1' - y_1'') + b_2y_2$

Subject to $a_{11}(y_1' - y_1'') + a_{21}y_2 \ge c_1$
$a_{12}(y_1' - y_1'') + a_{22}y_2 \ge c_2$

where y_1', y_1'' and y_2 all ≥ 0.

It is notable that the term $(y_1' - y_1'')$ occurs in the objective function as well as in all the constraints of the dual. This becomes true in case of equality constraints. If we put $y_1' - y_2'' = y_1$, then the new variable y_1, which is the difference between two non-negative variables $(y_1' - y_1'')$ will become unrestricted in sign and the dual problem becomes

Minimize $W = b_1y_1 + b_2y_2$

Subject to $a_{11}y_1 + a_{21}y_2 \ge c_1$
$a_{12}y_1 + a_{22}y_2 \ge c_2$

$y_2 \ge 0$ and y_1 is unrestricted in sign. This shows that the dual variable which corresponds to an equality constraint must be unrestricted in sign. Conversely, when a primal variable is unrestricted in sign, its dual constraint will be equation (=).

Example 4

Construct the dual of the problem

Maximize $Z = 3x_1 + 10x_2 + 2x_3$

Subject to $2x_1 + 3x_2 + 2x_3 \le 7$
$3x_1 - 2x_2 + 4x_3 = 3$

where x_1, x_2, x_3 *all* ≥ 0.

Solution:

Minimize $W = 7y_1 + 3y_2$

Subject to $2y_1 + 3y_2 \ge 3$
$3y_1 - 2y_2 \ge 10$
$2y_1 + 4y_2 \ge 2$

$y_1 > 0$, y_2 is unrestricted in sign.

Example 5

Construct the dual of the problem

Minimize $Z = x_2 + 3x_3$

Subject to $2x_1 + x_2 \le 3 \leftarrow$
$x_1 + 2x_2 + 6x_3 \ge 5$
$-x_1 + x_2 + 2x_3 = 2 \leftarrow$

where x_1, x_2, x_3 *all* ≥ 0.

Solution:

Let us change the 1st constraint to ≥ type by multiplying both sides with – 1.

i.e., $-2x_1 - x_2 \geq -3$

The dual problem of the given primal problem is

Maximize $W = -3y_1 + 5y_2 + 2y_3$

Subject to
$$-2y_1 + y_2 - y_3 \leq 0$$
$$-y_1 + 2y_2 + y_3 \leq 1$$
$$6y_2 + 2y_3 \leq 3$$

$y_1 \geq 0$, $y_2 \geq 0$ and y_3 are unrestricted in sign.

Example 6

Construct the dual of the primal problem

Maximize $Z = 2x_1 + x_2 + x_3$

Subject to
$$x_1 + x_2 + x_3 \geq 6 \leftarrow$$
$$3x_1 - 2x_2 + 3x_3 = 3$$
$$-4x_1 + 3x_2 - 6x_3 = 1$$

where x_1, x_2, x_3 *all* ≥ 0.

Solution:

Let us multiply 1st constraint by – 1,
$$-x_1 - x_2 - x_3 \leq -6$$

Minimize $W = -6y_1 + 3y_2 + y_3$

Subject to
$$-y_1 + 3y_2 - 4y_3 \geq 2$$
$$-y_1 - 2y_2 + 3y_3 \geq 1$$
$$-y_1 + 3y_2 - 6y_3 \geq 1$$

where $y_1 \geq 0$, y_2 and y_3 are unrestricted in sign.

6.4 PRIMAL-DUAL RELATIONSHIPS

The fundamental theorems of duality describe the relationships between the primal problem and its dual.

Theorem 1:

The dual of the dual is the primal

Proof: Let the primal problem in canonical form be

Maximize $Z = c_1x_1 + c_2x_2 + \ldots\ldots + c_nx_n.$

Subject to
$$a_{11}x_1 + a_{12}x_2 + \ldots\ldots + a_{1n}x_n \leq b_1,$$
$$a_{21}x_1 + a_{22}x_2 + \ldots\ldots + a_{2n}x_n \geq b_2,$$
$$\ldots\ldots \quad \ldots\ldots \quad \ldots\ldots \quad \ldots\ldots \quad \ldots\ldots$$
$$\ldots\ldots \quad \ldots\ldots \quad \ldots\ldots \quad \ldots\ldots \quad \ldots\ldots$$
$$a_{m1}x_1 + a_{m2}x_2 + \ldots\ldots + a_{mn}x_n \geq b_m,$$

where $x_1, x_2, \ldots\ldots, x_n,$ all ≥ 0 (1)

We find out the dual of the above primal problem

Minimize $W = b_1y_1 + b_2y_2 + \ldots\ldots + b_my_m,$

Subject to

$$a_{11}y_1 + a_{21}y_2 + \ldots\ldots + a_{m1}y_m \geq c_1,$$
$$a_{12}y_1 + a_{22}y_2 + \ldots\ldots + a_{m2}y_m \geq c_2$$
$$\ldots\ldots \quad \ldots\ldots \quad \ldots\ldots \quad \ldots\ldots \quad \ldots\ldots$$
$$\ldots\ldots \quad \ldots\ldots \quad \ldots\ldots \quad \ldots\ldots \quad \ldots\ldots$$
$$a_{1n}y_1 + a_{2n}y_2 + \ldots\ldots + a_{mn}y_m \geq c_n.$$

where all $y_1, y_2, \ldots\ldots, y_m,$ all $\geq 0.$ (2)

Multiplying each of the relations (2) throughout by – 1, we get

Minimize $-W = -b_1y_1 - b_2y_2 - \ldots\ldots - b_my_m,$

Subject to

$$-a_{11}y_1 - a_{21}y_2 - \ldots\ldots - a_{m1}y_m \leq -c_1$$
$$-a_{12}y_1 - a_{22}y_2 - \ldots\ldots - a_{m2}y_m \leq -c_2$$
$$\ldots\ldots \quad \ldots\ldots \quad \ldots\ldots \quad \ldots\ldots \quad \ldots\ldots$$
$$\ldots\ldots \quad \ldots\ldots \quad \ldots\ldots \quad \ldots\ldots \quad \ldots\ldots$$
$$-a_{1n}y_1 - a_{2n}y_2 - \ldots\ldots - a_{mn}y_m \leq -c_n$$

where $y_1, y_2, \ldots\ldots, y_m,$ all ≥ 0 (3)

Constructing the dual of the dual shown in equation and multiplying throughout by – 1, we obtain a system identical to relations (1). Thus, the theorem 1 is proved.

Theorem 2:

The value of the objective function Z for any feasible solution of the primal is ≤ the value of the dual objective function W for any feasible solution of the dual.

Proof. The canonical form of the primal linear programming problem of *n* decision variables and *m* constraints is given in equation (1) in theorem (1). The dual of this primal is given in equation (2) in theorem (1). The dual is having *m* decision variables and *n* constraints.

Let us multiply (consider primal) in equality of equation (1) by y_1, the second inequality by y_2; etc. and add them all, we get

$$(a_{11}x_1y_1 + a_{12}x_2y_1 + \ldots\ldots + a_{1n}x_ny_1) + (a_{21}x_1y_2 + a_{22}x_2y_2 + \ldots\ldots + a_{2n}x_ny_2) + \ldots\ldots$$
$$+ (a_{m1}x_1y_m + a_{m2}x_2y_m + \ldots\ldots + a_{mn}x_ny_m) \leq b_1y_1 + b_2y_2 + \ldots\ldots + b_my_m \quad (4)$$

Similarly, multiplying the first inequality of equation (2) by x_1, the second inequality of equation (2) by x_2; etc. and adding them all, we get

$$(a_{11}x_1y_1 + a_{21}x_1y_2 + \ldots\ldots + a_{m1}x_1y_m) + (a_{12}x_2y_1 + a_{22}x_2y_2 + \ldots\ldots + a_{m2}x_2y_m) + \ldots\ldots$$
$$+ (a_{1n}x_ny_1 + a_{2n}x_ny_2 + \ldots\ldots + a_{mn}x_ny_m) \geq c_1x_1 + c_2x_2 + \ldots\ldots + c_nx_n \quad (5)$$

The left hand side of equation (4) and (5) are equal, Hence

$$b_1y_1 + b_2y_2 + \ldots\ldots + b_my_m \geq c_1x_1 + c_2x_2 + \ldots\ldots + c_nx_n$$

or $W \geq Z$

Thus, $\boxed{Z \leq W}$

Hence the theorem (2) is proved.

Theorem 3:

If either the primal or the dual problem has an unbounded solution, then the solution to the other problem is infeasible.

Proof: We know $Z \leq W$. Thus, if the feasible solution to the dual approximates $\infty - \alpha$, the primal can have no feasible solution. Similarly, if the feasible solution to the primal approximates $+ \alpha$, the dual can have no feasible solution. In either case, there is no finite optimum for the primal or the dual. If, however, both problems have finite optimal solutions, it can be reasonably expected that these two solutions are the same. This proves the theorem (3).

Theorem 4:

If both the primal and the dual problems (Main duality theorem) have feasible solutions, then both have optimal solution and $Z_{max} = W_{min}$

Proof:

Primal;

Maximize $\quad Z = CX$

Subject to $\quad AX \leq b$

where $\quad X \geq 0$

Dual, Minimize $\quad W = Yb$

Subject to $\quad YA \geq C$

where $\quad Y \geq 0$

Let the finite optimal solution to the primal be $X_B = B^{-1}b$, we get

$$Z = C_B X_B = C_B B^{-1} b \tag{1}$$

Now $\quad Y_B = C_B B^{-1}$

Also $\quad [Z_j - C_j] \geq 0$ for all j

or $\quad [C_B B^{-1} A - C, C_B B^{-1}] \geq 0$

or $\quad C_B B^{-1} A - C \geq 0, C_B B^{-1} \geq 0$

Now to verify that the associated optimal dual solution is $Y_B = C_B B^{-1}$, only we observe that the above relation then demonstrates that the feasibility conditions for the dual problem is satisfied.

$$\overline{W} = Y_B b = C_B B^{-1} b = C_B X_B = Z_{max}$$

Now we have to show that $\overline{W}$ is also the optimal value of the dual objective function. From theorem (2), we have

$$Z \leq W$$

i.e., $\quad Z_{max} \leq W_{min}$

or $\quad \overline{W} \leq W_{min}$

But $\overline{W}$ can not be less than W_{min} $\overline{W} = W_{min}$

$\therefore \quad \max Z = \min W.$

Theorem 5:

Complementary slackness conditions:

(1) *If a primal variable is positive, then the corresponding dual constraint will be satisfied as an equation at the optimum.*

(2) *If a primal constraint is a strict inequality at the optimum, then the corresponding dual variable must be zero at the optimum.*

(3) *If a dual variable is positive, then the corresponding primal constraint will be satisfied as an equation at the optimum.*

(4) *If a dual constraint is a strict inequality, then the corresponding primal variable must be zero at the optimum.*

6.4.1 Summary of Primal-dual Pairs Relationship

Primal	*Dual*
(1) Maximization	Minimization
(2) No. of variable	No. of constraints
(3) No. of constraint	No. of variables
(4) ≤ type constraint	Non negative variables
(5) = type constraint	unrestricted variable
(6) Unrestricted variable	= type constraint
(7) Objective function coefficient for jth variable	RHS constant for jth constraint
(8) RHS constraint for ith constraint	Objective function coefficient for ith variable
(9) Coefficient (a_{ij}) for jth—variable in ith constraint.	Coefficient (a_{ij}) for ith–variable in jth constraint.

Example 7

A feed mixing operation can be described in terms of the two activities. The required mixture must contain four kinds of ingredients, w, x, y and z. Two basic feeds A and B, which contain the required ingredients are available in the market. One kg of A contains 0.1 kg of w, 0.1 kg of y and 0.2 kg of z. Likewise, one kg of feed B contains 0.1 kg of x, 0.2 kg of y and 0.1 kg of z. The daily per head requirement is of at least 0.4 kg of w, 0.6 kg of x, 2 kg of y and 1.8 kg of z. Feed A can be bought for Rs. 0.07 per kg and B can be bought for Rs. 0.05 per kg. The availabilities, requirements and costs are summarized in the table below.

Ingredient	*Feed A (kg)*	*Feed B (kg)*	*Requirements (kg)*
w	0.1	0.0	0.4
x	0.0	0.1	0.6
y	0.1	0.2	2.0
z	0.2	0.1	1.8
Cost	Rs. 0.07	Rs. 0.05	

Determine the quantities of feeds A and B in the mixture, so that the total cost is minimum.

Solution:

The **primal** linear programming is given below.

Minimize $Z = 0.07x_1 + 0.05\,x_2$ where x_1 is the quantity of feeds of A and x_2 of B.

Subject to
$$0.1\,x_1 + 0\,x_2 \ge 0.4$$
$$0\,x_1 + 0.1\,x_2 \ge 0.6$$
$$0.1\,x_1 + 0.2\,x_2 \ge 2.0$$
$$0.2\,x_1 + 0.1\,x_2 \ge 1.8$$

x_1, x_2, all ≥ 0 (1)

Step 1. Introducing slack or surplus variables, the problem may be written as

Minimize $Z = 0.07\,x_1 + 0.05\,x_2$

Subject to
$$0.1x_1 + 0\,x_2 - x_3 = 0.4$$
$$0\,x_1 + 0.1\,x_2 - x_4 = 0.6$$
$$0.1\,x_1 + 0.2\,x_2 - x_5 = 2.0$$
$$0.2\,x_1 + 0.1\,x_2 - x_6 = 1.8 \qquad (2)$$

where x_1 to x_6 all ≥ 0

$$A = \begin{pmatrix} 0.1 & 0 & -1 & 0 & 0 & 0 \\ 0 & 0.1 & 0 & -1 & 0 & 0 \\ 0.1 & 0.2 & 0 & 0 & -1 & 0 \\ 0.2 & 0.1 & 0 & 0 & 0 & -1 \\ x_1 & x_2 & x_3 & x_4 & x_5 & x_6 \end{pmatrix}$$

We find that there is no unit matrix of dimension $I_{4\times4} = \begin{pmatrix} 1 & 0 & 0 & 0 \\ 0 & 1 & 0 & 0 \\ 0 & 0 & 1 & 0 \\ 0 & 0 & 0 & 1 \end{pmatrix}$, so we put artificial variables

$$0.1\,x_1 + 0\,x_2 - x_3 + x_7 = 0.4$$
$$0\,x_1 + 0.1\,x_2 - x_4 + x_8 = 0.6$$
$$0.1\,x_1 + 0.2\,x_2 - x_5 + x_9 = 2.0$$
$$0.2\,x_1 + 0.1\,x_2 - x_6 + x_{10} = 1.8$$

All $x_{1 \text{ to } 10} \ge 0$ (3)

Now A becomes

$$A = \begin{pmatrix} 0.1 & 0 & -1 & 0 & 0 & 0 & 1 & 0 & 0 & 0 \\ 0 & 0.1 & 0 & -1 & 0 & 0 & 0 & 1 & 0 & 0 \\ 0.1 & 0.2 & 0 & 0 & -1 & 0 & 0 & 0 & 1 & 0 \\ 0.2 & 0.1 & 0 & 0 & 0 & -1 & 0 & 0 & 0 & 1 \\ x_1 & x_2 & x_3 & x_4 & x_5 & x_6 & x_7 & x_8 & x_9 & x_{10} \end{pmatrix}$$

$I_{4\times4} = \begin{pmatrix} 1 & 0 & 0 & 0 \\ 0 & 1 & 0 & 0 \\ 0 & 0 & 1 & 0 \\ 0 & 0 & 0 & 1 \end{pmatrix}$ is available with x_7, x_8, x_9 and x_{10} (Here $x_{7 \text{ to } 10}$ are artificial variables).

$$x_1 = x_2 = x_3 = x_4 = x_5 = x_6 = 0$$

So, $\quad x_7 = 0.4,\ x_8 = 0.6,\ x_9 = 2.0,\ x_{10} = 1.8$

Thus, we solve the problem by 'BIG 'M' Method.

$$Z_{min} = 0.07\,x_1 + 0.05\,x_2 + 0\,x_3 + 0\,x_4 + 0\,x_5 + 0\,x_6 + M\,x_7 + M\,x_8 + M\,x_9 + M\,x_{10}$$

where M is a large number.

Table 1

				0.07	0.05	0	0	0	0	M	M	M	M	
i	*Basis*	C	P_0	P_1	P_2	P_3	P_4	P_5	P_6	P_7	P_8	P_9	P_{10}	
1	P_7	M	0.4	0.1	0	−1	0	0	0	1	0	0	0	$\frac{0.4}{0} = \alpha$
2	P_8	M	0.6	0	(0.1)	0	−1	0	0	0	1	0	0	$\frac{0.6}{0.1} = 6$ ← Min ← Key row
3	P_9	M	2.0	0.1	0.2	0	0	−1	0	0	0	1	0	$\frac{2.0}{0.2} = 10$
4	P_{10}	M	1.8	0.2	0.1	0	0	0	−1	0	0	0	1	$\frac{1.8}{0.1} = 18$
			4.8M	0.4M −0.07	0.4M −0.05	−M	−M	−M	−M	0	0	0	0	

Key no. = 0.1 ↑ Key column

As the leaving vector P_8 is an artificial vector, P_8 column is subsequently dropped.

Table 2

				0.07	0.05	0	0	0	0	M	M	M	
i	*Basis*	C	P_0	P_1	P_2	P_3	P_4	P_5	P_6	P_7	P_9	P_{10}	
1	P_7	M	0.4	0.1	0	−1	0	0	0	1	0	0	$\frac{0.4}{0} = \alpha$
2	P_2	M	6	0	1	0	−10	0	0	0	0	0	
3	P_9	M	0.8	0.1	0	0	(2)	−1	0	0	1	0	$\frac{0.8}{2} = 0.4$ ← Min ← Key row
4	P_{10}	M	1.2	0.2	0	0	1	0	−1	0	0	1	$\frac{1.2}{1} = 1.2$
			2.4M +0.3	0.4M −0.07	0	−M	3M −0.5	−M	−M	0	0	0	

↑ Key column

As the leaving vector P_9 is an artificial vector, P_9 column is subsequently dropped.

Table 3

i	Basis	C	P_0	0.07	0.05	0	0	0	0	M	M	
				P_1	P_2	P_3	P_4	P_5	P_6	P_7	P_{10}	
1	P_7	M	0.4	0.1	0	−1	0	0	0	1	0	$\frac{0.4}{0} = \infty$
2	P_2	0.05	10	0.5	1	0	0	−5	0	0	0	$\frac{10}{-5} = -2$ not considered
3	P_4	0	0.4	$\frac{1}{20}$	0	0	1	$-\frac{1}{2}$	0	0	0	− 0.8 not considered
4	P_{10}	M	0.8	$\frac{3}{20}$	0	0	0	$\left(\frac{1}{2}\right)$	−1	0	1	1.6 ← Min ← Key row
			1.2M +0.5	$\frac{5M}{20}$ −0.045	0	−M	0	M/2 −0.25	−M	0	0	

↑ Key column

As the leaving vector P_{10} is an artificial vector, P_{10} column is subsequently dropped.

Table 4

i	Basis	C	P_0	0.07	0.05	0	0	0	0	M	
				P_1	P_2	P_3	P_4	P_5	P_6	P_7	
1	P_7	M	0.4	(0.1)	0	−1	0	0	0	1	$\frac{0.4}{0.1} = 4$ ← Min ← Key row
2	P_2	0.05	18	2	1	0	0	0	−10	0	$\frac{18}{2} = 9$
3	P_4	0	1.2	$\frac{1}{5}$	0	0	1	0	−1	0	$1.2 \times 5 = 6$
4	P_5	0	1.6	$\frac{3}{10}$	0	0	0	1	−2	0	$\frac{16}{3} = 5.3$
			0.4M + 0.9	0.1M + 0.03	0	−M	0	0	−0.5	0	

↑ Key column

As the leaving vector P_7 is an artificial vector, column P_7 is subsequently dropped.

$Z_{min} = 0.74 \qquad x_1 = \frac{16}{3},\ x_2 = \frac{22}{3},\ x_3 = \frac{2}{15},\ x_4 = \frac{2}{15}$

Minimum Cost of mixture = 0.74 (Rs.)

Feed $A = x_1 = \frac{16}{3}$ kg., Feed $B = x_2 = \frac{22}{3}$ kg.

Table 5

i	Basis	C	P_0	0.07	0.05	0	0	0	0	
				P_1	P_2	P_3	P_4	P_5	P_6	
1	P_1	0.07	4	1	0	–10	0	0	0	
2	P_2	0.05	10	0	1	20	0	0	–10	$\frac{10}{20} = 0.5$
3	P_4	0	$\frac{2}{5}$	0	0	2	1	0	–1	$\frac{1}{5} = 0.2$
4	P_5	0	$\frac{2}{5}$	0	0	(3)	0	1	–2	$\frac{2}{15} = 0.13$ ← Min ← Key row
			0.78	0	0	0.3	0	0	–0.5	

↑ Key column

Table 6

i	Basis	C	P_0	0.07	0.05	0	0	0	0
				P_1	P_2	P_3	P_4	P_5	P_6
1	P_1	0.07	$\frac{16}{3}$	1	0	0	0	$\frac{10}{3}$	$-\frac{20}{3}$
2	P_2	0.05	$\frac{22}{3}$	0	1	0	0	$-\frac{20}{3}$	$\frac{10}{3}$
3	P_4	0	$\frac{2}{15}$	0	0	0	1	$-\frac{2}{3}$	$\frac{1}{3}$
4	P_3	0	$\frac{2}{15}$	0	0	1	0	$\frac{1}{3}$	$-\frac{2}{3}$
			0.74	0	0	0	0	$-\frac{1}{10}$	$-\frac{27}{90}$

Dual programming of the above problem

The dual programming of the problem is given below

Maximize $W = 0.4\, y_1 + 0.6\, y_2 + 2y_3 + 1.8\, y_4$

Subject to $0.1y_1 + 0y_2 + 0.1y_3 + 0.2y_4 \le 0.07$

$0\, y_1 + 0.1\, y_2 + 0.2\, y_3 + 0.1\, y_4 \le 0.05$

y_1, y_2, y_3, y_4 all ≥ 0 (4)

The problem can be changed to minimization problem

Minimize $W = -0.4\, y_1 - 0.6\, y_2 - 2y_3 - 1.8\, y_4 + 0\, y_5 + 0\, y_6$

Subject to $0.1\, y_1 + 0\, y_2 + 0.1\, y_3 + 0.2\, y_4 + y_5 = 0.07$

$0\, y_1 + 0.1\, y_2 + 0.2\, y_3 + 0.1\, y_4 + y_6 = 0.05$ (5)

where y_5 and y_6 are slack variables, and $y_{1 \text{ to } 6} \ge 0$

$$\text{Now } A = \begin{pmatrix} y_1 & y_2 & y_3 & y_4 & y_5 & y_6 \\ 0.1 & 0 & 0.1 & 0.2 & 1 & 0 \\ 0 & 0.1 & 0.2 & 0.1 & 0 & 1 \end{pmatrix}$$

$I_{2\times2} = \begin{pmatrix}1 & 0\\ 0 & 1\end{pmatrix}$ is available y_5 and y_6. So $y_1 = y_2 = y_3 = y_4 = 0$, $y_5 = 0.07$, $y_6 = 0.05$ are the initial solution.

Table 1

i	Basis	C	P_0	−0.4	−0.6	−2.0	−1.8	0	0	
				P_1	P_2	P_3	P_4	P_5	P_6	
1	$Y_5 = P_5$	0	0.07	0.1	0	0.1	0.2	1	0	$\frac{0.07}{0.1} = 0.7$
2	$Y_6 = P_6$	0	0.05	0	0.1	(0.2)	0.1	0	1	$\frac{0.05}{0.2} = 0.25$ ← Min ← Key row
			[0]	0.4	0.6	2.0	1.8	0	0	

↑ Key column (Maximum positive) [under P_3]

Table 2

i	Basis	C	P_0	−0.4	−0.6	−2.0	−1.8	0	0	
				P_1	P_2	P_3	P_4	P_5	P_6	
1	P_5	0	0.045	0.1	−0.05	0	(0.15)	1	−0.5	0.3 ← Min ← Key row
2	P_3	−2	$\frac{1}{4}$	0	$\frac{1}{2}$	1	$\frac{1}{2}$	0	5	0.5
			[0.5]	0.4	−0.4	0	0.8	0	−10	

↑ Key column [under P_4]

Table 3

i	Basis	C	P_0	−0.4	−0.6	−2.0	−1.8	0	0	
				P_1	P_2	P_3	P_4	P_5	P_6	
1	P_4	−1.8	0.3	$\frac{2}{3}$	$-\frac{1}{3}$	0	1	$\frac{20}{3}$	$-\frac{10}{3}$	
2	P_3	−2.0	$\frac{1}{10}$	$-\frac{1}{3}$	$\frac{2}{3}$	1	0	$-\frac{10}{3}$	$\frac{20}{3}$	
			[−0.74]	$-\frac{0.4}{3}$	$-\frac{0.4}{3}$	0	0	$-\frac{16}{3}$	$-\frac{22}{3}$	

$$W_{max} = +0.74 \quad \therefore \quad W_{min} = -0.74 \text{ (Rs.)}$$

$$y_1 = 0,\ y_2 = 0,\ y_3 = 0.1,\ y_4 = 0.3,\ W_{max} = 0.74$$

We have solved the primal and dual solutions completely and the following properties are found:

(1) The value of the objective function is the same for primal and dual solutions, but of opposite sign.

(2) The values for the slack variables of the primal are given by the base row under the non-basic variables of the dual solution with changed sign.

(3) The values for the non-basic variables of the primal are given by the base row of the dual solution, under the slack variables (if any), with changed sign and under the artificial variables (if there is no slack variables in a constraint) with changed sign after deleting the constant M.

6.5 ECONOMIC INTERPRETATION OF THE 'DUAL VARIABLES'

We find an interesting interpretation of dual variables from the cost or economic point of view. To illustrate this point we refer to the problem given in example 7.

Optimal solution to the primal was found to be

$x_1 = \frac{16}{3}$ kg, $x_2 = \frac{22}{3}$ kg, Z_{min} = Rs. 0.74 and optimal solution to the dual was found to be

$$y_1 = 0, y_2 = 0, y_3 = 0.1, y_4 = 0.3, W_{max} = 0.74 \text{ (Rs.)}$$

As the right hand side of constraints of equation (3) denotes monetary units (*i.e.*, in rupees), Left hand side must also be in monetary units. In the first term $0.1\,y_1$ of the first constraint, 0.1 is the amount in kg of ingredient w in one kg of feed A and hence y_1 must denote the cost in rupee per kg of ingredient w.

Similarly, y_2 stands for the cost per kg of ingredient x and so on. Here y_1, y_2, y_3 and y_4 are called the *SHADOW* prices of ingredients w, x, y and z respectively. They represent not the actual market prices but the true accounting values or the imputed values of the respective ingredients.

Thus, the true accounting values per kg of ingredients w, x, y and z to the company preparing the mixture are $y_1 = 0$, $y_2 = 0$, $y_3 = 0.1$ and $y_4 = 0.3$, respectively. $y_1 = 0$ and $y_2 = 0$ means that the accounting values of ingredient w and x are zero each *i.e.*, they are produced as by products.

The objective function of the dual is to maximize the total accounting values of the feeds produced per day. The two constraints of equation (3) of the dual ensure that the total accounting value of the daily production of each feed must remain less than their market prices. The shadow prices represent the values that the company should set on the four ingredients in order to reflect their value to the society.

6.6 EXPLANATION OF TABLE 3 OF DUAL PROBLEM (REFERENCE EXAMPLE 7 DUAL SOLUTION)

Optimal values of x_1 and x_2 are given under the slack variables of the dual with changed sign

i.e., $x_1 = -\left(-\frac{16}{3}\right) = \frac{16}{3}$, $x_2 = -\left(-\frac{22}{3}\right) = \frac{22}{3}$, optimal values of dual variables y_3 and y_4 ($y_3 = 0.1$, $y_4 = 0.3$) could be obtained from the optimal primal solution (Table 6 of Problem 6.4.2) under the slack variables x_5 and x_6 with changed sign

$$\left(x_5 = \frac{1}{10} = 0.1, x_6 = \frac{27}{90} = \frac{3}{10} = 0.3\right).$$

Chapter 7

DUAL SIMPLEX METHOD AND SENSITIVITY ANALYSIS

7.1 INTRODUCTION

In the simplex algorithm, the problem starts at a basic feasible solution. All the successive iterations remain basic and feasible but move towards optimality until the optimal is reached at the last iteration. The algorithm is sometimes referred to as the primal simplex method. In dual simplex, the linear programming (L.P.) starts at a basic solution that is (better than) optimal but infeasible and successive iterations remain basic and (better than) optimal as they move towards feasibility. At the last iteration, the feasible (optimal) solution is found.

7.2 DUAL FEASIBILITY CONDITION

The leaving variable, x_r, is the basic variable having the most negative value (break ties arbitrarily). If all the basic variables are non-negative, the algorithm ends.

7.3 DUAL OPTIMALITY CONDITION

The entering variable is determined from among the non-basic variables as the one corresponding to

$$\text{Min. non basic } x_j \quad \left\{ \left| \frac{Z_j - C_j}{\alpha_{rj}} \right|, \alpha_{rj} < 0 \right\}$$

where $Z_j - C_j$ is the objective coefficient of the Z row in the tableau and α_{rj} is the negative constraint coefficient of the tableau associated with the row of the leaving variable, x_r, and the column of the non-basic variable, x_j. Ties are broken arbitrarily. Note that the dual optimality condition guarantees that optimality will be maintained throughout all iterations.

To start the L.P. both optimal and feasible, two requirements must be satisfied.

(1) The objective function must satisfy the optimality condition of the regular simplex method.

(2) All the constraints must be of the type (≤).

The second condition requires converting any (≥) type to (≤) type simply by multiplying both sides of the inequality (≥) by − 1. If the L.P. includes (=) constraints, the equation can be replaced by two inequalities, for example $x_1 + x_2 = 1$ is equivalent to

$$x_1 + x_2 \le 1 \quad (1)$$

$$x_1 + x_2 \ge 1$$

or

$$-x_1 - x_2 \le -1 \quad (2)$$

After converting all the constraints to (≤), the L.P. will have an infeasible starting solution if and only if, at least one of the right-hand sides of the inequalities is strictly negative. Else, if Z is optimal and none of the right hand sides are negative, there will be no need to apply the dual simplex method as the starting solution is already optimal and feasible.

Example 1

Minimize $Z = 3x_1 + 2x_2$

Subject to

$$3x_1 + x_2 \ge 3$$

$$4x_1 + 3x_2 \ge 6$$

$$x_1 + x_2 \le 3$$

$$x_1, x_2 \ge 0$$

In the example, the first two inequalities are multiplied by − 1 to convert them to (≤) constraints.

$$-3x_1 - x_2 \le -3 \quad (1)$$

$$-4x_1 - 3x_2 \le -6 \quad (2)$$

$$x_1 + x_2 \le 3 \quad (3)$$

$$x_1, x_2 \ge 0 \quad (4)$$

or,

$$-3x_1 - x_2 + x_3 = -3$$

$$-4x_1 - 3x_2 + x_4 = -6$$

$$x_1 + x_2 + x_5 = 3$$

$$x_{1 \text{ to } 5} \ge 0$$

$$A = \begin{pmatrix} -3 & -1 & 1 & 0 & 0 \\ -4 & -3 & 0 & 1 & 0 \\ 1 & 1 & 0 & 0 & 1 \\ \downarrow & \downarrow & \downarrow & \downarrow & \downarrow \\ x_1 & x_2 & x_3 & x_4 & x_5 \end{pmatrix}$$

Unit matrix $I_{3 \times 3}$ is available with x_3, x_4, and x_5 which are slack variables.

$$x_3 = -3,\ x_4 = -6,\ x_5 = 3$$

and $$Z = 3x_1 + 2x_2 + 0x_3 + 0x_4 + 0x_5$$

Table 1

i	Basis	C	P_0	3	2	0	0	0	
				P_1	P_2	P_3	P_4	P_5	
1	P_3	0	−3	−3	−1				
2	P_4	0	−6	−4	(−3)				← Key row (maximum negative in P_0 column − 6)
3	P_5	0	3	1	1				
	$Z_j -$	C_j →	[0]	−3	−2				
				$\frac{-3}{-4}$	$\frac{-2}{-3}$				

↑ Minimum

The tableau starts optimal (all $Z_j - C_j \le 0$) and the starting basic solution is infeasible ($x_3 = -3$, $x_4 = -6$, $x_5 = 3$). According to the dual feasibility condition ($x_4 = -6$) is the leaving variable.

The ratios shows that x_2 is the entering variable. Note that a variable x_j is a candidate for entering the basic solution only if its α_{ij} is strictly negative. This means that the variables x_3, x_4 and x_5 should not be considered.

Table 2

i	Basis	C	P_0	3	2	0	0	0	
				P_1	P_2	P_3	P_4	P_5	
1	P_3	0	−1	$\left(-\frac{5}{3}\right)$	0	1	$-\frac{1}{3}$	0	← Maximum negative (− 1) under P_0 column
2	P_2	2	2	$\frac{4}{3}$	1	0	$-\frac{1}{3}$	0	
3	P_5	0	1	$-\frac{1}{3}$	0	0	$\frac{1}{3}$	1	
			[4]	$-\frac{1}{3}$	0	0	$-\frac{2}{3}$	0	
				$\frac{-1/3}{-5/3} = \frac{1}{5}$			$\frac{-2/3}{-1/3} = 2$		

↑ Minimum

Table 3

i	Basis	C	P_0	3	2	0	0	0
				P_1	P_2	P_3	P_4	P_5
1	P_1	3	$\frac{3}{5}$	1	0	$-\frac{3}{5}$	$\frac{1}{5}$	0
2	P_2	2	$\frac{6}{5}$	0	1	$\frac{4}{5}$	$-\frac{3}{5}$	0
3	P_5	0	$\frac{6}{5}$	0	0	$-\frac{1}{5}$	$\frac{2}{5}$	1
			$\boxed{\frac{21}{5}}$	0	0	$-\frac{1}{5}$	$-\frac{3}{5}$	0

Now we find that there is no negative value of entries under P_0 column. So it is final table. The table 3 is feasible and optimal.

$$x_1 = \frac{3}{5}, x_2 = \frac{6}{5}, x_5 = \frac{6}{5}, Z_{min} = \frac{21}{5}$$

7.3.1 Graphical Solution of Problem Example 1

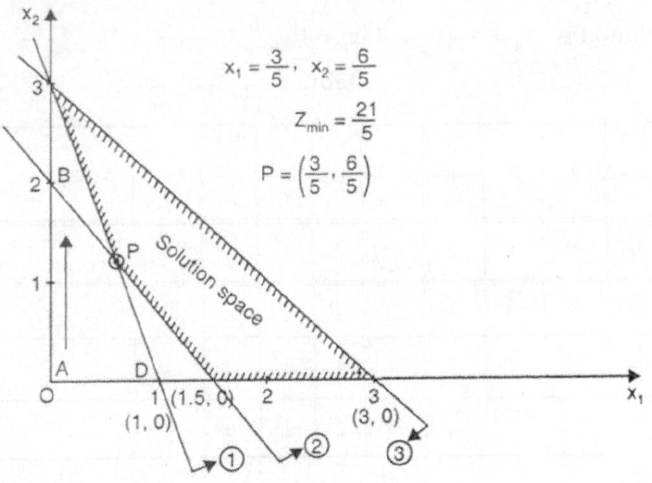

Fig. 1

For better understanding of the dual simplex approach, Fig. 1 shows graphically the path followed by the algorithm in the solution of the above problem. The algorithm starts at extreme point *A* (which is infeasible and better than optimum), then moves to *B* (which still is infeasible and better than optimum), and finally becomes feasible at *P*. At this point, the process ends with *P* as the feasible optimum solution.

7.4 GENERALISED SIMPLEX ALGORITHM (NON-OPTIMAL AND INFEASIBLE)

Example 2

Maximize $Z = 2x_3$

Subject to $-x_1 + 2x_2 - 2x_3 \geq 8$

$$-x_1 + x_2 + x_3 \leq 4$$

$$2x_1 - x_2 + 4x_3 \leq 10$$

$$x_1, x_2, x_3 \geq 0.$$

Solution:

Minimize $Z = -2x_3$

Subject to $x_1 - 2x_2 + 2x_3 \leq -8$ [Converted to ≤ type]

$$-x_1 + x_2 + x_3 \leq 4$$

$$2x_1 - x_2 + 4x_3 \leq 10$$

$$x_1, x_2, x_3 \geq 0$$

or,

$$x_1 - 2x_2 + 2x_3 + x_4 = -8$$

$$-x_1 + x_2 + x_3 + x_5 = 4$$

$$2x_1 - x_2 + 4x_3 + x_6 = 10$$

$$x_1, x_2, x_3 \geq 0$$

The initial solution is $x_4 = -8, x_5 = 4, x_6 = 10$

Table 1

i	Basis	C	P_0	0	0	−2	0	0	0	
				P_1	P_2	P_3	P_4	P_5	P_6	
1	P_4	0	−8	1	(−2)	2	1	0	0	← Maximum negative under P_0 column (− 8)
2	P_5	0	4	−1	1	1	0	1	0	
3	P_6	0	10	2	−1	4	0	0	1	
			[0]	0	0	2	0	0	0	
					(− 2)					

The model can be put in the above table in which starting basic solution ($x_4 = -8$, $x_5 = 4$, $x_6 = 10$) is both non-optimal (because of column under x_3) and infeasible (because of $x_4 = -8$). Let us remove infeasibility first by applying the dual simplex condition that selects x_4 as the leaving variable. To determine the entering variable, all we need is a non-basic variable whose constraint coefficient in the x_4 row is strictly negative here (− 2).

Table 2

i	Basis	C	P_0	0	0	−2	0	0	0	
				P_1	P_2	P_3	P_4	P_5	P_6	
1	P_2	0	4	$-\frac{1}{2}$	1	−1	$-\frac{1}{2}$	0	0	
2	P_5	0	0	$-\frac{1}{2}$	0	2	$\frac{1}{2}$	1	0	
3	P_6	0	14	$\frac{3}{2}$	0	3	$-\frac{1}{2}$	0	1	
			$\boxed{0}$	0	0	2	0	0	0	

The above table shows that $x_2 = 4$, $x_5 = 0$ and $x_6 = 14$ is a feasible solution but not optimal. So we can use the simplex algorithm to find out optimality.

7.5 POST OPTIMAL OR SENSITIVITY ANALYSIS

7.5.1 Graphical Sensitivity Analysis

An Linear Programming (L.P.) model is a snapshot of a real life situation in which the model parameters (objective and constraint coefficients) assume static values. To enhance the applicability of L.P. in practice, we need to add a dynamic dimension that investigates the impact of making changes in the model parameters (objective and constraint coefficients) on the optimal solution. This procedure is referred as sensitivity analysis because it studies the sensitivity of the optimal solution to changes made in the model.

Two cases of sensitivity analysis based on the graphical L.P. solution are (*i*) changes in the objective coefficients and (*ii*) changes in the right-hand side value of the constraints.

7.5.1.1 Sensitivity analysis based on changes in the objective function coefficients

The general objective function in a two variable L.P. problems can be written as

Maximize or minimize $Z = c_1x_1 + c_2x_2$.

Changes in the coefficients c_1 and c_2 will change the slope of Z and, hence, possibly, the optimal corner point. However, there is a range of variation for both c_1 and c_2 that will keep the current optimal unchanged. Specifically, we are interested in determining the range of optimality for the ratio $\frac{c_1}{c_2}$, $\left(\text{or } \frac{c_2}{c_1}\right)$ that will keep the present optimum solution unchanged.

Example: Consider

Maximum $\quad Z = 5x_1 + 4x_2$

Subject to $\quad 6x_1 + 4x_2 \leq 24 \qquad (1)$

$x_1 + 2x_2 \leq 6 \qquad (2)$

$$-x_1 + x_2 \le 1 \qquad (3)$$
$$x_2 \le 2 \qquad (4)$$
$$x_1, x_2 \ge 0, \text{ (5) and (6) respectively.} \qquad (5) \;\&\; (6)$$

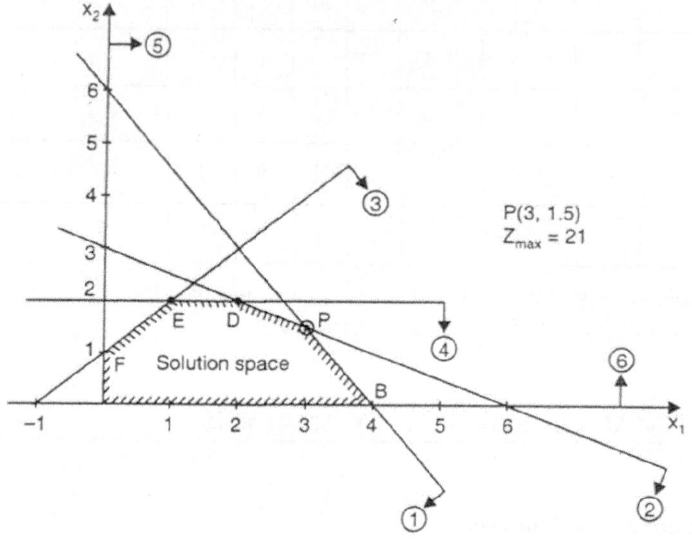

Fig. 1

The optimum solution at P provides the maximum value of $Z = 5x_1 + 4x_2$. If we change the objective to $Z = c_1x_1 + c_2x_2$ then the solution at P will remain optimum so long as the slope of Z lies between the slopes of the two lines intersecting at P.

For example here the lines are

$$6x_1 + 4x_2 = 24 \text{ and } x_1 + 2x_2 = 6$$

$$c_1x_1 + c_2x_2 = 21$$
$$6x_1 + 4x_2 = 24$$
$$x_1 + 2x_2 = 6$$

If $c_1 \neq 0$ then

$$\boxed{\frac{4}{6} \le \frac{c_2}{c_1} \le \frac{2}{1}}$$

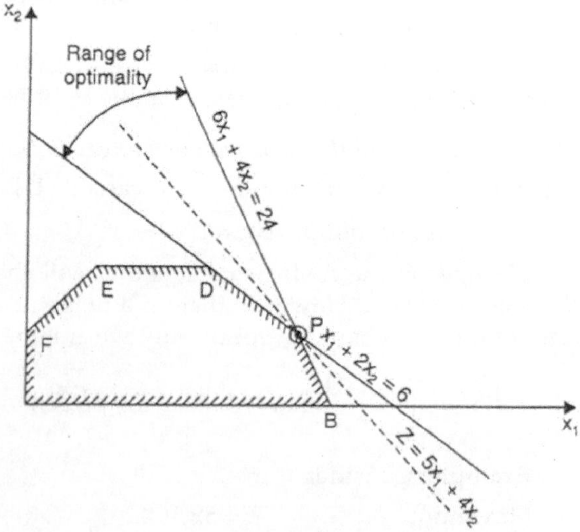

Fig. 2

and if $c_2 \neq 0$

$$\boxed{\frac{1}{2} \leq \frac{c_1}{c_2} \leq \frac{6}{4}}$$

In the first condition $c_1 \neq 0$ signifies that the objective function line cannot be horizontal. Similarly, in the second condition $c_2 \neq 0$ means that Z cannot be vertical. As can be seen from Fig. 2, the optimality range in this model (defined by the two lines intersecting at P) does not permit the objective function $Z = c_1x_1 + c_2x_2$ to be a horizontal or vertical line. As a result, either of the given two conditions is applicable to this example. For the cases where both c_1 and c_2 can assume zero values, the range for $\frac{c_1}{c_2}$ or $\frac{c_2}{c_1}$ must be partitioned into two sets in which the denominators are not allowed to be zero.

What the conditions for $\frac{c_1}{c_2}$ and $\frac{c_2}{c_1}$ say is that so long as these ratios are within specified limits, the optimum solution remains unchanged at P. Note that if $Z = c_1x_1 + c_2x_2$ happens to coincide with $x_1 + 2x_2 = 6$, then alternative optima can occur anywhere on the line segment PD. Similarly, if it coincides with $6x_1 + 4x_2 = 24$, then all the points on the line segment BP provide alternate optima. The observation, nevertheless, does not change the fact that P remains optimum in both cases. We can use the given conditions to determine the optimal range for one of the coefficients, given that the other remains as originally given in $Z = 5x_1 + 4x_2$. Thus, given $c_2 = 4$, the associated optimal range for c_1 is determined from the condition $\frac{1}{2} \leq \frac{c_1}{c_2} \leq \frac{6}{4}$ by substituting $c_2 = 4$, which yields

$$4 \times \frac{1}{2} \leq c_1 \leq 4 \times \frac{6}{4} \quad \text{or} \quad 2 \leq c_1 \leq 6$$

Similarly, given $c_1 = 5$, the conditions $\frac{4}{6} \leq \frac{c_2}{c_1} \leq \frac{2}{1}$ will yield $\frac{10}{3} \leq c_2 \leq 10$

7.5.1.2 Sensitivity analysis based on change in availability of resources

In Linear Programming models, constraints, directly or in directly, represent the usage of limited resources. In this case, the right hand side can be thought of as representing limits on the availability of the resources. We will investigate the sensitivity of the optimum solution to make changes in the amount of available resources.

Considering the present model, it shows that the current optimum occurs at P which is the intersection of the lines associated with raw materials (resources) M_1 and M_2. When the availability of M_1 changes (increases or decreases around its current level of 24 tons), and given $M_2 = 6$ tons, the optimum solution at point P will 'slide' along the line segment DG.

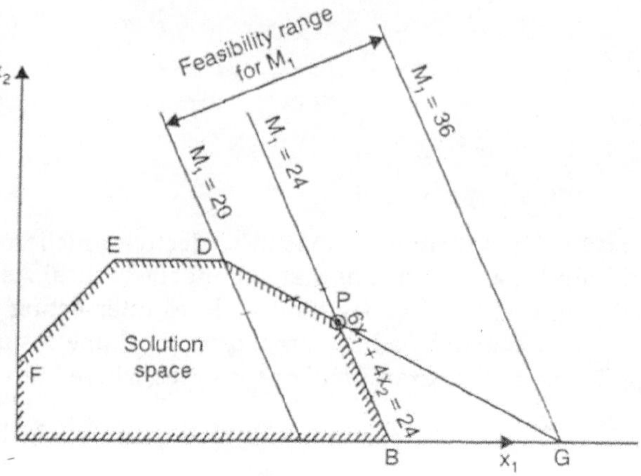

Fig. 3

Any change in M_1 outside the range of this segment will render point P (Intersection of the lines associated with M_1 and M_2) infeasible. For this reason, we say that the end points D (2, 2) and G (6, 0) delineate the feasibility range for M_1.

Thus, M_1 is given by at D (2, 2) $= 6 \times 2 + 4 \times 2 = 20$ tons

M_1 is given by at G (6, 0) $= 6 \times 6 + 4 \times 0 = 36$ tons

It then follows that given $M_2 = 6$, the feasibility range for M_1 is $20 \leq M_1 \leq 36$.

The result shows that M_1 can be decreased by as much as 4 tons or increased by as much as 12 (*i.e.*, 36 – 24) tons while guaranteeing that the optimum solution point will be given by the intersection of M_1 and M_2 lines. Indeed, given $M_2 = 6$, the associated general solution is obtained in terms of M_1 as

$$\left.\begin{aligned} x_1 &= \frac{1}{4} M_1 - 3 \\ x_2 &= -\frac{1}{8} M_1 + \frac{9}{2} \end{aligned}\right\}; \ 20 \leq M_1 \leq 36$$

Next consider raw material M_2. It shows that the feasibility range for M_2 ($M_1 = 24$) is delineated by the end points B and H, where B (4, 0) and $H\left(\frac{8}{3}, 2\right)$. H is defined by the intersection of lines ED with BP.

Thus, Amount of M_2 at $B = x_1 + 2x_2 = 4$ tons

Amount of M_2 at $H = \frac{20}{3}$ tons

When $M_1 = 24$, the feasibility range of M_2 is

$$4 \leq M_2 \leq \frac{20}{3} \quad \text{and} \quad x_1 = -\frac{1}{2} M_2 + 6$$

$$x_2 = \frac{3}{4} M_2 - 3$$

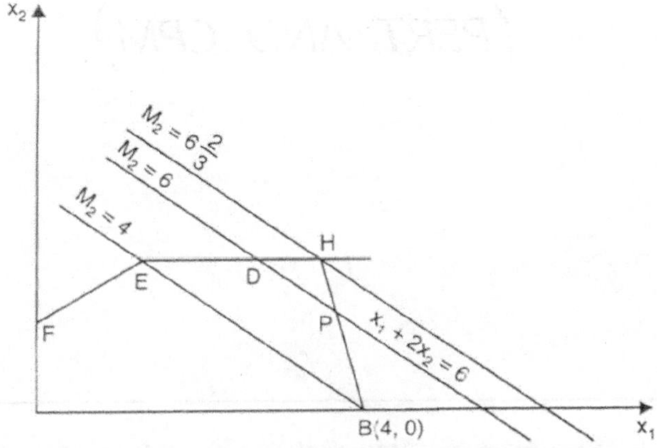

Fig. 4

Unit worth of resource:

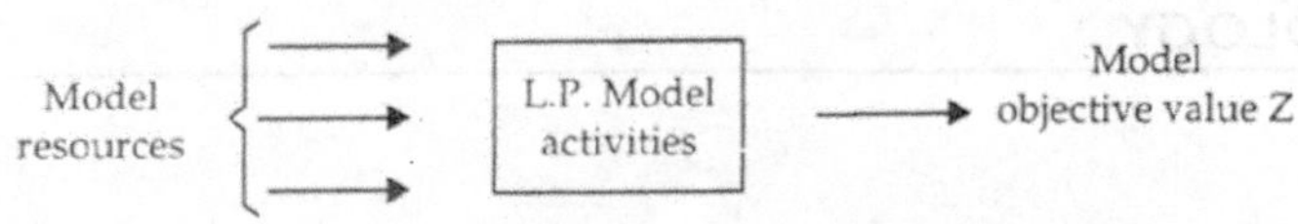

Figure above shows that an L.P. model can be thought of as an input-output model in which the limited resources represent the input and the value of the objective function summarizes the output. An useful measure of the model is to determine how changes in its input (resources) can impact its output (the objective value). Such a measure can be obtained as a by product of the calculation of the feasibility range presented in case (2). Specifically, we seek to determine the unit worth of a resource, which is defined as the rate of change in the optimum objective value that results from making changes in the available amount of a resource.

Let, y_i represents the worth per unit of resource i, the associated formula for computing this measure is

$$y_i = \frac{\text{Change in value of } Z \text{ corresponding to the feasible range of resource } i}{\text{feasible range of resource } i}$$

Fig. (3) shows $20 \le M_1 \le 36$

$$y_i = \frac{\text{Change in } Z \text{ from } D \text{ to } G}{\text{Change in } M_1 \text{ from } D \text{ to } G}$$

Given D (2, 2), G (6, 0) then

$$Z_D = 18, \quad y_i = \frac{30 - 18}{36 - 20} = 0.75 \text{ per ton of } M_1$$

$$Z_G = 30,$$

1 ton change in M_1 in the above range will change the optimum value of Z by 0.75.

Chapter **8**

PROJECT MANAGEMENT (PERT AND CPM)

8.1 PERT

Project analysis through systematic network showing various alternative paths is known as PERT (Programme evaluation and review technique).

8.2 TERMINOLOGY

8.2.1 Event

The starting and finishing of an activity is called event, event itself does not take any time. It is denoted by a circle with number inside, *e.g.*, event 1 is denoted by 1.

Event or events that immediately come before another event without any intervening events are called 'predecessor events' to that event. Event or events that immediately follow another event without any intervening events are called 'successor events' to that event.

8.2.2 Activity

It is the operation done between two events. It is denoted by an arrow →

e.g.,

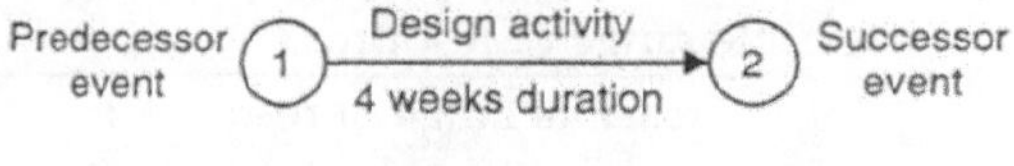

8.2.3 Dummy Activity

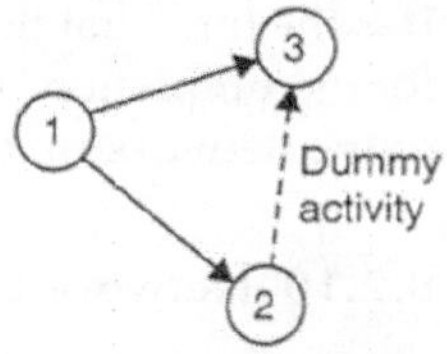

The activity which does not consume any time is called dummy activity. It is denoted as ···→ (dotted arrow).

(2) and (3) may be assumed to be the same place.

8.2.4 Optimistic Time (t_o)

It is the earlier completion time. It assumes that execution goes extremely well. It is denoted as t_o.

8.2.5 Pessimistic Time (t_p)

It is the later completion time. It assumes that execution goes extremely poor. It is denoted as t_p.

8.2.6 Normal Time (t_n)

It is the most likely time. It assumes that execution is done under normal conditions.

8.2.7 Estimated Time (t_e)

It is statistically determined time. It is denoted as t_e.

$$t_e = \frac{t_o + 4t_n + t_p}{6}$$

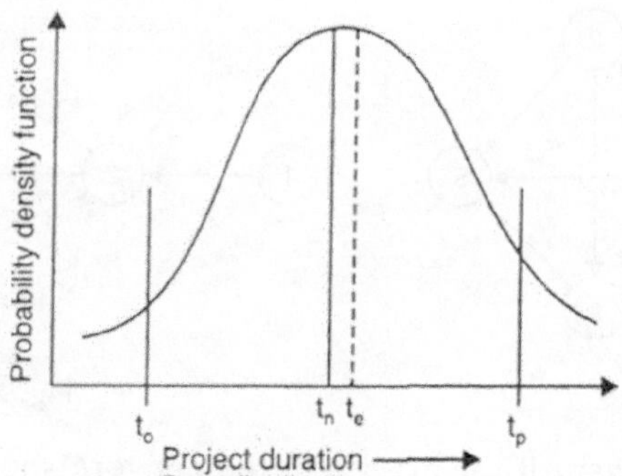

Beta distribution

8.2.8 Notation

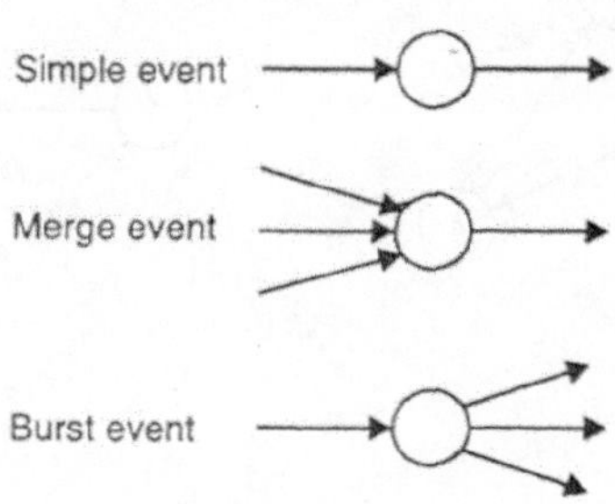

8.2.9 Earliest Expected Time (T_E)

It is the time that the activity consumes or it is the longest path that the activity ending event takes for its completion. This is calculated by adding the expected time of each activity through any path of the network up to that event. It is denoted as e.g. $\boxed{8}$, T_E = 8 weeks.

8.2.10 Network Drawing

It is desirable to draw a clear network. There is no formal rule. It depends on the project-planner. However, here we can discuss few points which help in drawing a better network.

(*a*) **Curved arrows:** We should not use any curved arrows in the network. With a little modification it can be converted into straight line artows. Refer Fig. 1(*a*) and Fig. 1(*b*).

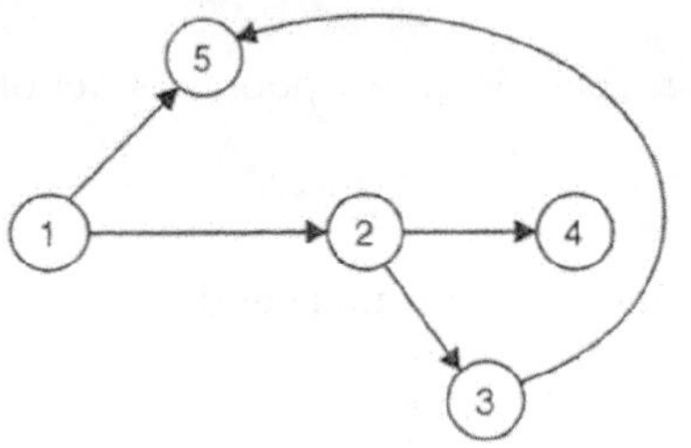

Fig. 1(*a*) 'No'

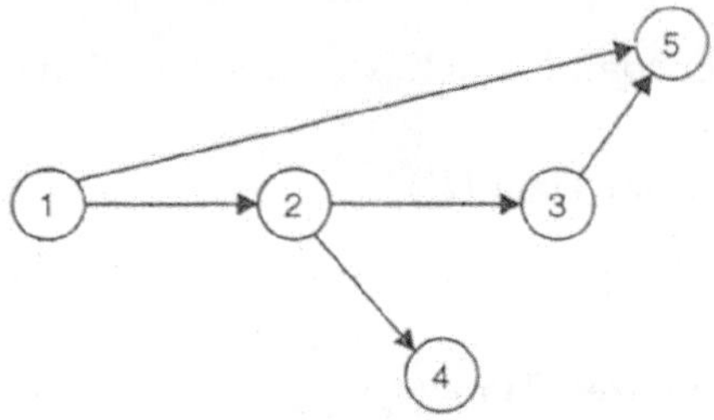

Fig. 1(*b*) Yes

(*b*) **Intersecting arrows:** Intersecting or crossed arrows should be avoided because it makes the network clumsy and difficult to analyse.

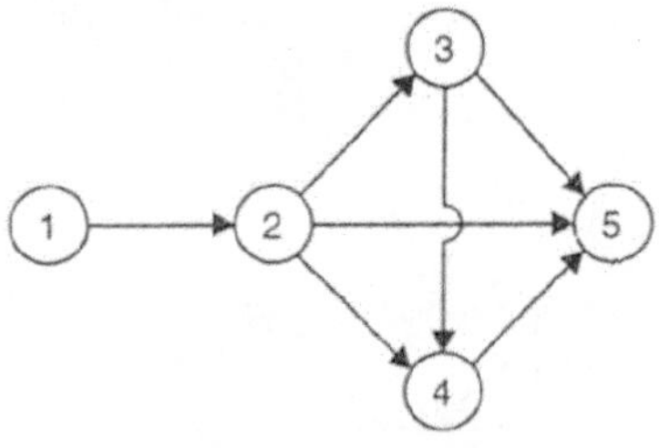

Fig. 2(*a*) No

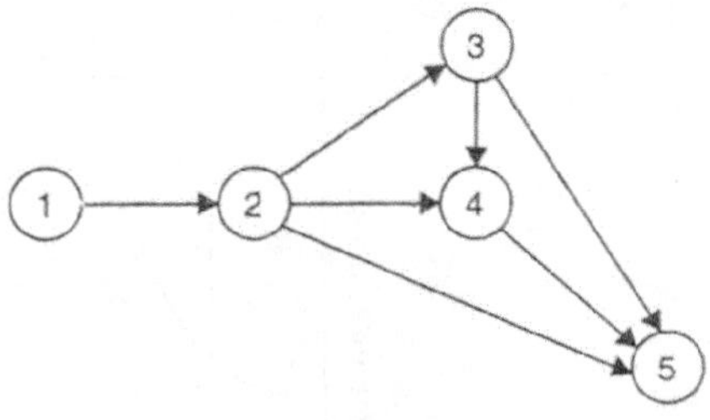

Fig. 2(*b*) Yes

(*c*) **Unidirectional arrows:** All the arrows of the network should be directed from left to right only. These are explained in Fig. 3(*a*) and 3 (*b*).

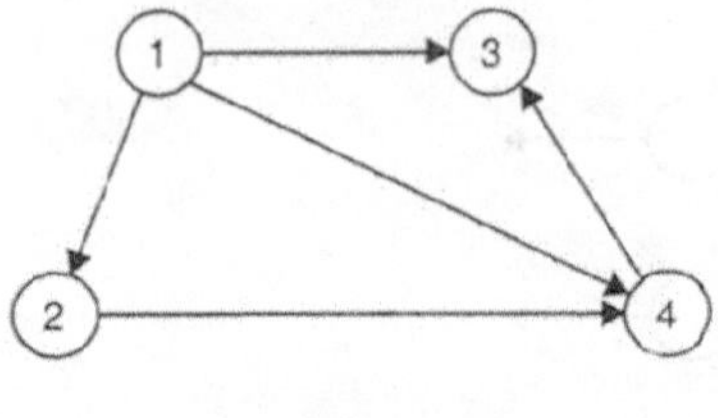

Fig. 3(*a*) No

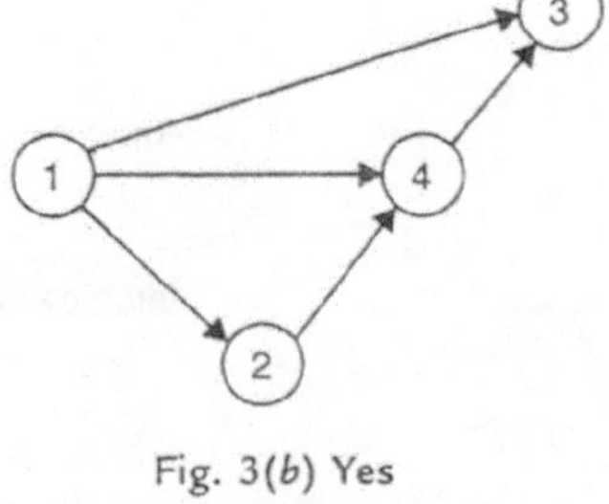

Fig. 3(*b*) Yes

(*d*) **Arrows of equal length:** As far as possible the arrows will be of equal length. This makes the network look better and clear as shown in Fig. 4(*a*), 4(*b*).

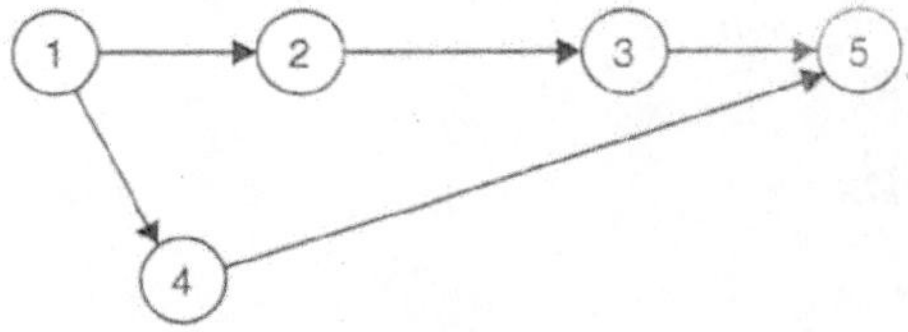

Fig. 4(*a*) No

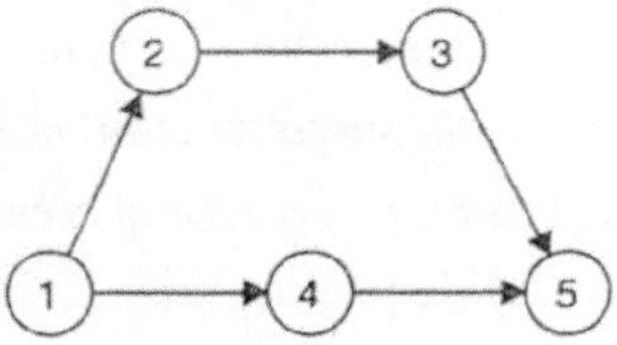

Fig. 4(*b*) Yes

(*e*) **Equal angle:** As far as possible it is a good practice to place the arrows at equal angles and make them as symmetric as practicable.

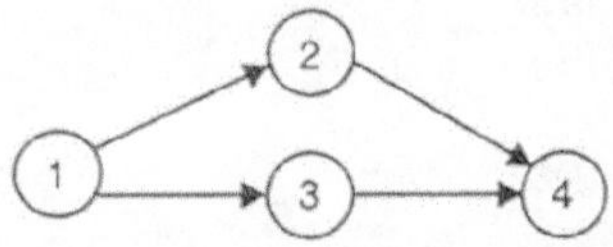

Fig. 5(*a*) No

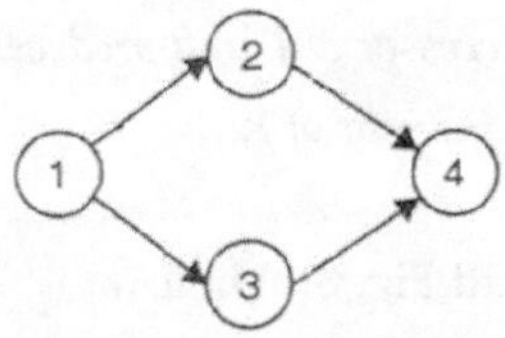

Fig. 5(*b*) Yes

(*f*) **Parallelism of arrows:** The arrows should be parallel to each other as far as possible. Dummies can be used to make arrows parallel. These dummies are called 'redundant dummies'.

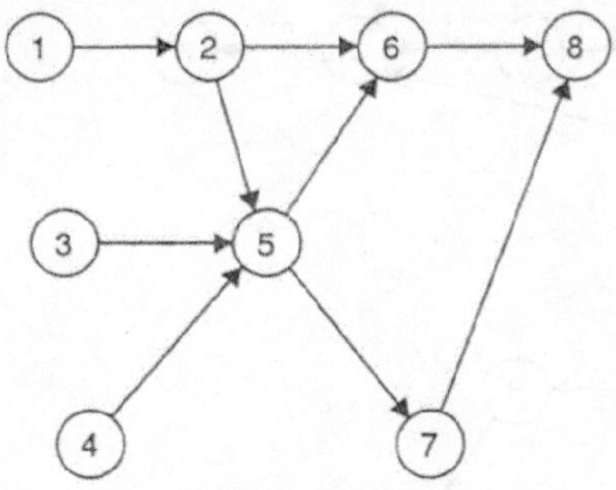

Fig. 6(*a*) No

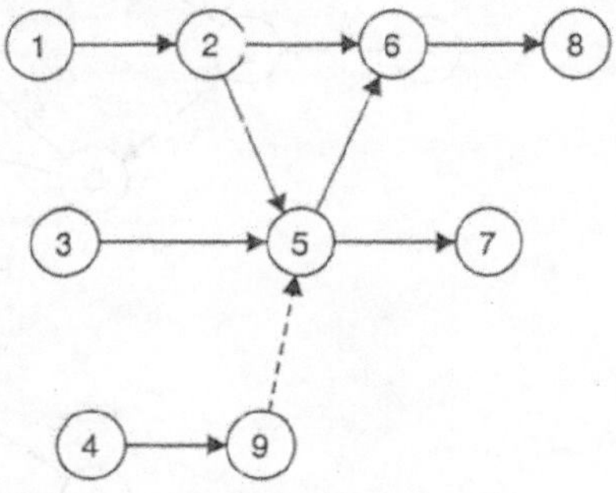

Fig. 6(*b*) Yes

(*g*) **Excessive dummies:** Use of excessive dummies should be avoided.

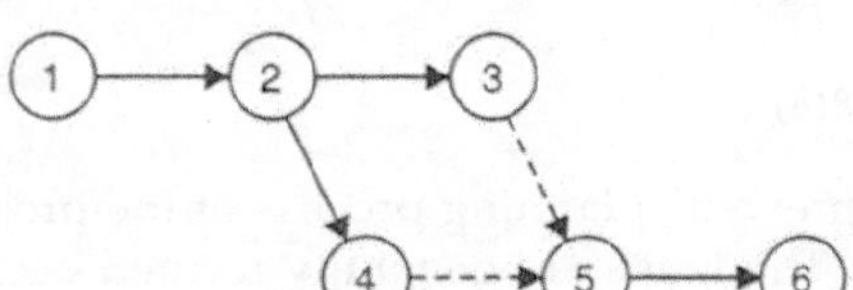

Fig. 7(*a*) No

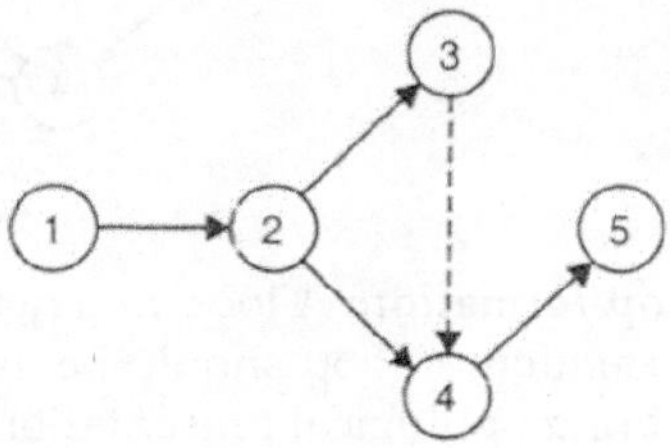

Fig. 7(*b*) Yes

Example 1

Draw a network for the following project and number the events according to Fulkerson's rule. (See 8.2.10).

Sr. No.	*Description*
(*a*)	*A is the starting event and K is the end event.*
(*b*)	*B is the successor event of A.*
(*c*)	*B is the predecessor of events C and D.*
(*d*)	*C is the predecessor of event F.*
(*e*)	*E is the successor of C and D.*
(*f*)	*E is the predecessor of G.*
(*g*)	*D is the predecessor of J.*
(*h*)	*G is the predecessor of J.*
(*i*)	*H is the successor of F and predecessor of J.*
(*j*)	*J is the predecessor of K.*

Solution:

Refer Fir. 8(*a*) and Fig. 8(*b*) below

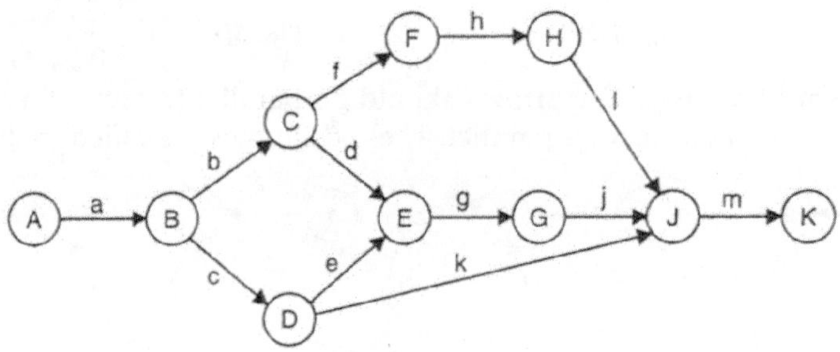

Fig. 8(*a*)

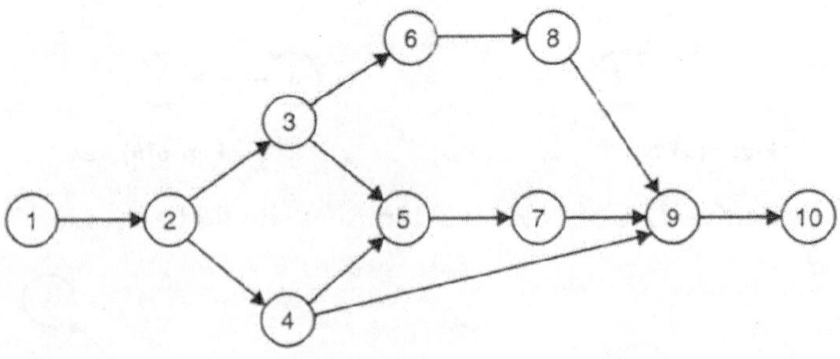

Fig. 8(*b*)

(*h*) **Loop formation:** A loop in a network prevents planning process of the project further. Hence the formation of loop should be avoided. The loops are generally formed because of the wrong numbering or illogical presentation of the activities. Refer Fig. 9.

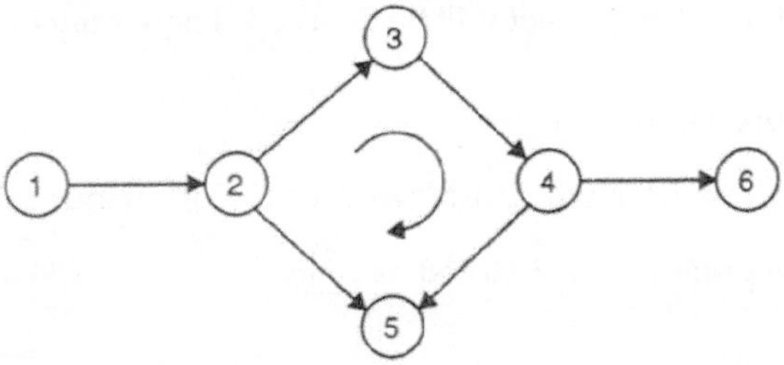

Fig. 9.

8.2.11 Numbering the Network: (Fulkerson's Rule)

D.R. Fulkerson proposed a rule which reduces the sequential numbering to the following steps.

(*i*) An 'initial' event is one which has arrows coming out of it (emerging arrows) and none entering it. In a network there will be one initial event. Number it as 1.

(*ii*) Delete all arrows emerging from event 1. This will create at least one more 'initial event'.

(*iii*) Number these initial events as 2, 3, ...

(*iv*) Delete all emerging arrows from these newly found numbered events which will create new initial event.

(*v*) Follow step (*iii*) and (*iv*).

(*vi*) Continue until the end-event is reached which has no emerging arrows.

Use of Fulkerson's rule: By applying Fulkerson's rule we get example 1. The explanation follows.

(*i*) Event A has no entering arrows, only one emerging arrow is there. Hence, it is an 'initial' event and we number it 1.

(*ii*) By deleting the emerging arrow *a*, another initial event B is found.

(*iii*) We number this new initial event B as 2.

(*iv*) There are two emerging arrows *b* and *c* from event B. By deleting these two emerging arrows we get two more initial events C and D.

(*v*) Number these initial events as 3 and 4 respectively.

(*vi*) This process of numbering is to continue until we reach the end - event K which has no emerging arrows. This is numbered as 10.

Though we have used the numbers serially from 1 to 10 to number these ten events, 'skip numbering system' can also be used to number the events in a practical project because we can enter any number in between. By 'skip-numbering' we mean numbers like 10, 20, 30, 40, ... or 5, 10, 15, 20, ... etc.

8.2.12 Critical Path

The path which consumes the maximum time is known as critical path and the activities following this path are critical activities. The importance to the critical path lies in the fact that any delay in the critical path will involve the delay in the project time but the delay in the other paths does not necessarily imply that the entire project will be delayed. There may be more than one critical path.

8.2.13 Latest Allowable Time (T_L)

It is the time we can allow after which no event could occur but still not interferring with the completion of the entire project. It is denoted as $\triangle T_L$.

8.2.14 Slack Time

Slack means more time to work, less to worry about and transfer of main machinery and supervision to the different activities on the critical path. Knowing the slacks in different activities is of paramount importance to management. It is mathematically calculated as

Slack $S = T_L - T_E$

Note that slack in the critical path is zero. So in the critical path $T_L = T_E$.

8.3 NUMERICAL EXAMPLES

Example 2

A 'PERT' network is shown below. It shows events, activities, t_o, t_n and t_p. The problem is

(i) To find out the earliest expected time (T_E) for different activities and for the project.

(ii) To determine also the latest allowable (T_L) for different activities and for the project showing the slacks for different activities.

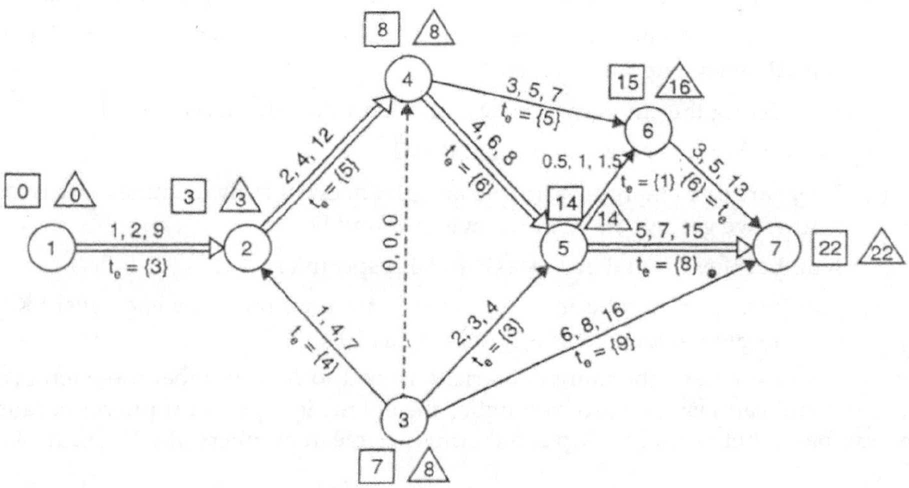

Fig.

Solution :

(1) **To find T_E:** For T_E, we have to find t_e's for different activities from the formula

$$t_e = \frac{t_o + 4t_n + t_p}{6}$$

Then T_E of an event is equal to the sum of the statistically calculated expected elapsed time (t_e) for the activities on the longest path from the beginning of the project to the given event whose T_E is to be calculated. Note that T_E for the starting event is zero. And T_L for the last event is equal to the T_E of the last event. When multiple activities lead into an event, the T_E of that event is always the **largest sum** of the preceding t_e's (for forward movement of the activity *i.e.*, → way). Thus, we can compute the T_E values for the different activities and for the project.

(2) **To find T_L:** The T_L value for a given event is calculated by subtracting the sum of the expected elapsed times (t_e's for the activities on the longest path from the given event to the end event of the project) from the latest date allowable for completing the project. T_L for the end event in a project is equal to the directed date of the project. If a directed date is not specified, then take $T_L = T_E$ for the end event. We have to proceed against the arrow to get T_L of different events. In short, T_L is the **minimum** value of all the T_L's calculated by different paths or activities (Note that T_L calculation is just opposite of T_E calculation). Thus, T_L's can be calculated by moving against the direction of arrow.

(3) **To find slacks:** Use formula $S = T_L - T_E$

(4) **To find the critical path:** The path which consumes the maximum time. For quick finding we choose the path where $T_L = T_E$ *i.e.*, $S = 0$.

In our example it is 1—2—4—5—7. It is denoted by ⇒ (Double line arrow) or Σt_e = maximum is to be chosen for critical path.

8.4 'PERT' PROBABILITY

Standard deviation of an activity is given by

$$\sigma = \frac{t_p - t_o}{6}$$

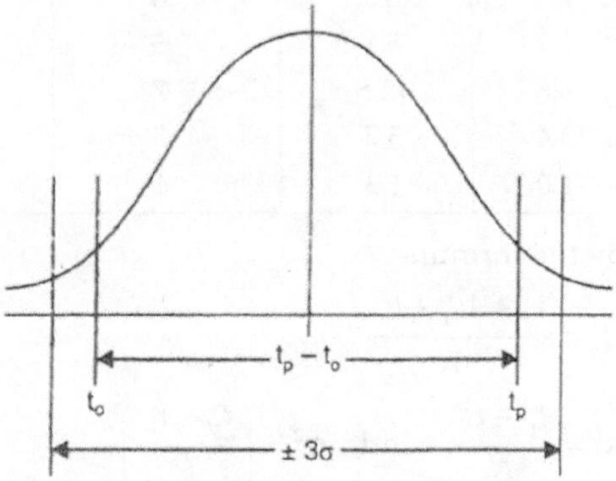

Normal curve

That is standard deviation is the deviation of t_e towards the right or towards the left. On probability, we can infer whether the project will be completed on due date or not.

± 1 % = 68 % (area under normal curve)
± 2 % = 95 % (area under normal curve)
± 3 % = 99.7 % (area under normal curve)

If probability is >60 % it will be assumed that the project will be completed in due dates; and if probability <40 % the project will not be completed in due time. If probability = 50 %. The project may or may not be completed in due date.

$$\text{Variance} = \sigma^2 = \left(\frac{t_p - t_o}{6}\right)^2$$

Standard deviation of the entire project

$$= \frac{T_P - T_E}{\sigma_{\text{entire}}} = \frac{T_P - T_E}{\sqrt{\Sigma \text{ variances of the activities on the critical path}}}$$

Where T_E = Earliest expected time of the project
T_P = Project time (Contractual obligation time).

Example 3

(a) *Find the probability of completion two days later of the following project problem.*

(b) *Suppose we are late by three days when we have completed the activity 2—3. What is the probability of completion of the project in time ?*

The following table is given with t_o, t_n and t_p.

Solution:

We calculate t_e, σ and variance of each activity.

				Calculated	*Calculated*	*Calculated*
Activity	t_o	t_n	t_p	t_e	σ	σ^2
1—2	0.7	1.0	1.3	1	0.1	0.01
2—3	3.8	5.6	9.8	6	1.0	1.00
2—4	5.2	7.6	12.4	8	1.2	1.44
3—4	2.1	2.7	5.1	3	0.5	0.25
3—5	2.0	6.8	12.8	7	1.8	3.24
4—5	0.7	3.4	3.7	3	0.5	0.25
5—6	0.7	1.0	1.3	1	0.1	0.01

We have calculated t_e by the formula.

$$t_e = \frac{t_o + 4t_n + t_p}{6}$$

and

$$\sigma = \frac{t_p - t_o}{6} \quad \text{and} \quad \sigma^2 = \left(\frac{t_p - t_o}{6}\right)^2$$

We have inserted t_e, σ and σ^2 in the table.

Now let us find out the critical path.

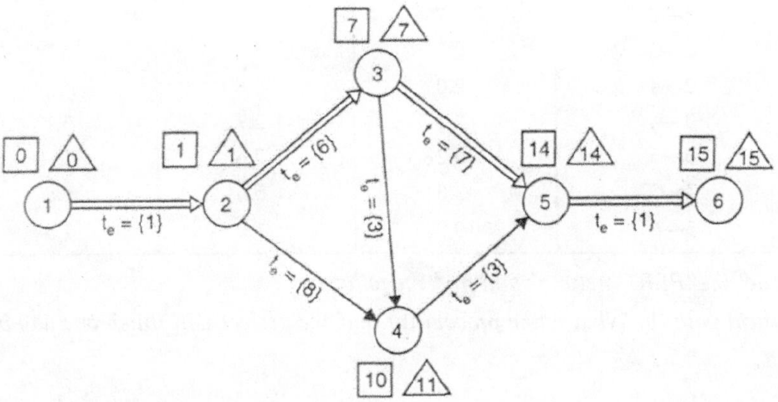

The critical path is 1—2—3—5—6

Variance of the finishing date along the critical path

$$\sigma^2 = 0.01 + 1.00 + 3.24 + 0.01 = 4.26$$

$$\sigma = \sqrt{4.26} = 2.064$$

Now $T_E = 15$ days

(*a*) $T_P = T_E + 2 = 15 + 2 = 17$ days

Standardised deviation of the entire project

$$Z = \frac{T_P - T_E}{\sigma_{\text{entire}}} = \frac{17 - 15}{2.064} = 0.968$$

Corresponding to this value 0.968, we get probability = 82.9 %.

(*b*) We should not consider the portion which has been completed. We have to consider only 3 — 5 — 6 path.

$$\sigma^2_{3-5-6} = 3.24 - 0.01 = 3.25$$

$$\sigma = \sqrt{3.25} = 1.8027$$

$$T_E = 15 + 3 = 18$$

$$T_P = 15$$

$$Z = \frac{T_P - T_E}{\sigma_{3-5-6}} = \frac{15 - 18}{1.8027} = -1.664$$

From the normal table probability = 5 %.

Example 4

The following table gives the optimistic, most likely and pessimistic times for the jobs in a network which has no dummies.

Activity	*Estimate of time duration in days*		
Start-Finish	*Optimistic*	*Most likely*	*Pessimistic*
1—2	0.7	1.0	1.3
2—3	0.7	3.4	3.7
2—4	2.0	6.8	12.8
3—4	2.1	2.7	5.1
3—5	5.2	7.6	12.4
4—5	3.8	5.6	9.8
5—6	0.7	1.0	1.3

Construct the 'PERT' network and find the following.

(a) Critical path (b) What is the probability that the project will finish one day before the expected time ?

Given

Standardised deviation	− 0.1	− 0.2	− 0.3	− 0.4	− 0.5	− 0.6
% Probability	46	42.1	38.2	34.5	30.8	27.4

Solution:

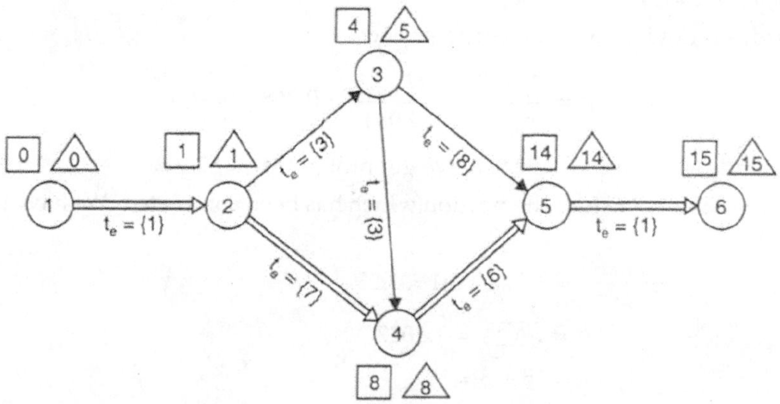

Table 1

Activity	*Estimate of duration in days*			*Standard deviation*	*Variance*	*Expected time*
	t_o	t_n	t_p	σ	σ^2	t_e
1—2	0.7	1.0	1.3	0.1	0.01	1
2—3	0.7	3.4	3.7	0.5	0.25	3

2—4	2.0	6.8	12.8	1.8	3.24	7
3—4	2.1	2.7	5.1	0.5	0.25	3
3—5	5.2	7.6	12.4	1.2	1.44	8
4—5	3.8	5.6	9.8	1.0	1.0	6
5—6	0.7	1.0	1.3	0.1	0.01	1

(*a*) Thus, the critical path is 1—2—4—5—6

(*b*) $$\sigma^2_{\substack{\text{entire project}\\ \text{on critical path}}} = 0.01 + 3.24 + 1.00 + 0.01 = 4.26$$

or $$\sigma_{\text{entire}} = \sqrt{4.26} = 2.064$$

Standardised deviation

$$Z = \frac{T_P - T_E}{\sigma_{\text{entire}}} = \frac{(15-1)-15}{2.064} = -0.48$$

From the table we get probability = 32% (between 34.5 and 30.8).

Example 5

The following table gives the optimistic (t_o), most likely (t_n) and pessimistic times (t_p) for the jobs which has no dummies.

Activity	*Given*			*Calculated*		
	t_o	t_n	t_p	t_e	σ	σ^2
1—2	1	2	3	2	0.33	0.11
2—3	1	4	7	4	1	1.00
2—4	1	2	9	3	1.33	1.77
3—5	1	2	9	3	1.33	1.77
4—5	2	3	4	3	0.33	0.11
5—6	2	3	4	3	0.33	0.11

Draw the 'PERT' network and find the following :

(a) The critical path

(b) The probabilities

(i) of completing the project in 12 days

(ii) of completing the project in 14 days.

(iii) of completing the project in 10 days.

Solution:

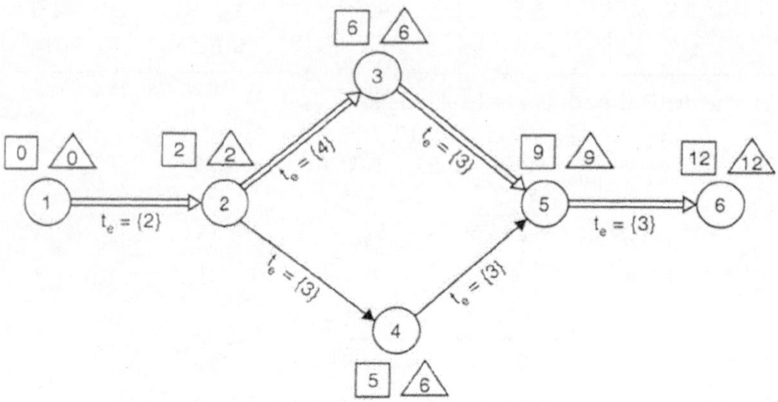

(*a*) The critical path is 1—2—3—5—6

(*b*)

$$\sigma^2_{entire} = \sigma^2_{1-2} + \sigma^2_{2-3} + \sigma^2_{3-5} + \sigma^2_{5-6}$$

$$= 0.11 + 1.00 + 1.77 + 0.11 = 2.99$$

$$\sigma_{entire} = \sqrt{2.99} = 1.73$$

(*i*) Standardised deviation

$$Z = \frac{T_P - T_E}{\sigma_{entire}} = \frac{12 - 12}{\sigma_{entire}} = 0$$

Probability $= 50\%$

(*ii*) $$Z = \frac{14 - 12}{\sigma_{entire}} = \frac{2}{1.73} = 1.156, \text{ Probability} = 87.7\ \%$$

(*iii*) $$Z = \frac{10 - 12}{\sigma_{entire}} = \frac{-2}{1.73} = -1.156$$

Probability $= (100 - 87.7)\ \% = 12.3\ \%.$

Example 6

The following table gives the optimistic, most likely and pessimistic times for the jobs in a network which has dummy between 3—4.

Draw the network and calculate.

(a) Critical path

(b) The probability when the contractual obligation time is one day later the expected time duration of the project.

Table 1

Activity	Given			Calculated		
	t_o	t_n	t_p	t_e	σ	σ^2
1—2	2	2	8	3	1	1
2—3	1	2.5	7	3	1	1
2—4	0.5	1	7.5	2	1.66	1.36
3—4	0	0	0	0	0	0
4—5	6	7	8	7	0.33	0.11
3—5	1	2.5	7	3	1	1
3—6	1	2	3	2	0.33	0.11
4—6	3	4	11	5	1.33	1.77
5—6	4	6	8	6	0.66	0.44

Solution:

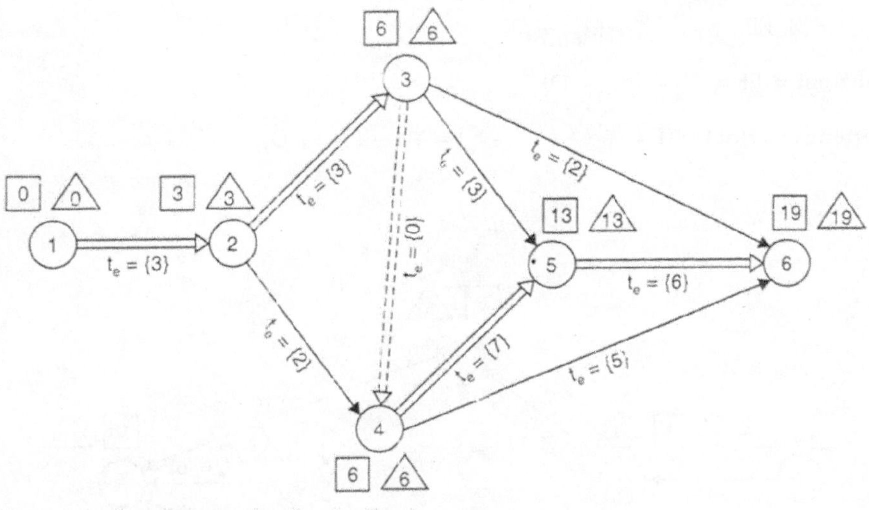

(*a*) The critical path is 1—2—3—4—5—6

(*b*) $T_P = T_E + 1 = 19 + 1 = 20$

$$Z = \frac{T_P - T_E}{\sigma_{entire}} = \frac{1}{\sqrt{1+1+0+0.11+0.44}} = 0.626$$

Probability = 72.6 % (From Normal Table).

8.5 CPM (CRITICAL PATH METHOD)

It has already been discussed that there are two basic elements of a network, the 'EVENT' and the 'ACTIVITY'. Event represents a significant point on time, while the activity is a time consuming element. The network technique which emphasizes more on 'events' is called 'PERT' and the other which emphasizes more on 'activity' is called CPM. The other point where CPM differs from PERT is that CPM does not take into account of uncertainties while estimating its activity times. In CPM, costs are related to time.

8.5.1 Float

The float of an activity has the same significance as the slack in PERT. Slack corresponds to events and hence to PERT; while the float corresponds to activities and hence to CPM. There are three types of floats:

8.5.1.1 Free float

Merged point activities which lie on the slack path have free float. It is the amount of time by which an activity can be delayed without affecting the earliest start or occurrence time of any other activity. It is denoted as FF.

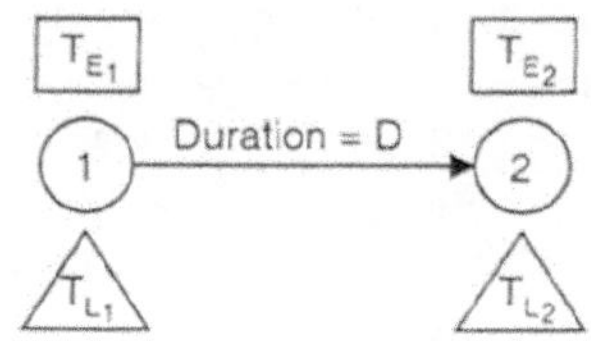

D = Activity duration (Take $D = t_{n}$ if t_o, t_p not given and take $D = t_e$ if t_o, t_n and t_p given)

$$FF_{(1-2)} = T_{E_2} - (T_{E_1} + D)$$

Total float = TF = $T_{L_2} - (T_{E_1} + D)$

Independent float = IF = $T_{E_2} - (T_{L_1} + t_e) = T_{E_2} - (T_{L_1} + D)$

Example 7

In the network shown below find out the different floats.

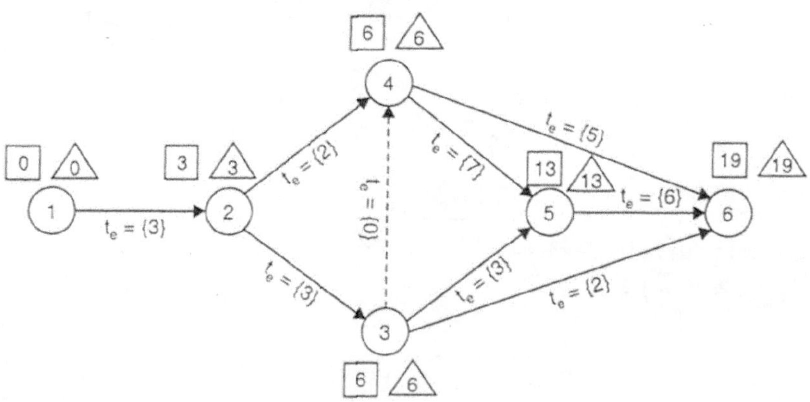

Activity	Activity duration	Earliest time T_E		Latest time (T_L)		Float ① → ②		
		Start	Finish	Start	Finish	TF	FF	IF
	D	T_{E_S}	T_{E_F}	T_{L_S}	T_{L_F}	$T_{L_2} - (T_{E_1} + D)$	$T_{E_2} - (T_{E_1} + D)$	$T_{E_2} - (T_{L_1} + D)$
1—2	3	0	3	0	3	0	0	0
2—3	3	3	6	3	6	0	0	0
2—4	2	3	5	4	6	1	1	1
3—4	0	6	6	6	6	0	0	0
3—5	3	6	9	10	13	4	4	4
3—6	2	6	8	17	19	11	11	11
4—5	7	6	13	6	13	0	0	0
4—6	5	6	11	14	19	8	8	8
5—6	6	13	19	13	19	0	0	0

Sample calculation

Activity

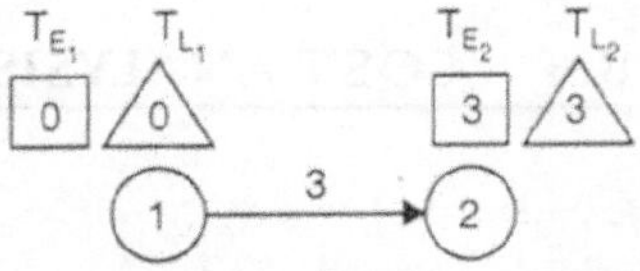

1—2

$T_{E_1} = 0, \quad T_{E_2} = 3$

$T_{L_1} = 0, \quad T_{L_2} = 3$

$D = 3$

$FF = T_{E_2} - (T_{E_1} + D) = 3 - (0 + 3) = 0$

$TF = T_{L_2} - (T_{E_1} + D) = 3 - (0 + 3) = 0$

$IF = T_{E_2} - (T_{L_1} + D) = 3 - (0 + 3) = 0$

Activity

2—3

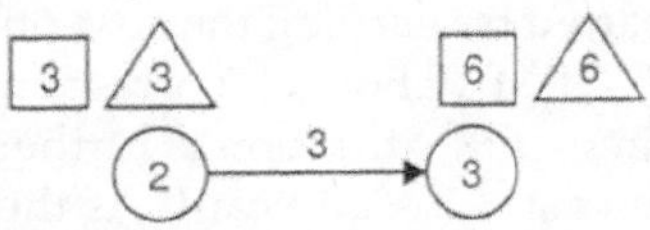

$T_{E_2} = 3, T_{L_2} = 3$

$T_{E_3} = 6, T_{L_3} = 6, D = 3$

$TF = T_{L_3} - (T_{E_2} + D) = 6 - (3 + 3) = 0$

$FF = T_{E_3} - (T_{E_2} + D) = 6 - (3 + 3) = 0$

$IF = T_{E_3} - (T_{L_2} + D) = 6 - (3 + 3) = 0$

Activity

4—6

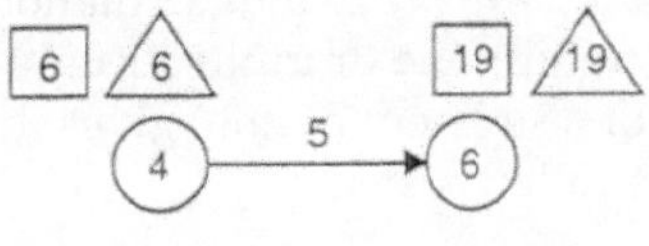

$T_{E_4} = 6 \quad T_{L_4} = 6$

$D = 5, \quad T_{E_6} = 19 \quad T_{L_6} = 19$

$TF = T_{L_6} - (T_{E_4} + D) = 19 - (6 + 5) = 8$

$FF = T_{E_6} - (T_{E_4} + D) = 19 - (6 + 5) = 8$

$IF = T_{E_6} - (T_{L_4} + D) = 19 - (6 + 5) = 8$

Activity

3—6

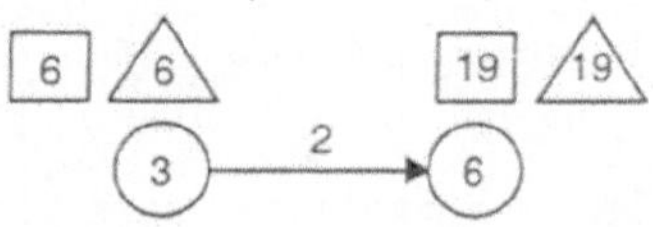

$$D = 2$$

$$T_{E_3} = 6 \quad T_{L_3} = 6$$

$$T_{E_6} = 19 \quad T_{L_6} = 19$$

$$TF = T_{L_6} - (T_{E_3} + D) = 19 - (6 + 2) = 11$$

$$FF = T_{E_6} - (T_{E_3} + D) = 19 - (6 + 2) = 11$$

$$IF = T_{E_6} - (T_{L_3} + D) = 19 - (6 + 2) = 11$$

8.6 COST ANALYSIS

Costs are of two types :

8.6.1 Direct cost

Direct costs are generally associated with individual activities. This is the cost of materials, equipment and labour required to perform the activity.

It can be seen from the direct cost time relationship shown (in Fig. 1), that the activity can be varied by varying the cost-point 'N' referred to as the 'NORMAL POINT' corresponds to the normal activity time. If the duration is further increased, the decrease in cost is insignificant. As the activity is compressed, the direct cost goes on increasing. If it is compressed beyond 'C', the cost increases very rapidly for insignificant change in the activity duration time. This point is called 'CRASH POINT'. Crash time is thus the minimum activity duration to which an activity can be compressed by increasing the resources and hence by increasing the direct cost.

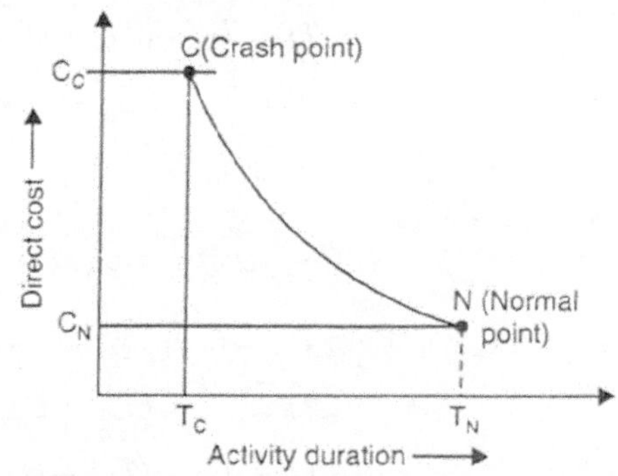

Fig. 1

To make the calculations simple, the direct cost-time curve is approximated to either a single straight line or multi straight line, as shown in Fig 1(*a*) and 1(*b*) respectively. The slope of the line (or a segment of line) gives the increase in direct cost per unit time for expediting the activity. This is called cost slope.

For straight line approximation (Fig. 1(*a*)), we have

$$\text{cost slope} = \frac{C_C - C_N}{T_N - T_C} = \frac{\Delta C}{\Delta C}.$$

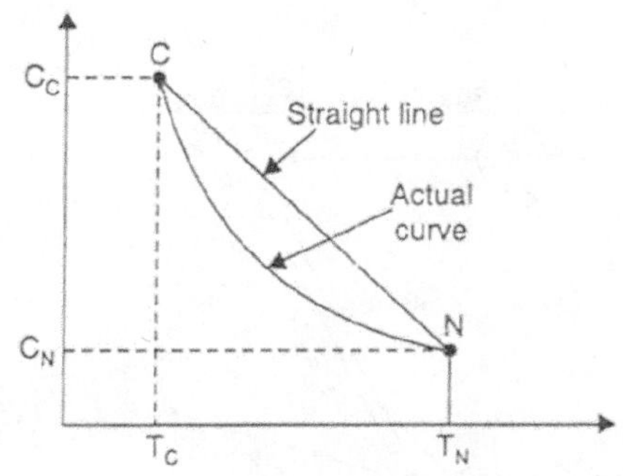

Fig. 1(a)

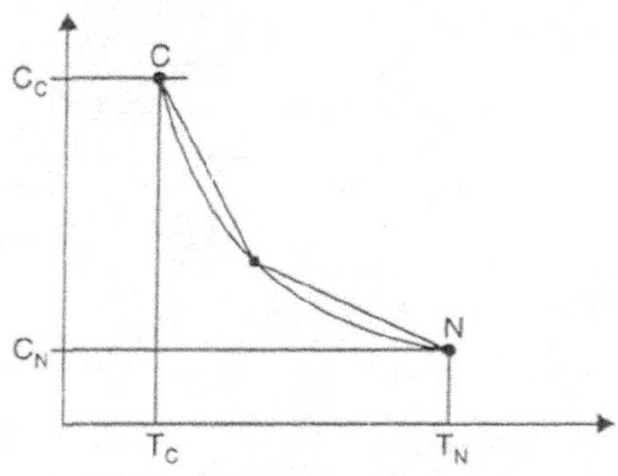

Fig. 1(b)

8.6.2 Indirect Cost

Project indirect cost can further be sub-divided into two parts. Fixed indirect cost and variable indirect cost. The fixed indirect cost is due to the general and administrative expenses, licence fee, insurance cost and taxes and does not depend upon the progress of the project. The variable indirect cost depends upon the time consumed by the project and consists of overhead expenditure, supervision, interest on capital and depreciation, etc. It is assumed that the indirect cost increases linearly with time as shown in Fig. 2.

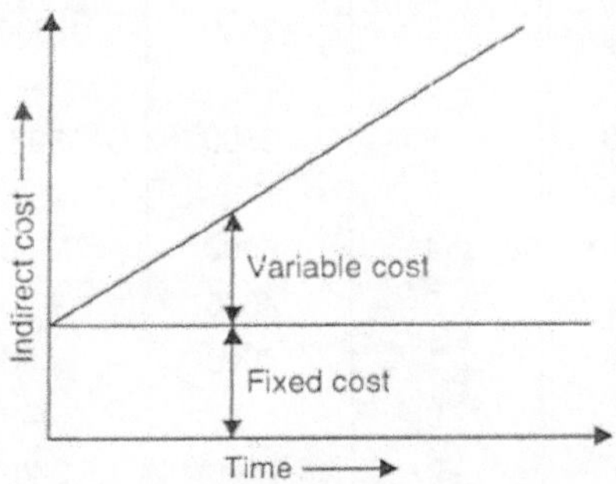

Fig. 2

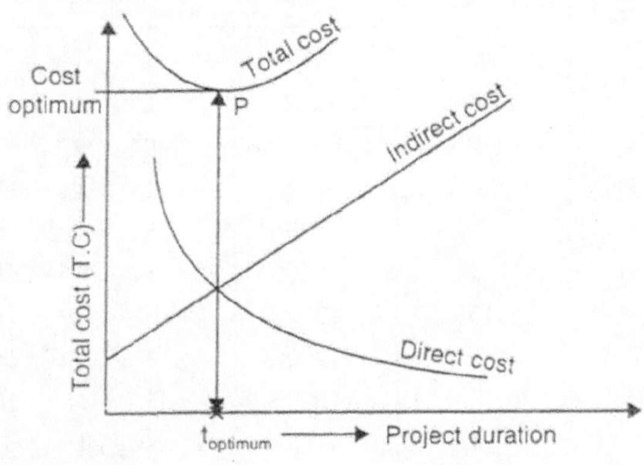

Fig. 2(a)

The sum of the indirect and direct costs gives the total project cost. As the direct cost decreases with time and the indirect cost increases with time, the total project cost curve will have a point P where the total cost will be minimum. The time corresponding to this point is called the optimum duration time and the cost is the optimum (minimum) cost.

8.7 CRASHING THE NETWORK

8.7.1 Introduction

To explain the process of crashing a network to reach the optimum project schedule, let us consider the network shown in the Fig.

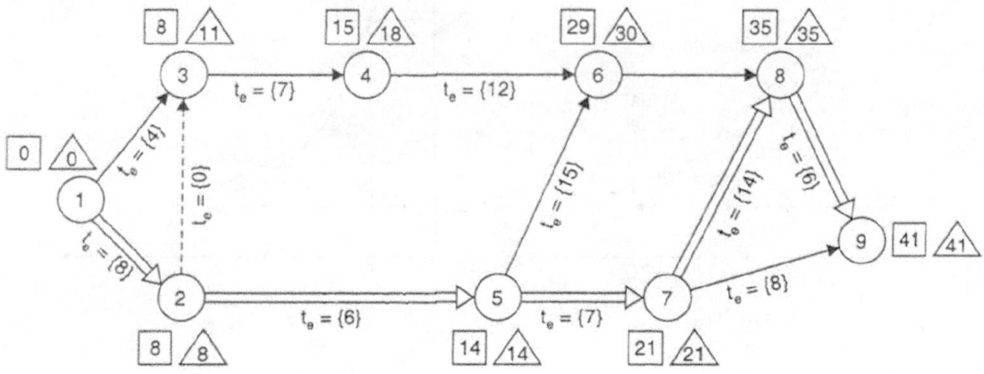

Fig.

Times are in weeks and cost in rupees.

Activity	Given				Calculated		
	Normal		Crash				
	T_N	C_N	T_C	C_C	ΔT	ΔC	$\frac{\Delta C}{\Delta T}$
1—2	8	7000	3	10000	5	3000	600
1—3	4	6000	2	8000	2	2000	1000
2—3	0	0	0	0	0	0	—
2—5	6	9000	1	11500	5	2500	500
3—4	7	2500	5	3000	2	500	250
4—6	12	10000	8	16000	4	6000	1500
5—6	15	12000	10	16000	5	4000	800
5—7	7	12000	6	14000	1	2000	2000
6—8	5	10000	5	10000	0	0	—
7—8	14	6000	7	7400	7	1400	200
7—9	8	6000	5	12000	3	6000	2000
8—9	6	6000	4	7800	2	1800	900
		86500		115700			

Given indirect cost = Rs. 1000 per week.
Entire project time should be = 38 weeks.

Solution:

Step 1: To determine the optimum schedule, the first step is to identify the critical path. Here we find that the critical path is 1—2—5—7—8—9 with project duration time = 41 weeks (T_E for entire project)

$\therefore$ Total cost of the project = Direct cost of all activities + Indirect cost for 41 weeks

$$= 86500 + 41 \times 1000 = \text{Rs. } 127500.00$$

Step 2: The next step is to identify those activities along the critical path which can be crashed. Crash at least expensive activities, *i.e.*, the activity with the least slope $\left(\frac{\Delta C}{\Delta T}\right)$. We find from the table that the activity 7—8 which is on the critical path, has got least slope of 200. It can be crashed by 7 weeks at an additional cost of Rs. 200 × 7 = Rs. 1400.00. The crashed network is shown below :

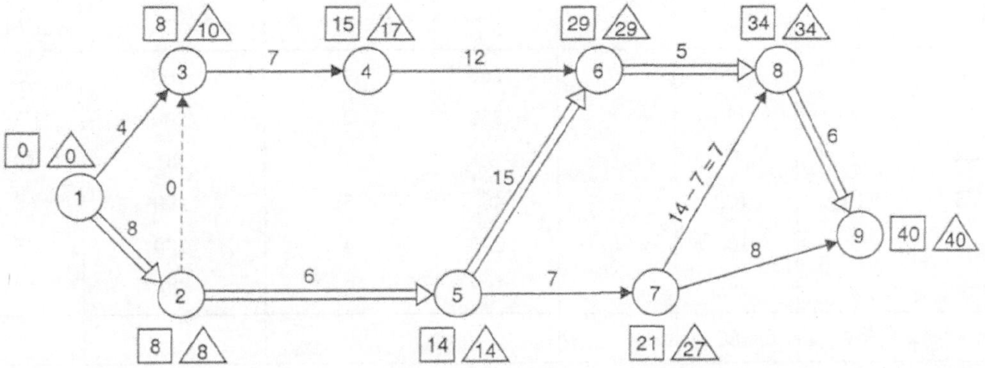

Now the critical path is 1—2—5—6—8—9

	∴ Direct cost of project	= Rs. (86500 + 7 × 200) = Rs. 87900.00
and,	Indirect cost	= Rs. 40 × 1000 = Rs. 40000.00
	Total cost of the project	= Rs. 87900 + Rs. 40000 = Rs. 127900.00

Step 3: In the new critical path, the activity with the lowest cost slope is activity 2—5 having a cost slope of 500. It can be crashed by 5 weeks. The crashed network is shown below :

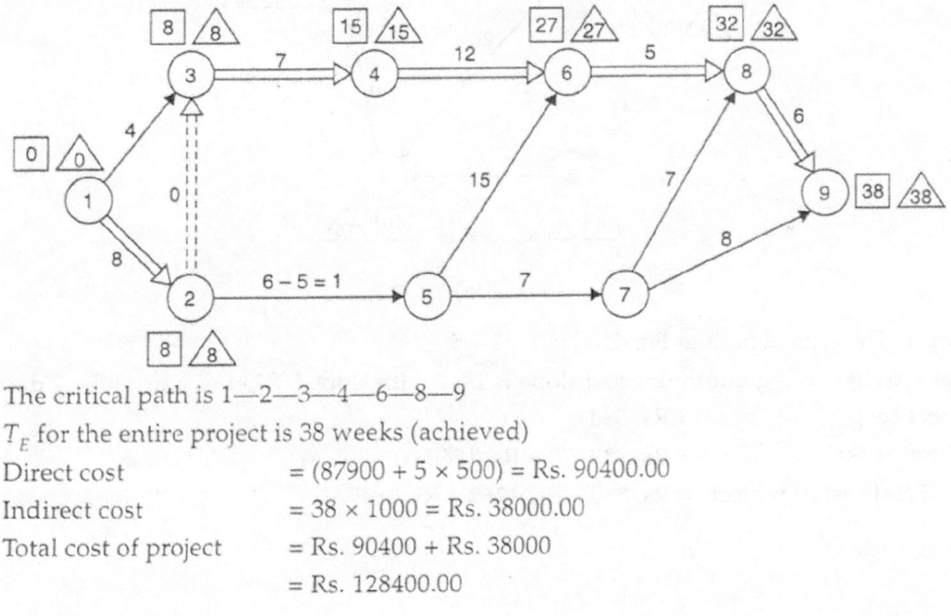

The critical path is 1—2—3—4—6—8—9

T_E for the entire project is 38 weeks (achieved)

Direct cost	= (87900 + 5 × 500) = Rs. 90400.00
Indirect cost	= 38 × 1000 = Rs. 38000.00
Total cost of project	= Rs. 90400 + Rs. 38000
	= Rs. 128400.00

Example 8

Time in days and cost in rupees.

Activity	Normal		Crash		$\Delta T = T_N - T_C$	$\Delta C = C_C - C_N$	$\Delta C/\Delta T$
	T_N	C_N	T_C	C_C			
1—2	8	100	6	200	2	100	50
1—3	4	150	2	350	2	200	100
2—4	2	50	1	90	1	40	40
2—5	10	100	5	400	5	300	60
3—4	5	100	1	200	4	100	25
4—5	3	80	1	100	2	20	10
		580					

Find out the total project cost and optimum project duration if the indirect cost is Rs. 70 per day.

Solution:

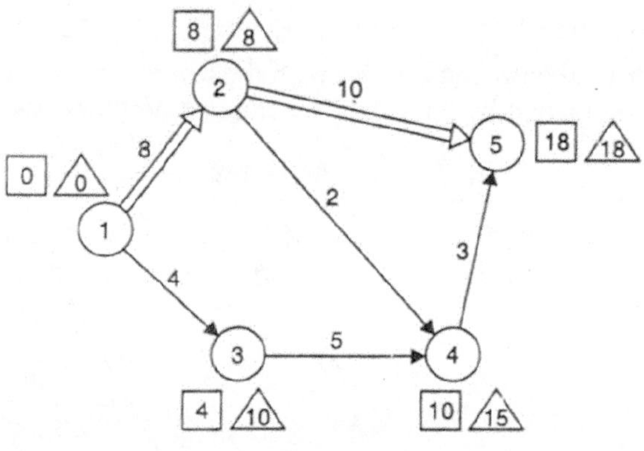

Fig. 2 (a)

Step 1: The critical path in Fig. 2 (*a*) is 1—2—5.

The activity having minimum cost slope is 1—2 with slope 50. Let us crash it by 2 days.

Direct cost = Rs. 580

Indirect cost = Rs. 18 × 70 = Rs. 1260.00

∴ Total cost of project = Rs. 580 + Rs. 1260 = Rs. 1840.

Step 2: After crashing, the network becomes (1—2 activity by 2 days).

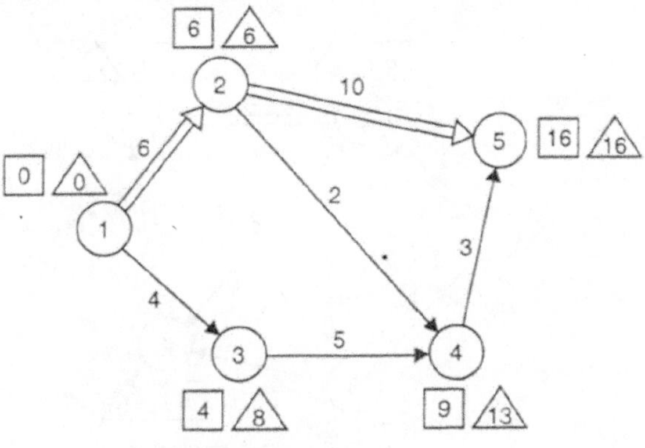

Fig. 2 (*b*)

Direct cost	= Rs. 580 + Rs. 2 × 50 = Rs. 680.00
Indirect cost	= Rs. 16 × 70 = Rs. 1120.
Total cost of project	= Rs. 680 + Rs. 1120 = Rs. 1800.

Step 3: In Fig. 2 (*b*), the critical path becomes 1—2—5 (unchanged). We have already crashed 1—2 activity, now we crash activity 2—5 by 5 days and the network becomes.

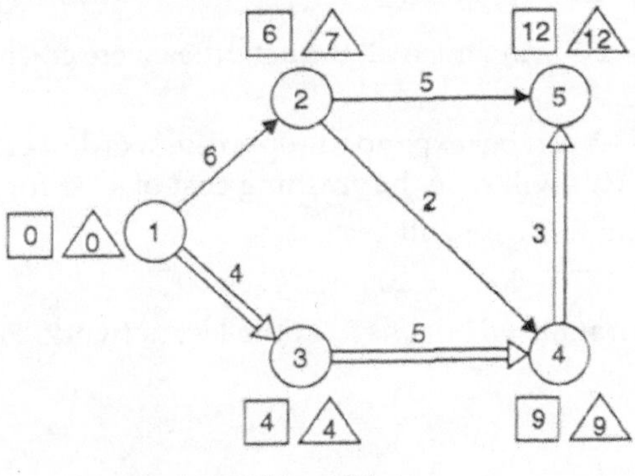

Fig. 2 (*c*)

The critical path becomes 1—3—4—5

Direct cost	= Rs. 680 + Rs. 5 × 60
	= Rs. 980
Indirect cost	= Rs. 12 × 70
	= Rs. 840
Total cost of project	= Rs. 980 + Rs. 840
	= Rs. 1820.

Step 4: We then crash the activity 4—5 by 2 days. The network becomes

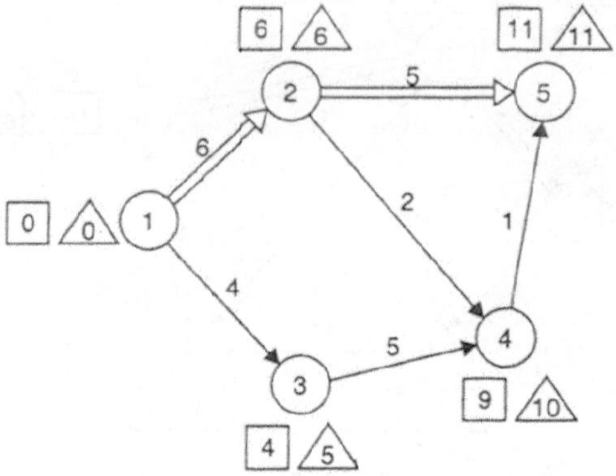

Fig. 2 (d)

The critical path is 1—2—5.

Direct cost = Rs. 980 + Rs. 2 × 10 = Rs. 1000

Indirect cost = Rs. 11 × 70 = Rs. 770

Total cost of the project = Rs. 1000 + Rs. 770

= Rs. 1770.

As the critical path is 1—2—5, in which all the activities were crashed, the project cannot be further contracted.

Note that the activity 4—5 can be expanded (opposite word of crash) by one day without affecting the project duration. This will save the crashing cost of 4—5 for one day.

The total cost of project in this case will be

= Rs. 1770 – Rs. 1 × 10 = Rs. 1760.00

The optimum project duration = 11 days (T_E of the last network, Fig. 2 (*d*))

i.e., T_E or T_L of the last event.

Example 9

Time in days, cost in rupees.

	Normal		*Crash*				
Activity	T_N	C_N	T_C	C_C	ΔT	ΔC	$\Delta C/\Delta T$
1—2	8	1800	6	2200	2	400	200
1—4	12	2400	9	3000	3	600	200
2—3	16	1500	11	2200	5	700	140
3—5	14	1800	9	2400	5	600	120
4—5	15	800	14	2000	1	1200	1200
5—6	10	2000	8	4000	2	2000	1000
		Rs. 10300					

Draw the part network and determine the least cost for 36 days schedule (Take indirect cost as zero).

Solution:

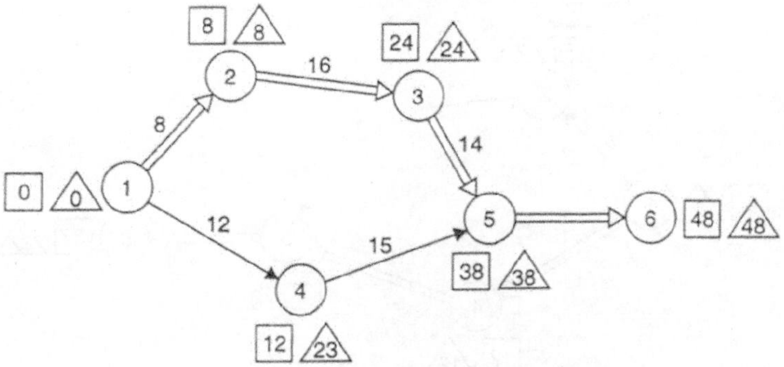

Fig. 3 (a)

Step 1: The critical path for network in Fig. 3 (*a*) is 1—2—3—5—6.

Direct cost = Rs. 10300, Indirect Cost = 0.

Step 2: We crash the activity (3—5) by 5 days and we get the following network.

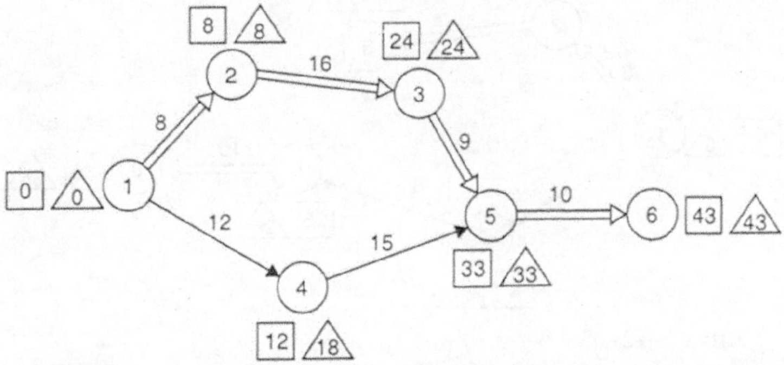

The critical path is the same as before *i.e.*, 1—2—3—5—6

Direct cost = Rs. 10300 + Rs. 5 × 120 = Rs. 10900.

Step 3: Then we crash the activity 2—3 by 5 days and we get the following network.

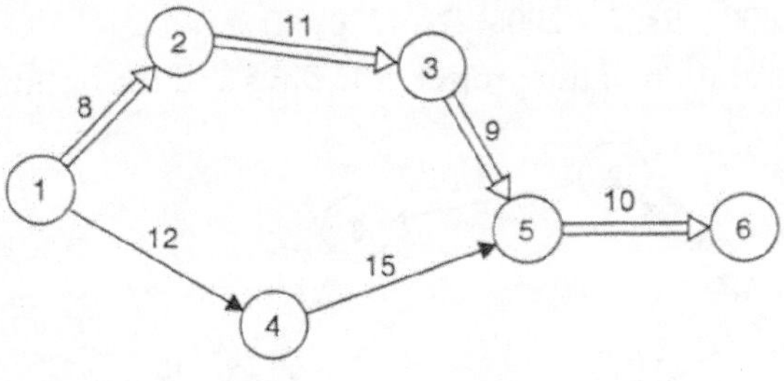

The critical path remains the same

Direct cost = Rs. 10900 + Rs. 5 × 140 = Rs. 11600.00.

Step 4: Then we crash the activity 1—2 by 2 days and the network becomes

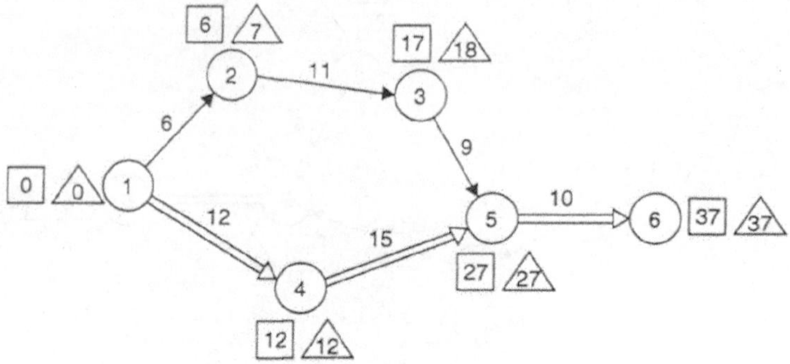

Direct cost = Rs. 11600 + Rs. 2 × 200 = Rs. 12000.00

The critical path is 1—4—5—6.

Step 5: Let us now crash the activity 1—4 by 3 days and we get the network as follows :

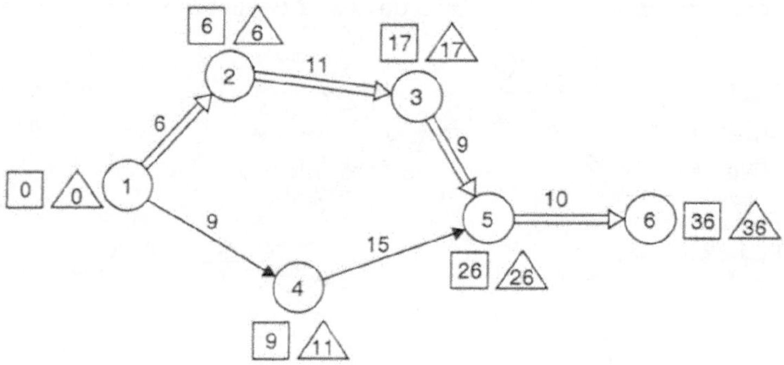

The critical path is 1—2—3—5—6.

Direct cost = Rs. 12000 + Rs. 3 × 200 = Rs. 12600.00

Note that the activity 1—4 can be expanded by 2 days without affecting the project duration. This will save the crashing cost of 1—4 for 2 days (Also note that we cannot expand 4—5 because for its normal time = 15 days and ΔT calculation will also be affected).

Direct cost = Rs. 12600 – Rs. 2 × 200 = Rs. 12200.00

And the optimum duration of the project is 36 days and the optimum network becomes :

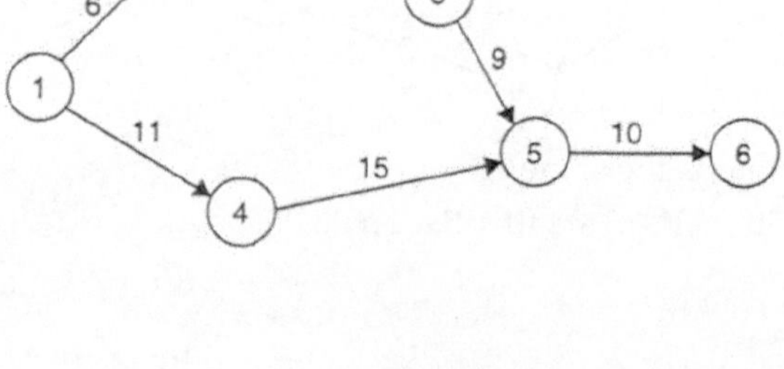

Example 10

A maintenance supervisor gives the following estimates of time and cost of overhauling electrical motors. The various activities involved are:

A = Disassemble the electric motor

B = Clean the stator and paint it

C = Remove the burnt windings and rewind the armature.

D = Replace the wornout bearings

E = Assemble the motor.

Activity A predeces activities B, C and D. And activity E can be taken up only when B, C, D have been completed. Activities A, B, C, D and E consume 6, 5, 10, 8 and 6 hours; and Rs. 60, 30, 80, 50 and 40 respectively for a lot. However activities A, C and D can be completed 2 hours before, whereas activities B and E can be finished one hour before their schedule time. But in doing so the firm will have to spend Rs. 90, 80, 160, 100 and 60 on activities A, B, C, D and E respectively. The problem is

(a) Plot the network

(b) Calculate earliest expected time; latest allowable time and floats

(c) Identify the critical path and calculate the project duration

(d) Crash the critical activities

(e) Find the optimum cost. Assume all missing data.

Solution:

Activity	Depends on activity
B, C, D	A
E	B, C, D

Step 1: Let us draw the 'PERT' network.

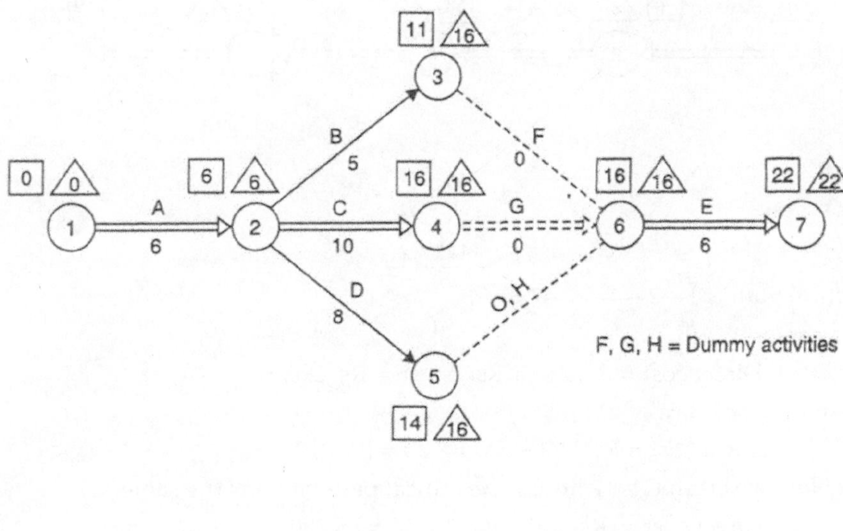

Time in hours, cost in Rupees

Activity	T_N	C_N	T_C	C_C	ΔT	ΔC	$\Delta C/\Delta T$
A(1—2)	6	60	4	90	2	30	15
B(2—3)	5	30	4	80	1	50	50
C(2—4)	10	80	8	160	2	80	40
D(2—5)	8	50	6	100	2	50	25
E(6—7)	6	40	5	60	1	20	20
F(3—6)	0	0	0	0	0	0	—
G(4—6)	0	0	0	0	0	0	—
H(5—6)	0	0	0	0	0	0	—
		Rs. 260					

Steps 2 and 3: The critical path is $1 \overset{(A)}{—} 2 \overset{(C)}{—} 4 \overset{(G)}{—} 6 \overset{(E)}{—} 7$

Direct cost = Rs. 260.00

Let us crash the activity 1—2 *i.e.*, A by 2 hours

The network becomes

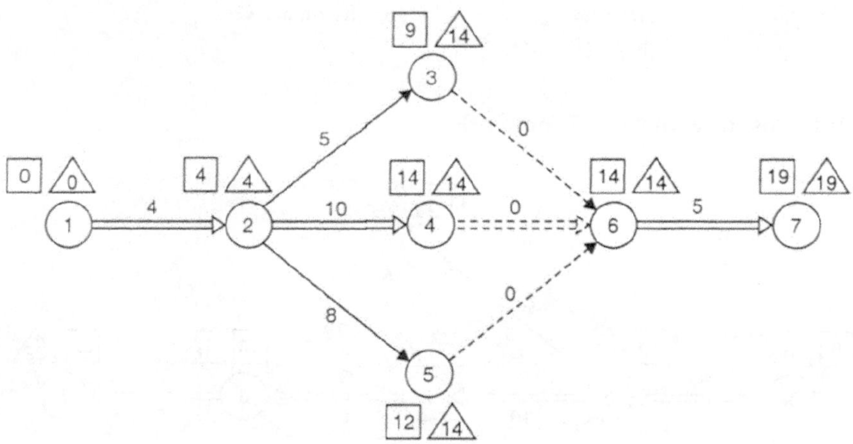

The critical path is 1—2—4—6—7

(same as before)

Direct cost = Rs. 260 + Rs. 2 × 15 = Rs. 290.

We crash *E* by one day.

Direct cost = Rs. 290 + Rs. 1 × 20 = Rs. 310.

Step 4: Now we crash *C* by 2 hours, the critical path remains the same.

Direct cost = Rs. 310 + Rs. 2 × 40 = Rs 390

The network becomes

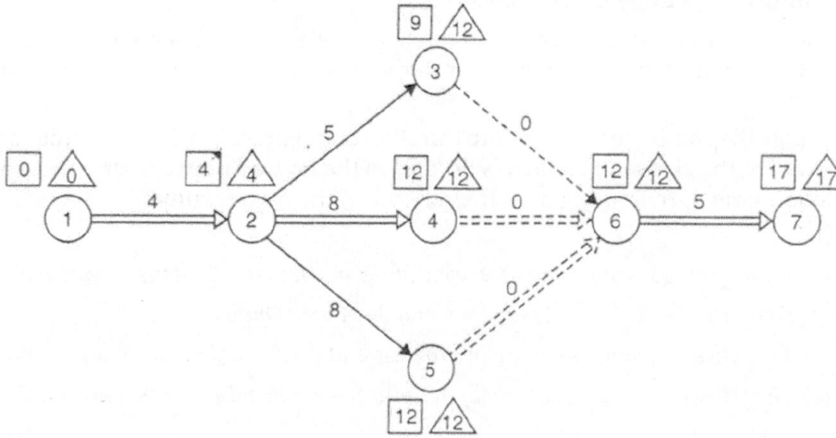

The critical paths are 1—2—4—6—7 or 1—2—5—6—7

We cannot crash any further.

The optimum cost is = Rs. 390.00

And optimum project duration = 17 hours.

8.8 UPDATING A PROJECT

8.8.1 Introduction

The project planner does the planning and scheduling in advance and the execution of the project starts thereafter. There are bound to be unexpected delays and difficulties in terms of delays when the project is actually executed. The delays may be due to late supply of material, non-availability of some machines and/or breakdown of machines, non-availability of skilled manpower, natural calamity, and so on. So it is necessary to review the progress of network planning and scheduling. After collecting the necessary informations and getting a good stock of the progress of the project, the planner makes changes in the initial schedule in terms of time and resources required by incomplete activities in the project.

There is no hard and fast rule about the time for updating a project network. The frequency of updating may be more when project duration is small because few slippages in detecting the progress will affect the project as a whole as the time for absorbing such slippages is less. But in case of large projects the frequency of updating may be less in the initial stages because a few initial slippages may be absorbed later in the project. To impart dynamism to progress of work, updating should be carried out as frequently as economically possible.

8.8.2 Definition

The process of revising the network diagram of a project by incorporating in it the changes which have occurred due to replanning and rescheduling is called updating.

Updating can be done in two ways :

1. Use the revised estimates of incomplete activities and calculate from the initial event the earliest and latest completion of each event in the usual manner to know the project completion time.

2. Change the complete work to zero duration and represent all the activities already finished by an arrow called the elapsed time arrow. Events in the revised network diagram are renumbered. The completion time of remaining activities are taken the revised time.

Example 11

The network for a project is shown below. A review of the project after 15 days reveals that :

(i) Activities 1—2, 1—3, 2—3, 2—4 and 3—4 are complete.

(ii) Activities 3—5 and 4—6 are in progress and need 2 and 4 days more, respectively.

(iii) The revised estimate shows that activity 8—9 will take only 8 days but 7—9 will need 10 days.

Draw the new network after updating the project and determine the new critical path. The work completed may be shown by an elapsed time activity.

Refer Example 11

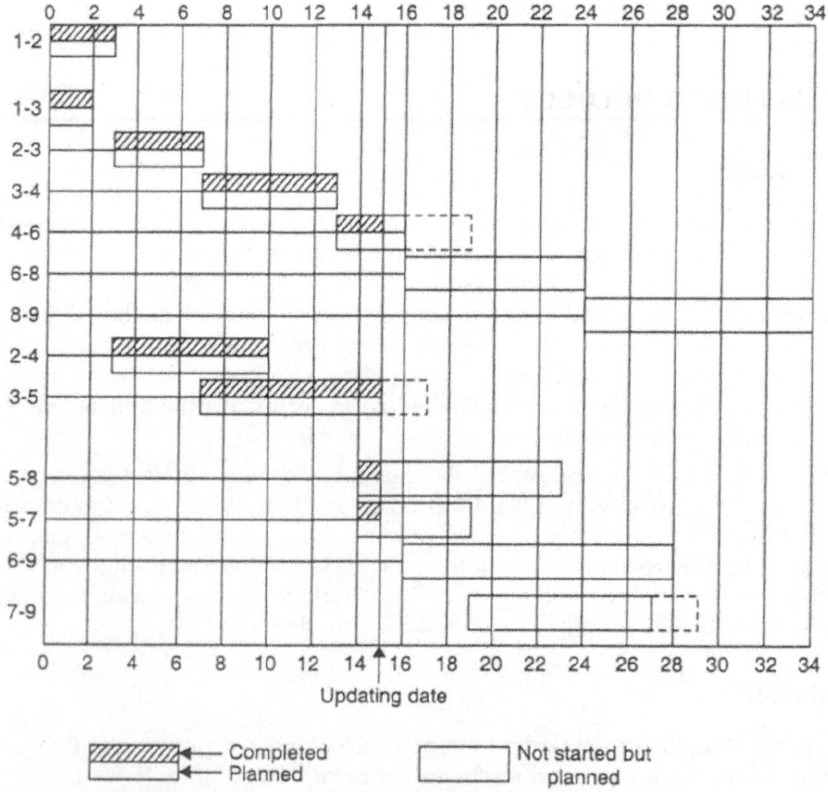

Fig. 1 Bar chart indicating the modification based on updating.

Solution:

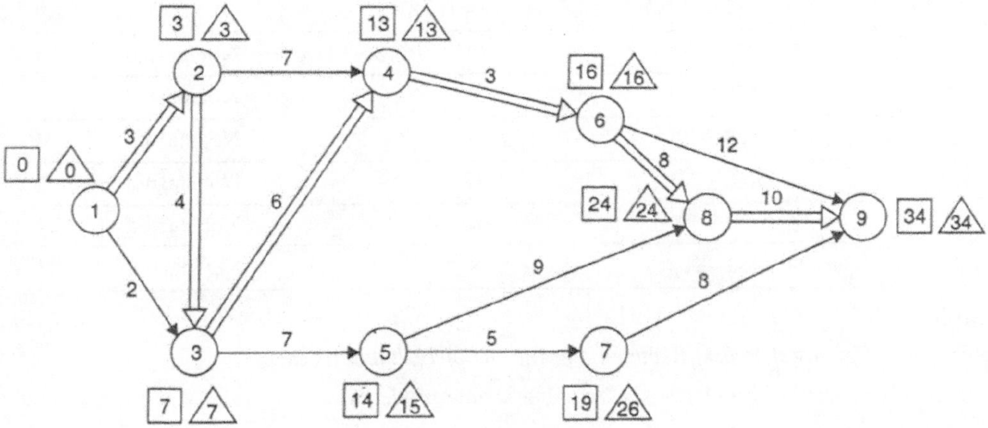

Fig. 2 Initial

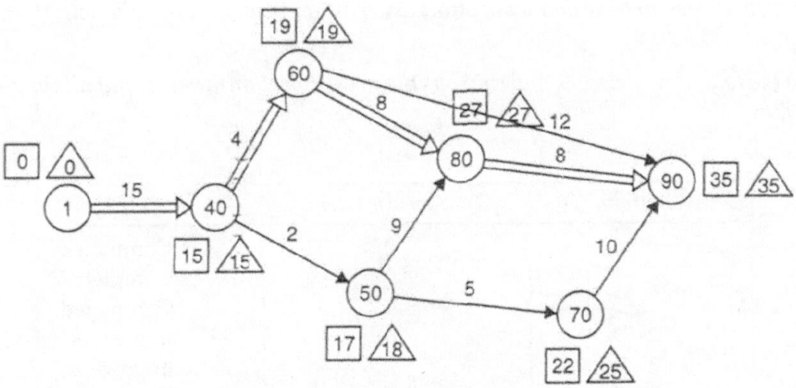

Fig. 3 Updated

The critical path is 1—40—60—80—90 is drawn by double lines. The project duration is increased by one day.

Table

Activity	*Time required (days)*	*Situation*
1—2	0	Complete
1—3	0	Complete
2—3	0	Complete
2—4	0	Complete
3—4	0	Complete
3—5(40—50)	2	In progress
4—6(40—60)	4	In progress

5—8(50—80)	9	Not started
5—7(50—70)	5	Not started
6—8(60—80)	8	Not started
6—9(60—90)	12	Not started
7—9(70—90)	10	Not started
8—9(80—90)	8	Not started

Example 12

Consider the following network. Reviewing at the end of 10th day reveals.

(i) activities (0—1), (0—2), and (1—3) are completed,

(ii) activity (2—3) is in progress and will take 6 days more,

(iii) activity (2—4) is in progress and will take 7 days more,

(iv) also, it is estimated that on account of arrival of new machine, the activity (3—5) will take 6 days only.

Update the following network and find out the new project duration & put all the above information into a tabular form.

Solution:

Activity	*Time required (days)*	*Situation*
0—1	0	Completed
0—2	0	Completed
1—3	0	Completed
2—3	6	In process
2—4	7	In process
3—5	6	Not started
4—5	6	Not started
4—6	9	Not started
5—6	8	Not started.

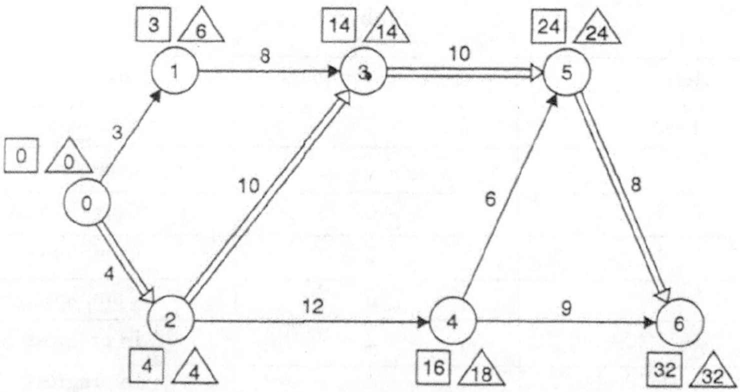

Fig. 1

The critical path is 0—2—3—5—6.

The updating can be performed by two methods:

(*i*) use the revised time estimates and calculate from the initial starting event.

(*ii*) Change the completed work to zero duration and put one activity called elapsed time activity.

The events are numbered in different manner with revised time.

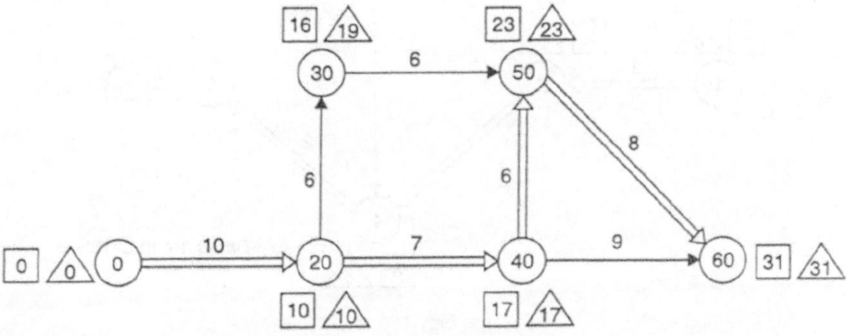

Fig. 2

The revised network in shown in Fig. (2). The new critical path is 0—20—40—50—60. The total duration is reduced by one day.

To represent the information regarding the original schedule, bar charts (Fig. 3) can be used in the process of updating.

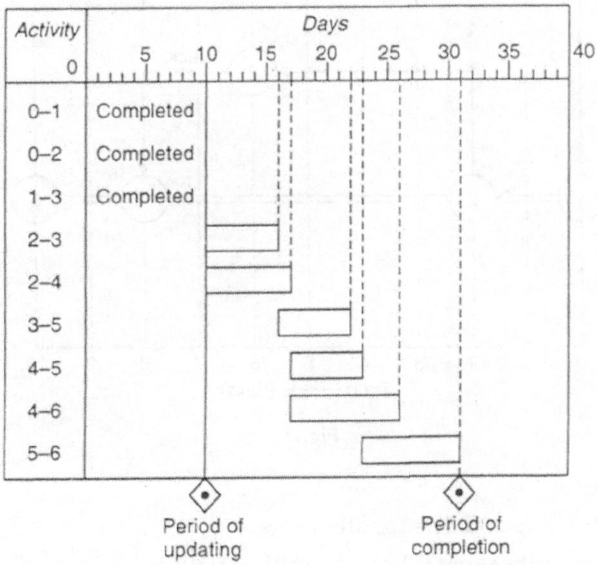

Fig. 3

8.9 'TIME-SCALED VERSION' OF NETWORKING

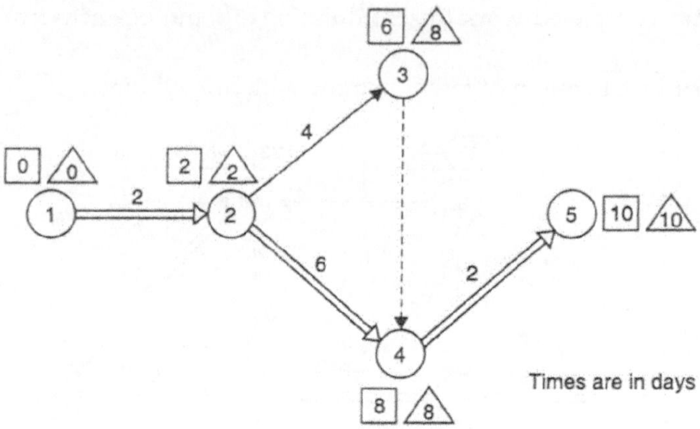

Fig. 1

Let us draw the time-scaled version of the network shown in Fig. 1. This is also called 'squared diagram'.

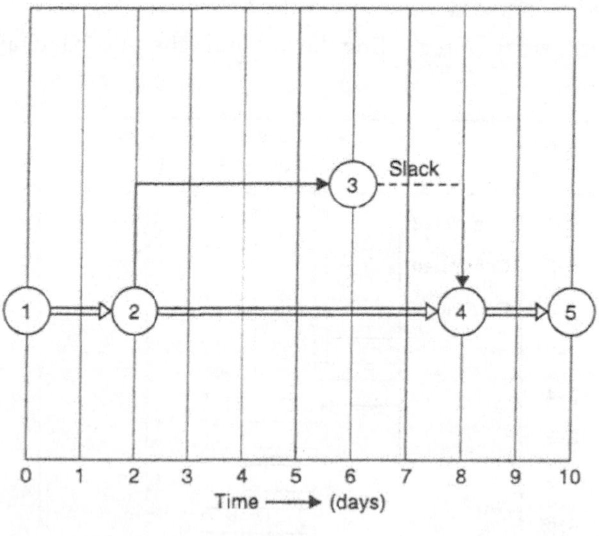

Fig. 2

Scale 1 cm = 1 day

Step 1: Find out the T_E's and T_L's for all events.

Step 2: Find out the critical path; here the critical path is 1—2—4—5.

Step 3: Draw the critical path horizontally into a scale. The length of the critical path in the drawing is equal to the project time.

Step 4: Next draw the non-critical paths in the same scale on the two sides of this critical path line.

Step 5: Show the slacks (if any) in a dotted line note that we have drawn the activity time in the same scale.

The time-scaled version of the network is shown in Fig. 2.

Example 13

Draw the following network in the time-scaled version. The time allotted is in weeks.

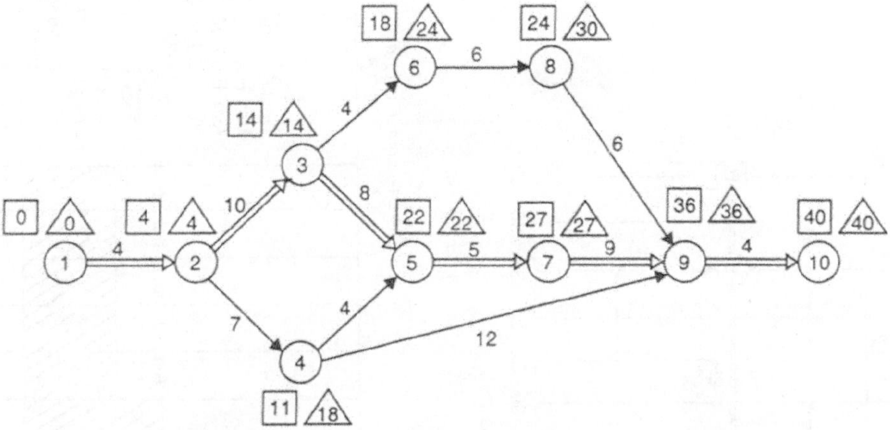

Fig. 3

Fig. 3 (*a*) shows the time-scaled version of the network shown in Fig. 3.

Fig. 3 (*b*) shows bar chart for number of helpers. Bar charts for fitters can also be drawn. In Fig. 3 (*a*) we have put the manpower required for each activity. Two types of manpower are shown here, namely, Fitters (*F*) and Helpers (*H*).

8.10 RESOURCE SMOOTHING AND LEVELLING

8.10.1 Resource Smoothing

Resource smoothing is a technique of maintaining resources as uniform as possible by using floats in activities. Intelligent utilization of floats can smoothen the demand of resources to the maximum possible extent. Resource smoothing is also called 'load smoothing'.

8.10.2 Resource Levelling

There are various activities in a project demanding varying levels of resources. The demand on certain specified resources should not go beyond the prescribed level. This operation of resource allocation is called 'Resource Levelling' or 'Load levelling'.

Fig. 3(*b*) shows that there is large variation of human resources. The requirement of number of helpers is as high as 5 in the 14—15 week of the project whereas one helper is required during 18th to 27th week with an average of 2.32 helpers during the project period. This means that resource utilization (RU) $= \frac{2.32}{5} \times 100 = 46.4\%$ indicating low utilization of resources. Hence the project should be planned in such a way that this type of unsteady requirement of resources is smoothened for economy of the project. This can be achieved by shifting the activities with floats on the time-scaled-version of the network. By doing so, it is not necessary that the non-critical activities should start at their latest start-time because it may not also result in a steady requirement of the resources.

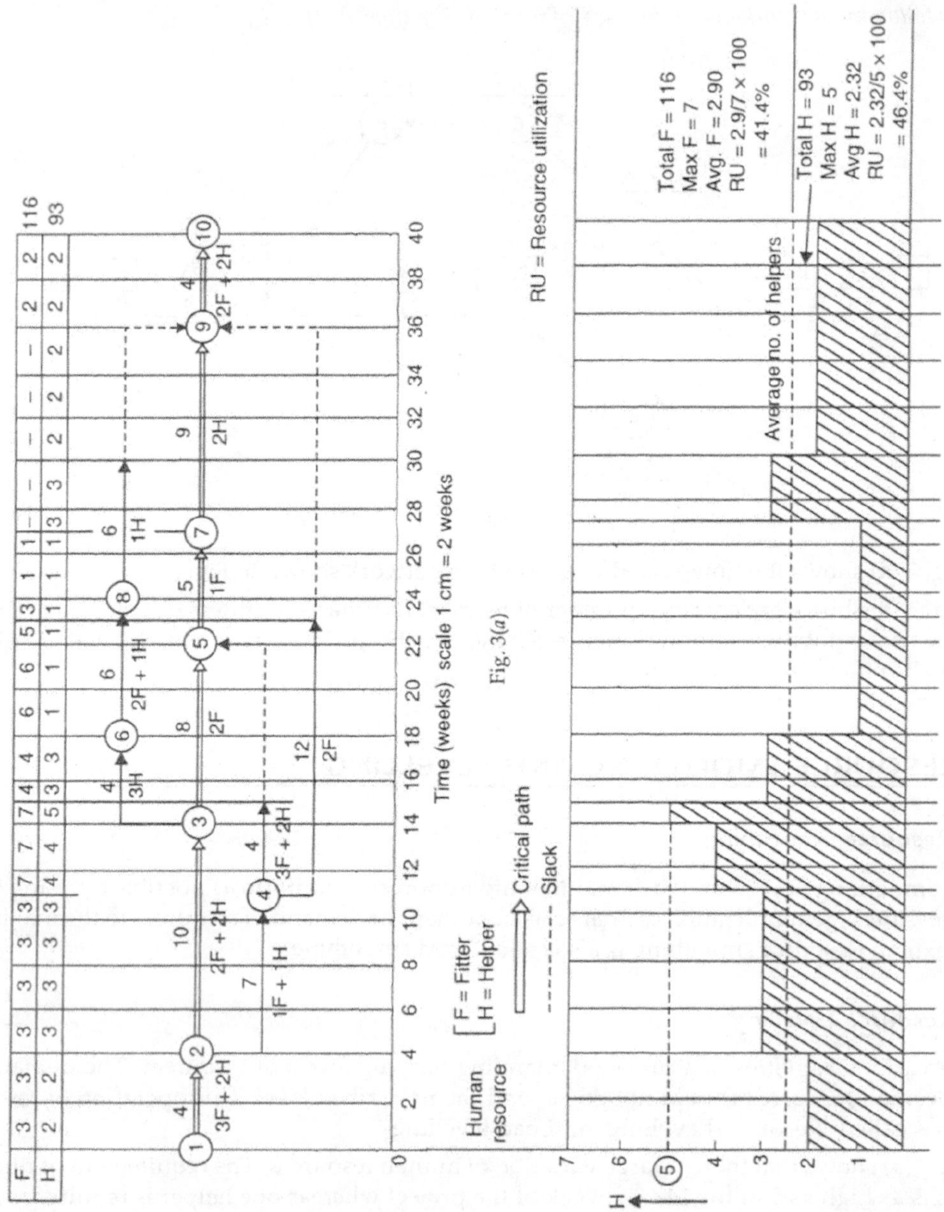

Fig. 3(a)

Fig. 3(b)

Shifting of activity: (1) Shift the activity 4—9 to right side *i.e.*, firm line goes towards right touching event (9) with a length of 12 weeks with 2F.

(2) Shift 4—5 activity towards right with a similar fashion.

(3) Shift event (8) towards right thus its right side will be firm line and the event (8) will be positioned at 30 week. In doing so the event (6) will have dotted line at the start of activity 6—8.

The above shifting will smoothen the resource requirement.

The RU (F) will be = $\frac{2.9}{5} \times 100 = 58\ \%$ → This is much higher than before. Thus, utilization of fitter (as well as helper also) is more than before.

Chapter 9

DECISION ANALYSIS

9.1 DECISION UNDER UNCERTAINTY

There are uncertainty about outcome. A single decision can be drawn from more than one outcome. The decision maker cannot assign probability to the various states of nature.

Example: (*a*) Launching a new motor cycle in the market

(*b*) Investing money in the share market.

9.1.1 Maximin Criterion

This is a pessimistic approach. We will go about the minimum pay off and out of different minimum alternatives the maximum of the minimum pay off is choosen. This is also called wald decision criterion. Let us understand this criterion with an example.

Example 1

The VCS company's R and D cell has recommended to the marketing manager to launch room freshner with three different perfumes. The marketing manager is to decide the type of perfumes considering the following payoff conditions on sales.

Table 1

	Estimated levels of sales (units)		
Type of perfume	*25000*	*15000*	*3000*
A	30 (= pay off)	20	15
B	45	25	10
C	65	30	8

Solution:

As per the criterion we first find out the minimum pay off from each type.

Minimum pay off of type $A = 15 \leftarrow$ Maximum

Minimum pay off of type $B = 10$

Minimum pay off of type $C = 8$

Now the maximum of (15, 10, 8) is 15. Thus type *A* perfume is the choice according to this maximin criterion.

9.1.2 Minimax Criterion

This is an optimistic approach. We will go about the maximum pay off and out of different maximum alternatives, the minimum of the maximum pay off is choosen. Thus this strategy is exactly opposite to that under maximin criterion. Referring to example 1 of 9.1.1, we find out first the maximum pay off from each type.

Maximum pay off of type $A = 30 \leftarrow$ minimum

Maximum pay off of type $B = 45$

Maximum pay off of type $C = 65$

Now the minimum of (30, 45, 65) is 30.

Thus type *A* perfume is also the choice according to this minimax criterion.

9.1.3 Maximax Criterion

This is a completely optimistic approach of the decision maker. We will go about the maximum pay off and out of different maximum alternatives, the maximum of the maximum pay off is choosen. Thus the decision maker chooses a strategy that is expected to give the best of the best pay off.

Referring to example 1 of 9.1.1, we find out first the maximum pay off from each type which is (30, 45, 65).

Now the maximum of (30, 45, 65) is 65. Thus type C perfume is the choice according to this maximax criterion.

9.1.4 Minimin Criterion

When we are dealing with costs, the minimum for each alternative is considered and then we choose the minimum of the alternatives found in the first mentioned step (*i.e.*, minimum of minimum alternatives). If the example 1 of 9.1.1 is having cost matrix (Pay off represent cost) we have minimum of (15, 10, 8) is 8. Thus type *C* perfumes will be the choice according to this criterion.

9.1.5 Laplace Criterion

Here we assume equal probability of various events. This is called criterion of rationality. This is also named Jacob Bernoulli method, using the example 1 of 9.1.1 we have the following table 2.

Table 2

Type	Probability	Expected pay off
A	$\frac{1}{3}$	$\frac{1}{3} \times 30 + \frac{1}{3} \times 20 + \frac{1}{3} \times 15 = \frac{65}{3}$
B	$\frac{1}{3}$	$\frac{1}{3} \times 45 + \frac{1}{3} \times 25 + \frac{1}{3} \times 10 = \frac{80}{3}$
C	$\frac{1}{3}$	$\frac{1}{3} \times 65 + \frac{1}{3} \times 30 + \frac{1}{3} \times 8 = \frac{103}{3} \longleftarrow$ MAX

The maximum of $\left(\frac{65}{3}, \frac{80}{3}, \frac{103}{3}\right)$ is $\frac{103}{3}$. Thus type C perfume is the choice for launching the product.

9.1.6 Hurwicz Criterion

It is the combination of maximin and maximax criteria. Hurwicz introduced the following formula.

$$D_i = \alpha M_i + (1 - \alpha)\, m_i$$

where D_i = Decision index of ith strategy

M_i = Maximum pay off from any of the outcomes resulting from the ith strategy.

m_i = minimum pay off from any of the outcomes resulting from the ith strategy.

α = Degree of optimism

$1 - \alpha$ = Degree of pessimism

Thus $\alpha = 0$ indicates total pessimism

$\alpha = 1$ indicates total optimism.

Referring to example (a) of 9.1.1, Let $\alpha = 0.6$

$$\therefore \quad D_1 = 0.6 \times 30 + (1 - 0.6)\, 15 = 24$$

$$D_2 = 0.6 \times 45 + (1 - 0.6)\, 10 = 31$$

$$D_3 = 0.6 \times 65 + (1 - 0.6)\, 8 = 42.2 \leftarrow \text{MAX}$$

Maximum of (24, 31, 42.2) is 42.2. Thus the decision will be to launch type C perfume.

In case of cost: The formula is

$$HC_i = \alpha(\text{Minimum}) + (1 - \alpha)\,(\text{Maximum}).$$

HC_i = Hurwicz cost in ith strategy.

If the pay off represents cost, example 1(a) of 9.1.1 will be calculated as follows:

$$HC_1 = 0.6(15) + (1 - 0.6)\, 30 = 21 \leftarrow \text{MIN}$$

$$HC_2 = 0.6(10) + (1 - 0.6)\, 45 = 24$$

$$HC_3 = 0.6\,(8) + (1 - 0.6)\, 65 = 30.8$$

Thus the minimum of (21, 24, 30.8) is 21. Thus type A perfume will be the choice.

9.1.7 Minimax Regret Criterion

Here regret means opportunity loss. L.J. Savage developed this criterion. He calls for selecting the course of action that minimises the maximum opportunity loss (regret). The all other decisions do not take into account the cost of opportunity lost making the wrong decision, this criterion does so.

For profit:

*i*th regret = max pay off – *i*th pay off for the *j*th event.

we have to choose minimum of the maximum regret.

For cost:

*i*th regret = *i*th pay off – maximum pay off (*i.e.*, minimum cost) for the *j*th event

we have to choose minimum of the maximum regret.

This criterion will be cleared from the following example.

Example 2

A marketing manager has 3 alternatives open to him each of which can be followed by any of the 4 possible events. The conditional pay off (in Rs.) for each action event combinations are given below:

Alternatives	*Pay offs conditional on events*			
	I	*II*	*III*	*IV*
A	8	1	– 9	6
B	– 3	12	19	– 1
C	14	6	1	8

Find out which alternative should be adopted, if the manager adopts the maximum regret criterion.

Solution:

Alternatives	*Regret pay off amount*				*Maximum regret*
	I	*II*	*III*	*IV*	
A	14 – 8 = 6	12 – 1 = 11	19 – (– 9) = 28	8 – 6 = 2	28
B	14 – (– 3) = 17	12 – 12 = 0	19 – 19 = 0	8 – (– 1) = 9	17 ← MIN
C	14 – 14 = 0	12 – 6 = 6	19 – 1 = 18	8 – 8 = 0	18

The minimum of (28, 17, 18) is 17. So the decision maker (marketing manager) would choose alternative *B*.

Example 3

M/S VCS company has 3 alternatives open, each of which can be followed by any of the 4 possible events. The conditional pay offs (in Rs.) for each action event combination are given below:

Alternative	*Pay offs conditional on events*			
	A	*B*	*C*	*D*
X	8	0	– 10	6
Y	– 4	12	18	– 2
Z	14	6	0	8

Determine which alternative should the company choose, if they adopt the
(i) maximin criterion
(ii) maximax criterion
(iii) Hurwicz criterion (α = 0.70)
(iv) Laplace criterion
(v) minimax regret criterion.

Solution.

(*i*)

	A	*B*	*C*	*D*	MIN
X	8	0	– 10	6	– 10
Y	– 4	12	18	– 2	– 4
Z	14	6	0	8	0 ← MAX

Ans. = Z

(*ii*)

	A	*B*	*C*	*D*	MAX
X	8	0	– 10	6	8
Y	– 4	12	18	– 2	18 ← MAX
Z	14	6	0	8	14

Ans. = *Y*

(*iii*)

Alternative	MAX^m	MIN^m	D = α (max) + (1– α) min (α = 0.7)
X	8	– 10	2.6
Y	18	– 4	11.4 ← MAX
Z	14	0	9.8

Ans. = *Y*

(*iv*)

Alternative	*A*	*B*	*C*	*D*	Expected pay off values = (*A*/4 + *B*/4 + *C*/4 + *D*/4)
X	8	0	– 10	6	1
Y	– 4	12	18	– 2	6
Z	14	6	0	8	7 ← MAX

Ans. = *Z*

(*v*)

Alternative	*A*	*B*	*C*	*D*	MAX^m Regret
X	14 – 8 = 6	12 – 0 = 12	18 – (– 10) = 28	8 – 6 = 2	28
Y	14 – (– 4) = 18	12 – 12 = 0	18 – 18 = 0	8 – (– 2) = 10	18 ← MIN
Z	14 – 14 = 0	12 – 6 = 6	18 – 0 = 18	8 – 8 = 0	18 ← MIN

Ans. = *Y* or *Z*

9.2 DECISION UNDER RISK

Here the probabilities of occurrence are known and the decision maker has to choose among several possible options. The past data and experience help the decision maker to take a judgement under the condition of risk. There are two popular decision criteria; one is EMV (expected monetary value and the other is EOL (expected opportunity loss).

9.2.1 Expected Monetary Value (EMV) Criterion

The following steps are followed:

(*a*) Conditional pay off table for each decision-event combination is to be prepared first alongwith the corresponding probabilities.

(*b*) Secondly the EMV for each decision alternative is to be determined by multiplying the conditional profit, by assigned probabilities. Additions of conditional values are done.

(*c*) Finally, the alternative that yields the maximum EMV is to be selected for decision.

Example 4

ABC company finds from the past data that the cost of making an item is Rs. 35, the selling price of the item is Rs. 40 if it is sold within a week, and it could be disposed off at Rs. 30 per item at the end of the week if unsold.

Weekly sales	4	5	6	7
Probabilities	0.1	0.2	0.4	0.3

Find the optimum number of items per week the company should produce for sale.

Solution:

Cost of producting one item	= Rs. 35
Selling price of one item	= Rs. 40
Profit if sold	= Rs. 40 – Rs. 35 = Rs. 5 per item.
If unsold, disposal price	= Rs. 30.
Loss if an item is unsold	= Rs. 35 – Rs. 30 = Rs. 5

Step (*a*)

Conditional Profit Table

Sales	*Probability*	*Production*			
		4	5	6	7
4	0.10	Rs. 20	20 – 5 = 15	20 – 2 × 5 = 10	20 – 3 × 5 = 5
5	0.20	20	25	25 – 1 × 5 = 20	25 – 2 × 5 = 15
6	0.40	20	25	30	30 – 1 × 5 = 25
7	0.30	20	25	30	35

Step (*b*)

Possible demand	*Probability*	*Expected profit for producing (Rs.)*			
		4	5	*6	7
4	0.10	20 × 0.1 = 2.0	15 × 0.1 = 1.5	10 × 0.1 = 1.0	5 × 0.1 = 0.5
5	0.20	20 × 0.2 = 4.0	25 × 0.2 = 5.0	20 × 0.2 = 4.0	15 × 0.2 = 3.0
6	0.40	20 × 0.4 = 8.0	25 × 0.4 = 10.0	30 × 0.4 = 12.0	25 × 0.4 = 10.0
7	0.30	20 × 0.3 = 6.0	25 × 0.3 = 7.5	30 × 0.3 = 9.0	35 × 0.3 = 10.5
Total expected Profit (Total EMV)		20.0	24.0	*26.0 (MAXIMUM)	24

Step (c)

*Hence the optimum number of items to be produced = 6 **Ans.**

9.2.2 Expected Opportunity Loss (EOL) Criterion

Minimizing EOL is equivalent to maximizing EMV.

The expected opportunity loss or expected value of regrets represents the amount by which maximum possible profit will be reduced under various possible stock actions.

The following steps are followed:

Step (*a*): Conditional pay off table for each decision event combination is to be prepared first alongwith the corresponding probabilities.

(*b*) Secondly, for each event the COL (conditional opportunity loss) is to be found out by subtracting the pay off from the maximum payoff for that event.

(*c*) Thirdly, the EOL for each decision alternative is to be found out by multiplying the COL's by the corresponding probabilities and then the results are added.

(*d*) Finally select the alternative that yields the lowest EOL.

Example 5

Solve the example 4 by EOL criterion.

Solution:

Step (*a*) same as before (see example (4))

Step (*b*) **Conditional loss table**

Sales	*Probability*	*Possible production action (alternative)*			
		4	5	6	7
4	0.1	20 – 20 = 0	20 – 15 = 5	20 – 10 = 10	20 – 5 = 15
5	0.2	25 – 20 = 5	25 – 25 = 0	25 – 20 = 5	25 – 15 = 10
6	0.4	30 – 20 = 10	30 – 25 = 5	30 – 30 = 0	30 – 25 = 5
7	0.3	35 – 20 = 15	35 – 25 = 10	35 – 30 = 5	35 – 35 = 0

Step (*c*) **Expected loss table**

Sales	*Probability*	*Possible production action (alternative)*			
		4	5	*6	7
4	0.10	0 × 0.1 = 0	5 × 0.10 = 0.50	10 × 0.10 = 1.0	15 × 0.10 = 1.5
5	0.20	5 × 0.2 = 1.0	0 × 0.20 = 0	5 × 0.2 = 1.0	10 × 0.20 = 2.0
6	0.40	10 × 0.4 = 4.0	5 × 0.40 = 2.0	0 × 0.4 = 0	5 × 0.4 = 2.0
7	0.30	15 × 0.3 = 4.5	10 × 0.3 = 3.0	5 × 0.3 = 1.5	0 × 0.3 = 0
Expected EOL		9.50	5.50	*3.50 MINIMUM	5.50

Step (*d*)

*The optimum number of items = 6 **Ans.**

N.B:

The EMV criterion is based on either largest EMV or smallest EMV depending on the problem of maximization or minimization respectively, but EOL criterion is based on finding the minimum EOL irrespective of maximizing expected profit or minimizing expected loss.

9.3 EXPECTED VALUE OF PERFECT INFORMATION (EVPI)

Here there is a complete and accurate (*i.e.*, perfect) information about the future demand which would remove all uncertainty from the problem.

In the event of accurately knowing the demand, the company would stock exactly the same number and realise a known profit. For the previous problem if the company keep stock of 4 items and all sold, it will realise a profit of Rs. 20, if 5 items sold then Rs. 25 and so on. We need two tables one for conditional profit under perfect information (certainty) and expected profit with perfect information.

Conditional profit table under certainty (Rs.)

Possible demand (event)	*Possible stock action (alternatives)*			
	4	5	6	7
4	20	—	—	—
5	—	25	—	—
6	—	—	30	—
7	—	—	—	35

The expected profit under perfect information (EPPI) can be calculated as follows:

EPPI

Market size (No. of items)	*Conditional profit under certainty*	*Probability of market size*	*Expected profit with perfect information*
4	20	0.1	20 × 0.1 = 2.0
5	25	0.2	25 × 0.2 = 5.0
6	30	0.4	30 × 0.4 = 12.0
7	35	0.3	35 × 0.3 = 10.5
			EPPI = 29.5

Thus with perfect information the profit is Rs. 29.5 and in case of uncertainty the best expected profit was Rs. 26.0 *i.e.*, a difference of Rs. 3.50. This difference *i.e.*, Rs. 3.50 is called the expected value of perfect information *i.e.*, EVPI.

It is noted that the minimum EOL (it is Rs. 3.50 in the previous problem) equals to EVPI.

Thus, EVPI = Minimum EOL = EPPI – Maximum EMV.

9.4 EMV FOR ITEMS THAT HAVE A SALVAGE VALUE

If an item is unsold, we have assumed its salvage value as zero *i.e.*, there is no salvage value. If there is salvage value, we have to take it into account and recalculate the EMV.

Example 6

A fruit seller buys apple at a cost of Rs. 6 per apple and sells it for Rs. 9 per apple. At the end of day the unsold apple has a salvage value of Rs. 3 per apple. Past sales figure range from 15 to 18 apples per day. Find EMV if the sale history has the following probabilities:

Market Size	< 15	15	16	17	18	> 18
Probability	0	0.10	0.20	0.40	0.30	0

Solution:

Let S = stock,

D = market demand.

Here the conditional profit, $CP = (9 - 6)\ S = 3\ S$, when $D \geq S$.

and $CP = 9D - 6S + 3(S - D)$, when $D < S$.

A stock of 15 apples each day will result in daily profit of Rs. 15 × 3 = Rs. 45. A stock of 16 apples each day will result in a profit of Rs. 16 × 3 = Rs. 48 when the demand is 16 apples or more. But when the demand is 15 nos., the conditional profit will be [9 × 15 – 6 × 16 + 3(16 – 15)] = Rs. 42. The resulting pay off matrix is given in the following table 1.

Table 1

Conditional profit

Possible demand (event)	*Probability* (i)	*Possible stock action* 15 (ii)	16 (iii)	17 (iv)	18 (v)
15	0.10	45	42	39	36
16	0.20	45	48	45	42
17	0.40	45	48	51	48
18	0.30	45	48	51	54

The expected pay off and the EMV for each stock action are calculated as given in table 2.

Table 2

Expected Profit

Possible demand (event)	*Probability* (i)	*Possible stock action (alternatives)* 15 (i × ii)	16 (i × iii)	*17 (i × iv)	18 (i × v)
15	0.10	4.50	4.20	3.90	3.60
16	0.20	9.00	9.60	9.00	8.40

17	0.40	18.00	19.20	20.40	19.20
18	0.30	13.50	14.40	15.30	16.20
	EMV → (Rs.)	45.00	47.40	*48.60 MAXIMUM	47.40

∴ *Maximum EMV = Rs. 48.60 for stock action of 17 apples each day.

9.5 INCREMENTAL OR MARGINAL ANALYSIS

We have observed in example of section 9.4 that if there are 4 demand levels and 5 possible stock actions, calculation of 4 ×5 = 20 conditional profit is to be done. So if there are 100 demand levels and 105 possible stock actions there will be 100 × 105 = 10500 computations which are cumbersome. This excessive computational work can be avoided by using incremental or marginal approach. According to this approach if P represents the probability of selling one additional unit, then $(1-p)$ must be the probability of not selling it. If the additional unit is sold, the conditional profit will increase as a result of the profit earned from this unit. This is known as incremental (marginal) profit, IP. If the additional unit is unsold, the conditional profit reduces and the amount of reduction is known as incremental (marginal) loss, IL, resulting from stocking of an item that is not sold. We can stock additional units so long the expected incremental profit is more than the expected incremental loss. In the limiting case

$$p(IP) = (1-p)\,IL \quad \text{or} \quad p = \frac{IL}{IP + IL}.$$

The letter P represents the minimum required probability of selling at least an additional unit to justify the stocking of that additional unit. Additional units should be stocked so long as the probability of selling at least an additional unit is greater than p.

Example 7

A milkman buys milk at Rs. 4 per litre, and sells for Rs. 5.00 per litre. Unsold milk has to be thrown away. The daily demand has the following probability distribution.

Demand (litres)	46	48	50	52	54	56	58	60	62	64
Probability	0.01	0.03	0.06	0.10	0.20	0.25	0.15	0.10	0.05	0.05

The demands are independent with each other. How many litres should be ordered every day?

Solution:

$$p = \frac{IL}{IP + IL} = \frac{4}{(5-4)+4} = \frac{4}{5} = 0.8$$

We will go on stocking to the cumulative probability ≥ 0.8.

Cumulative probabilities of sales

Sales (litres of milk)	*Probability of this sales level*	*Cumulative probability that sales will be at this level or higher*
46	0.01	1.00
48	0.03	0.99
50	0.06	0.96
52	0.10	0.90
54	0.20	0.80 ←
56	0.25	0.60
58	0.15	0.35
60	0.10	0.20
62	0.05	0.10
64	0.05	0.05

The optimum number of litres of milk to be stocked is 54.

Expected *IP* for $p = 0.8 = p(IP) = 0.8 \times 1.00 =$ Rs. 0.8

Expected *IL* for $p = 0.8 = (1 - p)\ IL = 0.2 \times 4 =$ Rs. 0.8.

Example 8

A newspaper boy gets newspapers from the local office at the rate of Rs. 0.60 each and sells from his shop at Rs. 1.10 each. However, he has to tell the office in advance as to how many copies he will buy. The office takes back the copies he is not able to sell and pays him only 15 paise for each copy. Determine how many copies should he take everyday. The daily demand has the following probability distribution.

Demand	30	31	32	33	34	35
Probability	0.10	0.20	0.20	0.30	0.10	0.10

Solution:

$$IP = \text{Rs. } (1.10 - 0.60) = \text{Rs. } 0.50$$

$$IL = \text{Rs. } (0.60 - 0.15) = \text{Rs. } 0.45$$

$$p = \frac{IL}{IP + IL} = \frac{0.45}{0.50 + 0.45} = 0.473$$

Sales	*Probability*	*Cumulative Probability*
30	0.10	1.00
31	0.20	0.90
32	0.20	0.70
33 ←	0.30	0.50 ←
34	0.10	0.20
35	0.10	0.10

As 0.50 > 0.473. The optimum decision is to order 33 copies everyday.

9.6 MAXIMUM LIKELIHOOD CRITERION

This criterion is based on the highest probability of occurrence. The decision maker chooses the state of nature which is having the highest probability. For example (6), table 1, the decision maker would choose the demand level of 17 apples that corresponds to the highest probability of 0.40 and having largest conditional profit of Rs. 51 in that state of nature. This criterion works well when there is much more difference between probabilities without having significant difference in conditional values.

9.7 EXPECTED VALUE CRITERION FOR CONTINUOUSLY DISTRIBUTED RANDOM VARIABLES

Previously we had situations involving discrete random variables. Here we will discuss continuously distributed random variables of known probability density function.

Example 9

A fruit dealer buys oranges for Rs. 300 a box and sells them for Rs. 800 per box. If the box is not sold on the first selling day, it has a salvage value of Rs. 100. The past records indicate that demand pattern follows normal distribution with a mean of 30 boxes daily and a standard deviation of 9 boxes. How many boxes should the fruit dealer stock?

Solution:

$$p = \frac{IL}{IP + IL} = \frac{300 - 100}{(800 - 300) + (300 - 100)} = \frac{200}{700} = 0.285$$

$$Z_A = \frac{x - \bar{x}}{\sigma} = \frac{x - 30}{9}$$

$$0.57 = \frac{x - 30}{9}$$

or $x = 0.57 \times 9 + 30 = 35$, Z is normal deviate.

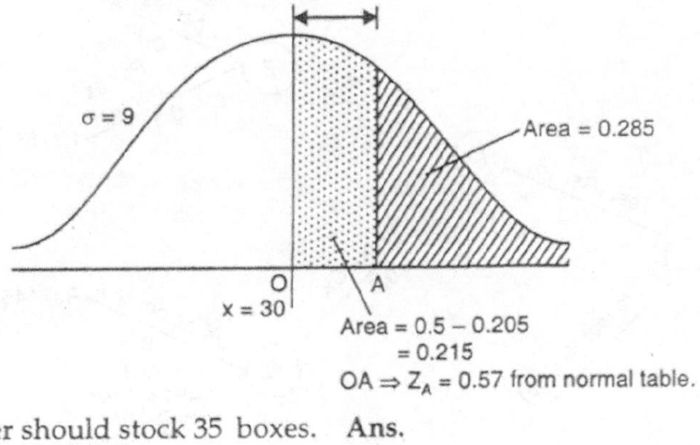

The fruit dealer should stock 35 boxes. **Ans.**

9.8 DECISION TREES

Decision tree is a graphical presentation of the decisions in a step by step indicating all parameters of decisions like decision alternatives, states of nature, probabilities attached to states of nature, conditional profit or loss.

Steps in decision tree analysis:

(1) Locate on papers the decision points and the alternative courses of action against decision points.

(2) Insert probability and associated pay off (EMV) for each course of action.

(3) Start calculating EMV from extreme right end.

(4) Choose the best EMV.

(5) Trace backward to the next stage of decision points.

(6) Repeat above steps till the first decision point is reached.

(7) Identify the path to be followed from beginning to the end under different possible outcomes for the situation as a whole.

Example 10

The manager of inspection department takes the following strategies against assembly of parts.

(i) *Testing costs Rs. 15, No test incorporates Rs. 55 as guarantee accuracy with probabilities.*

(ii) *After test, assembly actually OK, 70% and not OK 30%.*

(iii) *If assy OK, it is passed as per test, the probability is 70%. and if fails it is 30% and cost zero and Rs. 55 respectively.*

(iv) *If any faulty, it is having prob of 30%.*

(v) *Faulty assy, it will be OK 20% and not OK 80% and costs associated are Rs. 145 and Rs. 55 respectively.*

Draw the decision tree and find optimal EMV at starting node.

Solution:

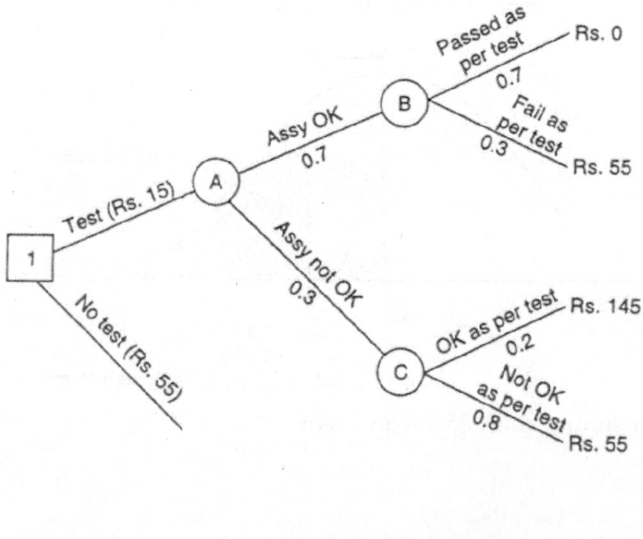

EMV of node $B = 0.7 \times 0 + 0.3 \times 55 =$ Rs. 16.5

EMV of node $C = 0.2 \times 145 + 0.8 \times 55 =$ Rs. 73.0

EMV of node $A = 0.7 \times 16.5 + 0.3 \times 73 =$ Rs. 33.45

EMV of node 1 via the branch testing $= 15 + 33.45 =$ Rs. 48.45

EMV of node 1 via the branch 'no test' $=$ Rs. 55 $>$ Rs. 48.45

Here we are dealing with cost, so optimal EMV of node 1 is Rs. 48.45 corresponding to the decision of testing the assembly.

9.9 BAYESIAN ANALYSIS

Let us understand this with the following example:

Example 11

Super Action International buys a petroleum derivative as a raw material input. The purchase executive Samuel La Porte expects an increase in the prices of the raw material following a meeting of the OPEC countries, which he feels in likely to take place in the near future, resulting in an increase in the petroleum prices. Mr. La Porte is also of the view that even if the meeting does not materialise, the supplying company may increase the price of the raw materials, in any case, though this would not be as high as the price increase consequent to the OPEC meeting taking place. Mr. La Porte weighs the various probabilities of the price hike as it concerns the purchase cost incurred by his company as:

1. *Probability of OPEC meeting occurring: 60%*
2. *If the OPEC meeting takes place, the probability of a*
   - *(i) 10% rise in raw material prices is 50%*
   - *(ii) 5% rise is 30%*
   - *(iii) 15% rise is 30%.*
3. *If the meeting is postponed, the probability of a*
   - *(i) 5% rise in the raw material prices is 30%*
   - *(ii) 2% rise in the raw material prices is 30%*
   - *(iii) No rise in the raw material prices is 40%.*

Mr. La Porte is assessing the impact of the hike in the prices of the raw material due to reasons given above on the financial requirement for the procurement of the raw material. At present, the company buys Rs. 1 crore worth of this material.

Solution:

We use the Bayesian analysis to determine the impact of the probable rise in raw material prices to various levels on the ultimate financial needs of the organization. The Bayes' theorem states that the probability of a certain event occurring, if it is conditional on the occurrence of the previous event, is given by the product of the probability of the previous event and that of the present event. For instance, the probability of a 10% price rise, in the event of OPEC meeting taking place, is computed to be $P(M) \times P(0.10/M) = 0.6 \times 0.5 = 0.30$.

The conditional probabilities tree for Mr. La Porte can be drawn as shown below.

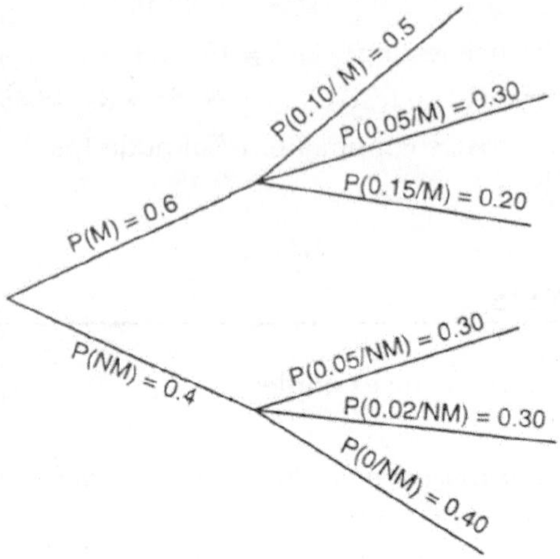

Note. M = OPEC meeting takes place

NM = No meeting of the OPEC

P = Probability.

Likewise, the probabilities of various prices increase can be computed as follows.

$$P(0.10) = 0.60 \times 0.50 = 0.3$$
$$P(0.05) = (0.30 \times 0.60) + (0.3 \times 0.4) = 0.30$$
$$P(0.15) = (0.2 \times 0.6) = 0.12$$
$$P(0.02) = 0.3 \times 0.4 = 0.12$$
$$P(0) = 0.4 \times 0.4 = 0.16.$$

Based on the above probabilities, the following calculations are made for the expected price to be paid for the same quantity of the raw material.

10% rise	⇒	Rs. 11000000 × 0.3 = Rs. 3300000
5% rise	⇒	Rs. 10500000 × 0.3 = Rs. 3150000
15% rise	⇒	Rs. 11500000 × 0.12 = Rs. 1380000
2% rise	⇒	Rs. 10200000 × 0.12 = Rs. 1224000
0% rise	⇒	Rs. 10000000 × 0.16 = Rs. 1600000
		Expected value = Rs. 10654000

Therefore; given the probability of a rise in raw material prices due to certain developments cited above Mr. La Porte should advise the company to be prepared for an average additional expenditure of Rs. 654000. *i.e.*, 6.54% more than at present. This necessitates a judicious selection of vendors so as to ensure the availability of the raw material at minimum cost.

Chapter **10** *GAME THEORY*

10.1 INTRODUCTION

A 'game' is not merely for pleasure but also to specify that a competitive situation exists at least between two parties. Game theory can be applied to the situation of war, business etc.

There are three types of game:

(1) Two person game
(2) Multi person game
(3) Games against Nature

→ Zero sum game.
→ Non-zero sum game.

In this chapter we will consider 'Two persons zero sum game'.

10.2 GOVERNING RULES

(1) Finite number of players take part in the game.

(2) The number of possible alternatives (called strategies) open to each player is finite.

(3)

Player B

Player A	B_1	B_2	B_3
A_1	P_{11}	P_{12}	P_{13}
A_2	P_{21}	P_{22}	P_{23}
A_3	P_{31}	P_{32}	P_{33}

Each player's decision may affect his own benefit as well as others.

(4) All players take their decisions simultaneously.

(5) The outcomes (called pay off) for all possible combinations of choices are known.

(6) The possible choices open to each player are known to other players.

(7) Players do not communicate (they play fair games).

(8) Players are assumed to have similar motivations and they are supposed to behave rationally.

10.3 TO FIND SADDLE POINT

Example 1.

Table 1

Player A \ Player B	B_1	B_2	B_3	Min. Gain : worst outcome for player A
A_1	1	−1	10	−1
A_2	−5	0	−4	−5
A_3	2	(1)	5	(1) → Maxi-min
Worst outcome for player B (Max. Loss)	2	(1)	10	

Saddle point = value of the game

(Loss) Mini-max

Maxi-min: This means maximum of row player's minimum pay off. In table 1, assuming row player's strategy as A_1, his minimum pay off is – 1; similarly minimum pay off the row player playing strategy A_2 is 5.

Similarly, if all the elements in a row are less than or equal to the corresponding elements in another row, that row is dominated.

Example 2.

Player A \ Player B	B_1	B_2	B_3
A_1	−3	7	4
A_2	−2	−2	7
A_3	3	−2	5

It is seen that there is no saddle point. Let us consider player B's' B_1 and B_2 strategies. B_3 column is having elements greater than all the elements of B_1 column. From B_3's point of view, player B will take B_1 rather B_3, regardless of player's A's strategy. Since B_3 is dominated (by B_1) it can be deleted, thereby reducing the size of the matrix as

	B_1	B_2
A_1	−3	7
~~A_2~~	~~−2~~	~~−2~~
A_3	3	−2

Let us now consider the strategy of player A's A_2, A_3. A_2 is dominated by A_3. Thus A_2 is dropped is – 5 and that while playing strategy A_3 is 1. Therefore maxi-min in this case is 1.

Mini-Max: This means minimum of column players maximum pay off. Referring to table (1) assuming column players strategy B_1, maximum pay off is 2 and for B_2 is 1 and for B_3 is 10. Therefore minimax in this case is 1 which is equal to maxi-min and the 'Game' is called zero-sum-Game.

Saddle point: Intersection of maximin and minimax if they are equal is called saddle point. In this case players adopt pure strategy.

Dominance: When in the problem of a game, we find a saddle point, we call it a pure strategy game. If this is not applicable, the step would be to find out dominance of strategies in order to reduce the size of pay-off matrix.

Rule of dominance: If all the elements in a column are greater than or equal to the corresponding elements in another column, then that column is dominated.

The matrix size reduces to

	B_1	B_2
A_1	−3	7
A_3	3	−2

Solution of the above last matrix:

Step 1: Write down the absolute value of difference in row and column.

Step 2: Then calculate the ratio, $\frac{\text{absolute value}}{\text{sum}}$.

Step 3: Interchange the fractions.

Step 4 and final: Interchanged fraction are solution.

	B_1	B_2	Absolute Difference			
A_1	−3	7	−3	10	$\frac{10}{15}$	$\frac{5}{15}\left(=\frac{1}{3}\right)$
A_3	3	−2	−2	5	$\frac{5}{15}$	$\frac{10}{15}\left(=\frac{2}{3}\right)$
	3	7				
	6	9		15 / 15		
	$\frac{6}{15}$	$\frac{9}{15}$				
	$\frac{9}{15}$	$\frac{6}{15}$				
	$\left(=\frac{3}{5}\right)$	$\left(=\frac{2}{5}\right)$				

The results are

Player A plays $\left(\frac{5}{15}, 0, \frac{10}{15}\right)$ and player B plays $\left(\frac{9}{15}, \frac{6}{15}, 0\right)$ *i.e.*, player A plays $\left(\frac{1}{3}, 0, \frac{2}{3}\right)$ and player B plays $\left(\frac{3}{5}, \frac{2}{5}, 0\right)$.

Value of the game = V

or,
$$V = (-3)\left(\frac{1}{3}\right)\left(\frac{3}{5}\right) + 7\left(\frac{1}{3}\right)\left(\frac{2}{5}\right) + 3\left(\frac{2}{3}\right)\left(\frac{3}{5}\right) + (-2)\left(\frac{2}{3}\right)\left(\frac{2}{5}\right)$$

$$= -\frac{3}{5} + \frac{14}{15} + \frac{6}{5} - \frac{8}{15} = \frac{-9 + 14 + 18 - 8}{15} = 1.$$

10.4 MIX-STRATEGY GAME

2 × 2 game: Example 3.

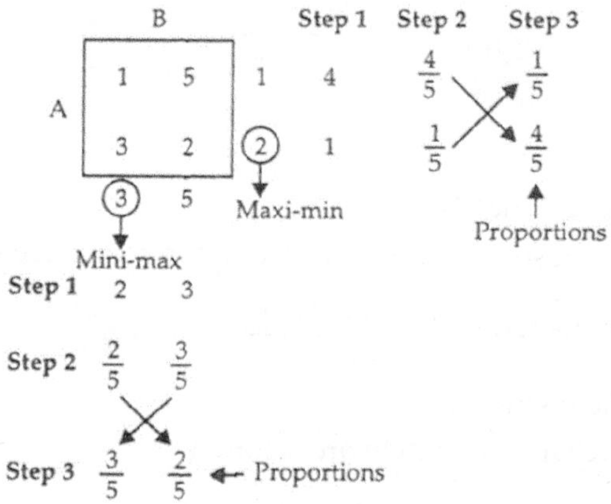

Note that the value of the game will lie between 2 and 3.

Value of the game:

$$V = 1\left(\frac{1}{5}\right)\left(\frac{3}{5}\right) + 5\left(\frac{1}{5}\right)\left(\frac{2}{5}\right) + 3\left(\frac{4}{5}\right)\left(\frac{3}{5}\right) + 2\left(\frac{4}{5}\right)\left(\frac{2}{5}\right)$$

= + 2.6 which lies between 2 and 3. Player A will gain + 2.6 units.

10.5 GRAPHICAL METHOD FOR 2 × n GAME OR m × 2 GAME

Example 4.

player A	B_1	B_2	B_3	B_4	
x, A_1	4	−2	3	−1	−2
$(1-x), A_2$	−1	2	0	1	(−1) ← Maxi-min
	4	2	3	(1)	
				↑ Minimax-max	

(Columns: player B)

Graphical method is applicable for those games in which one of the players has two strategies only. In the above example there is no saddle point and the value of the game lies between – 1 and 1.

Let A mixes x and $(1 - x)$

$$V = 4x + (-1)(1 - x) = 5x - 1$$

$$\therefore \quad \boxed{V = 5x - 1}$$

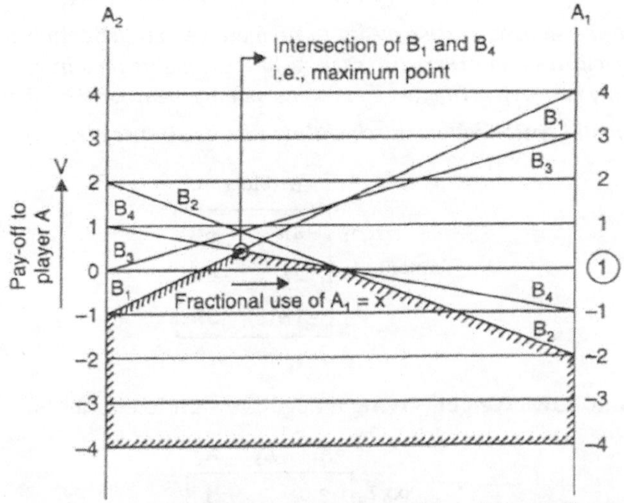

Intersection point must be on opposite slope lines. Here B_1 and B_4 are of opposite slope. Thus the game reduces to 2 × 2 game as given below:

	B_1	B_4	Step 1	Step 2	Step 3
A_1	4	– 1	$\frac{1}{5}$	$\frac{2}{5/7}$	$\frac{2}{7}$
A_2	– 1	1	2	$\frac{2}{7}$	$\frac{5}{7}$
Step 1	5	2			
Step 2	$\frac{5}{7}$	$\frac{2}{7}$			
Step 3	$\frac{2}{7}$	$\frac{5}{7}$			

The value of the game is

$$V = 4\left(\frac{2}{7}\right)\left(\frac{2}{7}\right) + (-1)\left(\frac{2}{7}\right)\left(\frac{5}{7}\right) + (-1)\left(\frac{5}{7}\right)\left(\frac{2}{7}\right) + (1)\left(\frac{5}{7}\right)\left(\frac{5}{7}\right)$$

$$= \frac{16}{49} - \frac{10}{49} - \frac{10}{49} + \frac{25}{49}$$

$$= \frac{16 - 10 - 10 + 25}{49}$$

$$= \frac{21}{49} = \frac{3}{7} \quad \text{Ans}$$

Example 5

A new 'Restora Antons' has been opened in a city where the main competition is from 'Blue Restora'. Antons' management has observed that Blue's promotional effort varies between reduced prices B_1 on certain night and special menu B_2 on other nights. To attract customers from Blue's, Anton can also reduce price A_1; serves special meal A_2 or can emphasis a new strategy which is a take out service A_3.

Both restora use the same advertise media to promote special attraction on each week. Because of differences in physical facilities and experience each restora excells in certain specialities. Percentage (%) gain or loss in net revenue has been estimated by Antons management for the different outcomes.

What strategy should Anton follow in scheduling its weekly specials.

		B_1 (Blues)	B_2
	A_1	–3%	6%
(Anton)	A_2	2%	–6%
	A_3	–1%	5%

Solution:

By changing column into rows we get (giving a negative sign to elements)

	A_1	A_2	A_3
(x), B_1	3	–2	1
(1 – x), B_2	–6	6	–5

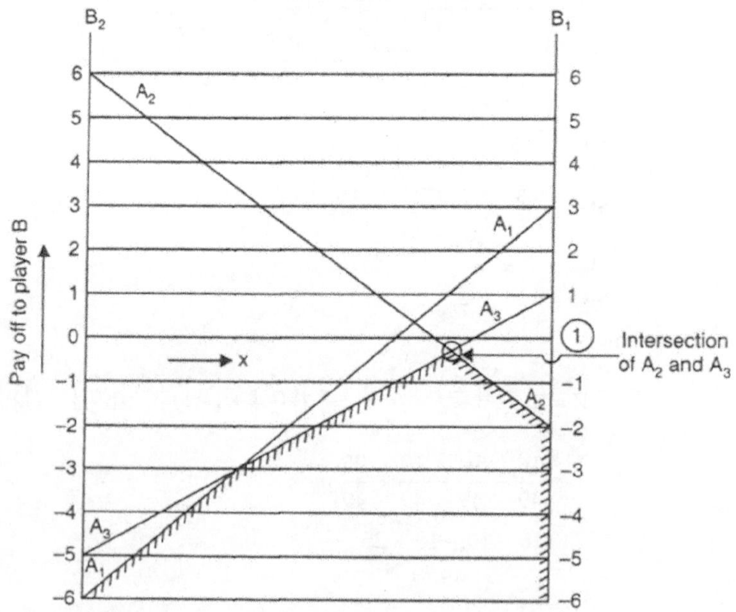

Thus the size of the game reduces to 2 × 2 game.

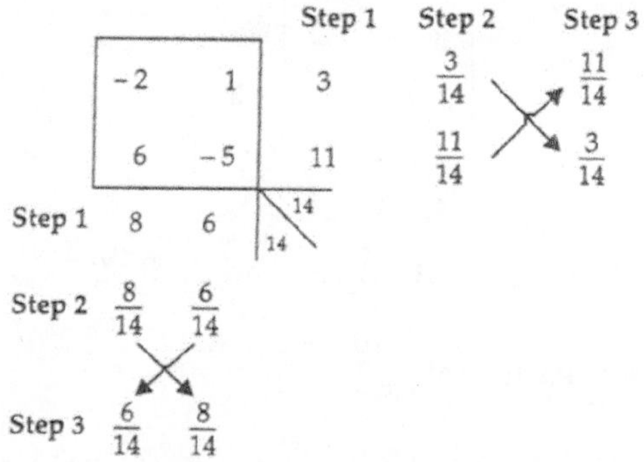

Value of the game (V) is given by

$$V = (-2)\left(\frac{11}{14}\right)\left(\frac{6}{14}\right) + (1)\left(\frac{11}{14}\right)\left(\frac{8}{14}\right) + 6\left(\frac{3}{14}\right)\left(\frac{6}{14}\right) + (-5)\left(\frac{3}{14}\right)\left(\frac{8}{14}\right)$$

$= -0.2857$ (to Blues)

i.e., Gain of Restora Antons by 0.2857 % **Ans.**

10.6 METHOD OF MATRICES (3 × 3 GAME)

Solve the following game:

Example 6

	B_1	B_2	B_3	
A_1	8	2	8	2
A_2	10	0	2	0
A_3	6	8	7	6 ← Maxi-min
	10	8	8	

Mini-max (8, 8)

Solution:

Step 1: <u>To find saddle point</u>. There is no saddle point: Value of the game lies between 6 and 8.

Step 2: Reduction of the matrix by method of dominance: It can not be reduced.

Step 3: Subtract each row from the row above ($A_1 - A_2$ and $A_2 - A_3$) and write it below the matrix.

Step 4: Subtract each column from the column to its left ($B_1 - B_2$ and $B_2 - B_3$) and write down the results to the right of the matrix. We get the following table 1.

$$
\begin{array}{c|ccc|cc}
 & B_1 & B_2 & B_3 & & \\
\hline
A_1 & 8 & 2 & 8 & 6 & -6 \\
A_2 & 10 & 0 & 2 & 10 & -2 \\
A_3 & 6 & 8 & 7 & -2 & 1 \\
\hline
 & -2 & 2 & 6 & & \\
 & 4 & -8 & -5 & &
\end{array}
$$

Step 5: Calculate the oddments for A_1, A_2, A_3 and B_1, B_2, B_3.

Oddment for $A_1 = \text{determinant}\begin{vmatrix} 10 & -2 \\ -2 & 1 \end{vmatrix} = |\,6\,| = 6$

Oddment for $A_2 = \text{determinant}\begin{vmatrix} 6 & -6 \\ -2 & 1 \end{vmatrix} = |\,-6\,| = 6$

Oddment for $A_3 = \text{determinant}\begin{vmatrix} 6 & -6 \\ 10 & -2 \end{vmatrix} = |\,48\,| = 48$

Oddment for $B_1 = \text{determinant}\begin{vmatrix} 2 & 6 \\ -8 & -5 \end{vmatrix} = 38$

Oddment for $B_2 = \text{determinant}\begin{vmatrix} -2 & 6 \\ 4 & -5 \end{vmatrix} = 14$

Oddment for $B_3 = \text{determinant}\begin{vmatrix} -2 & 2 \\ 4 & -8 \end{vmatrix} = 8$

Step 6: Put these oddments neglecting their signs. Since both the sums of oddments are same (*i.e.*, 6 + 6 + 48 = 60 = 38 + 14 + 8), we get result in matrix method otherwise the method of matrix fails.

$$
\begin{array}{c|ccc|cc}
 & B_1 & B_2 & B_3 & & \\
\hline
A_1 & 8 & 2 & 8 & 6 & \frac{6}{60} \\
A_2 & 10 & 0 & 2 & 6 & \frac{6}{60} \\
A_3 & 6 & 8 & 7 & 48 & \frac{48}{60} \\
\hline
 & 38 & 14 & 8 & 60 \diagdown 60 & \\
 & \frac{38}{60} & \frac{14}{60} & \frac{8}{60} & &
\end{array}
$$

$$
V = 8\left(\frac{6}{60}\right)\left(\frac{38}{60}\right) + 2\left(\frac{6}{60}\right)\left(\frac{14}{60}\right) + 8\left(\frac{6}{60}\right)\left(\frac{8}{60}\right) + 10\left(\frac{6}{60}\right)\left(\frac{38}{60}\right) + 0\left(\frac{6}{60}\right)\left(\frac{14}{60}\right) + 2\left(\frac{6}{60}\right)\left(\frac{8}{60}\right)
$$
$$
+ 6\left(\frac{48}{60}\right)\left(\frac{38}{60}\right) + 8\left(\frac{48}{60}\right)\left(\frac{14}{60}\right) + 7\left(\frac{48}{60}\right)\left(\frac{8}{60}\right)
$$

$$= \frac{23760}{3600} = 6.6 \text{ (Player } A \text{ will gain). } \textbf{Ans.}$$

10.7 METHOD OF LINEAR PROGRAMMING

This is the general method applicable to all situation, where there is no saddle point, the dominance and matrix fail.

Example 7

	$B_1(y_1)$	$B_2(y_2)$	$B_3(y_3)$
$A_1(x_1)$	5	2	–2
$A_2(x_2)$	4	2	7
$A_3(x_3)$	–2	5	–1

Solution:

Let A (x_1, x_2, x_3) and B (y_1, y_2, y_3) are their pure strategies. The value of the game (to A) be V. Considering the game from B's point of view, we get that B is trying to minimize V.

Minimize V, subject to

$$5y_1 + 2y_2 - 2y_3 \le V$$
$$4y_1 + 2y_2 + 7y_3 \le V$$
$$-2y_1 + 5y_2 - y_3 \le V$$
$$y_1 + y_2 + y_3 = 1 \text{ (Sum of probabilities equal to unity)}$$

Thus we have

Objective function Z (minimize) = V, subject to

$$\frac{y_1}{V} + \frac{y_2}{V} + \frac{y_3}{V} = \frac{1}{V}$$

$$\frac{5y_1}{V} + \frac{2y_2}{V} - \frac{2y_3}{V} \le 1$$

$$\frac{4y_1}{V} + \frac{2y_2}{V} + \frac{7y_3}{V} \le 1$$

$$-\frac{2y_1}{V} + \frac{5y_2}{V} - \frac{y_3}{V} \le 1$$

i.e., Maximize = $\frac{1}{V}$. *i.e.*,

$$Z = Y_1 + Y_2 + Y_3 \text{ where } Y_1 = \frac{y_1}{V}$$

$$Y_2 = \frac{y_2}{V}$$

$$Y_3 = \frac{y_3}{V}$$

Subject to

$$5Y_1 + 2Y_2 - 2Y_3 \leq 1$$
$$4Y_1 + 2Y_2 + 7Y_3 \leq 1$$
$$-2Y_1 + 5Y_2 - Y_3 \leq 1$$
$$Y_1, Y_2, Y_3 \geq 0$$

The above can be solved by Linear Programming method.

Chapter **11** *QUEUING THEORY*

11.1 INTRODUCTION

If we want to get our service done, in many situation we have to wait. Queuing is nothing but waiting for getting our service done. A facility or a group of facilities is/are kept ready to meet the demands for service created by customers. The size of customers *i.e.*, population may be finite or infinite; as well as the demands for service may be finite or infinite. A few places where we may have to wait in a queue are (*i*) Post offices (*ii*) Banks (*iii*) Hospitals (*iv*) Doctor's chamber (*v*) Bus stops (*vi*) Railway reservation counter (*vii*) Before a traffic signal (*viii*) Petrol pump.

11.2 COSTS ASSOCIATED WITH QUEUING PROBLEM

By increasing service facilities (investment of more labour and equipments), waiting time cost decreases (Fig. 1).

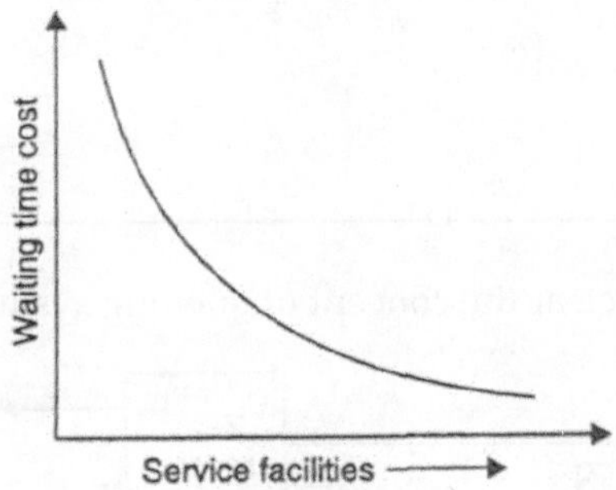

Fig. 1

It is obvious that cost of providing service increases with increase of labours and equipments (by increasing service facilities) (Fig. 2).

Fig. 2

Now both the situations happen simultaneously in the queuing system. Thus Fig. 1 and Fig. 2 are combined to get total cost as given in Fig. 3.

The total cost is minimum at service facilities S.

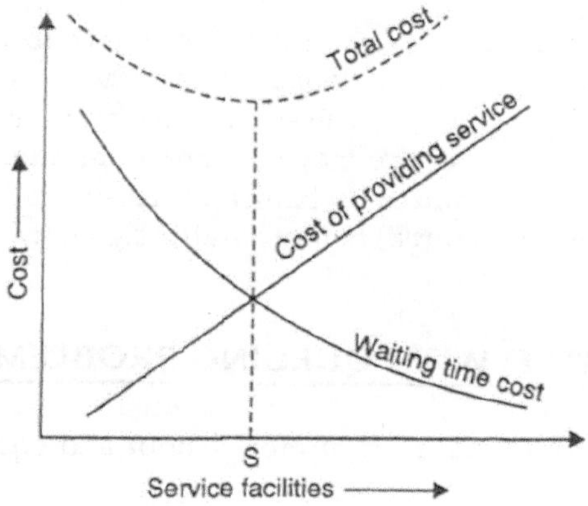

Fig. 3.

11.3 QUEUING SYSTEM

The following Fig. 4 will clear the concept of queuing system.

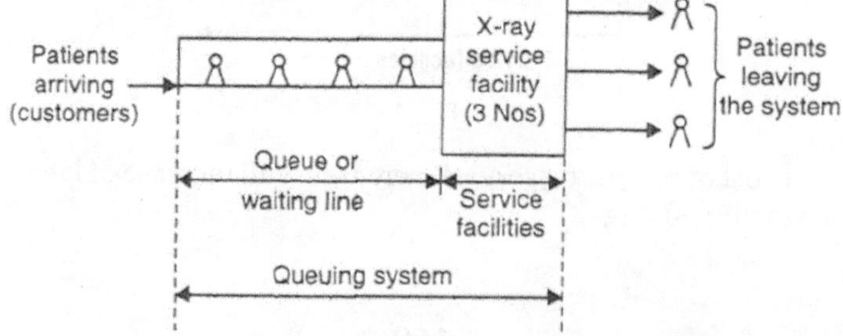

Fig. 4

11.4 THE ARRIVAL AND THE SERVICE MECHANISM

We assume that the number of arrivals per period to the queue is a random variable which follows a Poisson discrete distribution.

Poisson Probability mass function $P(X = x) = \dfrac{e^{-\frac{1}{\lambda}}\left(\frac{1}{\lambda}\right)^x}{x!}, \lambda > 0, x = 0, 1, 2, ..., n, ...)$

where mean or expected value $E(x) = \dfrac{1}{\lambda}$.

And the pattern according to which the customers are served follows exponential continuous distribution.

Exponential probability density function

$$f(x) = \mu e^{-\mu x}, \mu > 0, x \geq 0$$

Mean or expected value $E(X) = \dfrac{1}{\mu}$.

Under the above assumptions λ and μ are the rate of arrival and the rate of service completion respectively.

11.5 THE PROBABILITY OF n UNITS (CUSTOMERS) IN THE SYSTEM

[Model $(M/M/1: (FCFS/\infty/\infty)]$

Let n = number of units in the system at time t including the unit being served, if any.

$P_n(t)$ = Probability of n units in the system.

λdt = The probability that an arrival occurs between the time t and $t + \Delta t$.

μdt = The probability that a service completion occurs between t and $t + \Delta t$, given that one unit being serviced at time t.

For n $\geq$ 1

Event {n units in the system at time $t + \Delta t$}

= Event {n units in the system at time t, no arrival during the interval Δt and no service completion during that interval Δt}.

or

Event {$(n + 1)$ units in the system at time t, no arrival during the interval Δt, one service completion during the interval Δt}.

or

Event {$(n - 1)$ units in the system at time t, one arrival during the interval Δt, no service completion during the interval Δt}.

For three mutually exclusive events as mentioned above, we can mathematically write;

$P_n(t + \Delta t) = P_n(t)(1 - \lambda\Delta t)(1 - \mu\Delta t) + P_{n+1}(t)(1 - \lambda\Delta t)\mu\Delta t + P_{n-1}(t) . \lambda\Delta t(1 - \mu\Delta t)$ for $n \geq 1$

After simplification and neglecting $(\Delta t)^2$ terms, we get

$$P_n(t + \Delta t) = P_n(t) - (\lambda + \mu) P_n(t)\Delta t + \mu P_{n+1}(t)\Delta t + \lambda P_{n-1}(t)\Delta t.$$

or $$\frac{P_n(t+\Delta t)-P_n(t)}{\Delta t} = -(\lambda+\mu)\,P_n(t) + \mu P_{n+1}(t) + \lambda P_{n-1}(t).$$

Taking limit $\Delta t \to 0$, we get

$$\frac{d\,P_n(t)}{dt} = -(\lambda+\mu)\,P_n(t) + \mu P_{n+1}(t) + \lambda P_{n-1}(t). \quad (1)$$

for $n \geq 1$

for n = 0

Event {0 unit in the system at time $t + \Delta t$}

= Event {0 unit in the system at time t, no arrival during the interval Δt}

or

Event {one unit in the system at time t, no arrival during the interval Δt, one service completion during the interval Δt}

For events are mutually exclusive, we can mathematically write,

$$P_0(t+\Delta t) = P_0(t)\,(1-\lambda\Delta t) + P_1(t)\,(1-\lambda\Delta t)\,\mu\Delta t$$
$$= P_0(t) - \lambda P_0(t)\,\Delta t + \mu P_1(t)\,\Delta t \quad \text{(neglecting } (\Delta t)^2)$$

or $$\underset{\Delta t\to 0}{\text{Lt}} \frac{P_0(t+\Delta t)-P_0(t)}{\Delta t} = \frac{dP_0(t)}{dt} = -\lambda P_0(t) + \mu P_1(t). \quad ...(2)$$

for $n = 0$

The equations (1) and (2) are known poisson arrival and exponential service governing equations for single channel queue.

In practice $P_n(t)$ is independent of time t, thus $\frac{dP_n(t)}{dt} = 0$

equation (1) $\Rightarrow$ $$0 = -(\lambda+\mu)\;P_n + \mu P_{n+1} + \lambda P_{n-1}$$

or $$(\lambda+\mu)\,P_n = \mu P_{n+1} + \lambda P_{n-1} \text{ for } n \geq 1 \quad ...(3)$$

equation (2) $\Rightarrow$ $$0 = -\lambda P_0 + \mu P_1$$

or $$\lambda P_0 = \mu P_1 \text{ for } n = 0 \quad ...(4)$$

Let us assume $P_n = \rho P_{n-1}$ where ρ is a constant

(3) $\Rightarrow$ $$(\lambda+\mu)\,P_{n-1}\rho = \mu P_{n-1}\,\rho^2 + \lambda P_{n-1}$$

or $$(\lambda+\mu)\,\rho = \mu\rho^2 + \lambda, \quad [\text{assuming } P_{n-1} \neq 0]$$

or $\rho = \frac{\lambda}{\mu} > 0$, [assuming $\rho \neq 1$]

ρ is called traffic intensity.

The equation (4) $\Rightarrow P_1 = \frac{\lambda}{\mu} P_0 = \rho P_0$ which is obvious. The solution of (3) and (4) is a particular solution. We have the following indentities,

$$P_1 = P_0\rho, \quad P_2 = P_1\rho,$$
$$P_1\rho = P_0\rho^2, \;......,\; P_n = P_0\rho^n \quad ...(5)$$

We also have sum of all the probabilities of a certain event is unity.

$$P_0 + P_1 + P_2 + \ldots\ldots + P_n + \ldots\ldots \infty = 1$$

or $$P_0 (1 + \rho + \rho^2 + \ldots\ldots + \rho^n + \ldots\ldots + \infty) = 1$$

or $$\frac{P_0}{1-\rho} = 1 \qquad \text{[Sum of G.P. infinity series]}$$

or $$P_0 = 1 - \rho$$

$\therefore$ $$P_n = P_0 \rho^n = (1 - \rho)\, \rho^n \text{ where } \rho = \frac{\lambda}{\mu}.$$

As $0 < \rho < 1$

so $\frac{\lambda}{\mu} < 1$ or $\lambda < \mu$ for steady state of the queue.

*The above model M $\Rightarrow$ Markovian (Poisson) arrival or exponential service time distribution

* see section 11.5. FCFS = First time First, service

11.5.1 Kendall's Notation

$(a/b/c) : (d/e/f)$

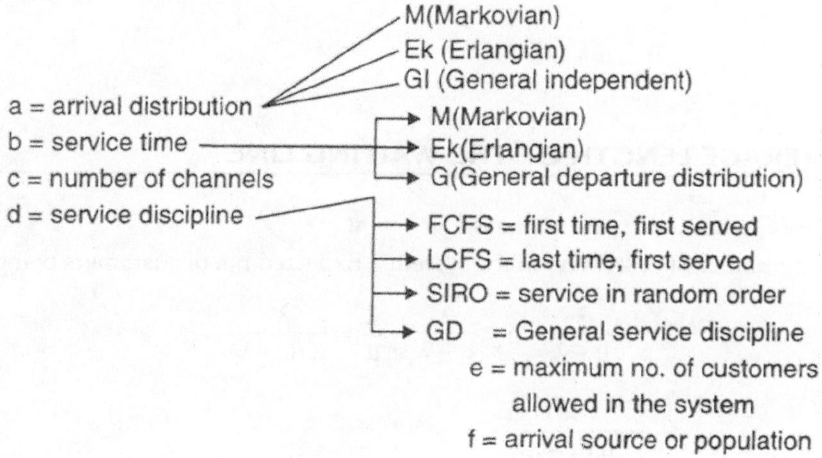

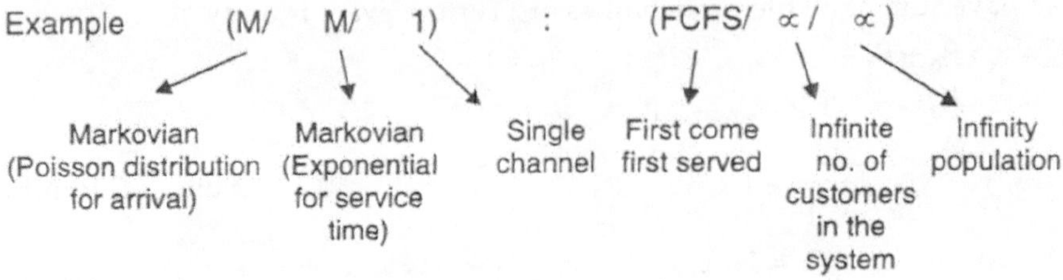

11.6 THE AVERAGE OR MEAN NUMBER OF UNITS IN THE SYSTEM

Expected number of customers (units) in the system (waiting + being served) is L_S given by

$$L_S = \sum_{n=0}^{\infty} nP_n = \sum_{n=0}^{\infty} n(1-\rho)\rho^n$$

$$= \rho(1-\rho)\sum_{n=0}^{\infty} n\rho^{n-1} = \rho(1-\rho)(1-\rho)^{-2}, \text{ [From binomial expansion]}$$

$$= \frac{\rho}{1-\rho} \qquad [\because\ 0<\rho<1]$$

$$= \frac{\lambda/\mu}{1-\lambda/\mu} = \frac{\lambda}{\mu-\lambda} > 0 \qquad \left[\text{as } \rho = \frac{\lambda}{\mu}\right]$$

$$\therefore \qquad L_S = \frac{\lambda}{\mu-\lambda} \tag{6}$$

11.7 THE AVERAGE LENGTH OF THE WAITING LINE

Expected number of customers in the queue is L_q

= Expected number of customers in the system – Expected no. of customers being served.

$$= \frac{\lambda}{\mu-\lambda} - \rho = \frac{\lambda}{\mu-\lambda} - \frac{\lambda}{\mu} = \frac{\lambda^2}{\mu(\mu-\lambda)}$$

$$\therefore \qquad L_q = \frac{\lambda^2}{\mu(\mu-\lambda)} \tag{7}$$

11.8 EXPECTED TIME A CUSTOMER SPENDS IN THE SYSTEM

W_S = (waiting time) + (service time).

We have λ the average arrival time and hence the average time between any two arrivals $= \frac{1}{\lambda}$.

$\therefore$ W_S = Mean waiting time in the system.

= average time between arrivals × average no. of customers in the system.

$$= \frac{1}{\lambda} \times L_S = \frac{1}{\lambda} \times \frac{\lambda}{\mu - \lambda} = \frac{1}{\mu - \lambda}.$$

11.9 EXPECTED TIME A CUSTOMER SPENDS IN THE QUEUE

W_q = Average time between arrivals × average number of customers in the queue.

$$= \frac{1}{\lambda} \times L_q = \frac{\lambda}{\mu(\mu - \lambda)}.$$

11.10 THE PROBABILITY OF THE QUEUE BEING NON-EMPTY

Average length of non-empty queue = L_n

Probability that the queue in non-empty

= Probability of at least one unit in the line and one unit being served at that time

= Probability of at least two units in the system

$= P_2 + P_3 + P_4 + \ldots\ldots = 1 - P_0 - P_1 = 1 - P_0 - P_0\rho$

$= 1 - (1 + \rho) P_0 = 1 - (1 + \rho)(1 - \rho) = \rho^2.$

11.11 THE AVERAGE LENGTH OF THE NON-EMPTY QUEUE

$$L_n = \frac{L_q}{\rho^2} = \frac{\lambda^2 . \mu^2}{\mu(\mu - \lambda) \times \lambda^2} = \frac{\mu}{\mu - \lambda}.$$

11.12 AVERAGE WAITING TIME OF A CUSTOMER IN NON-EMPTY QUEUE

Average waiting time of a customer who has to wait in a non-empty queue = W_n

$$W_n = \int_0^{\alpha} t(\mu - \lambda)\, e^{-(\mu - \lambda)t}\, dt$$

$$= \frac{1}{\mu - \lambda} = \frac{1}{\mu(1 - \rho)}.$$

11.13 PROBABILITY THAT THERE ARE MORE THAN *K* CUSTOMERS IN THE SYSTEM

$$= P(n > k) = \rho^{k+1} = 1 - (P_0 + P_1 + P_2 + \ldots\ldots + P_k).$$

11.14 PROBABILITY THAT THERE ARE ≥ *K* CUSTOMERS IN THE SYSTEM

$$= P(n \geq k) = \rho^k = 1 - (P_0 + P_1 + P_2 + \ldots\ldots + P_{k-1}).$$

11.15 PROBABILITY THAT THERE ARE EXACTLY *K* CUSTOMERS IN THE SYSTEM

$$P_k = \rho^k P_0 = \rho^k(1 - \rho).$$

11.16 PROBABILITY THAT A CUSTOMER SPENDS MORE THAN '*t*' TIME IN THE SYSTEM

$$= W_s(t) = P(T > t) = e^{-(\mu-\lambda)t}.$$

11.17 PROBABILITY THAT A CUSTOMER SPENDS LESS THAN '*t*' TIME IN THE SYSTEM

$$= 1 - W_s(t) = 1 - e^{-(\mu-\lambda)t}$$

11.18 PROBABILITY THAT A CUSTOMER SPENDS MORE THAN '*t*' IN THE QUEUE (WAITING LINE)

$$= W_q(t) = \rho e^{-(\mu-\lambda)t}.$$

Example 1

A self-service store employs one cashier at its counter. 10 customers arrive on an average 5 minutes while the cashier can serve 12 customers in the same time. Assuming Poisson distribution for arrival and exponential distribution for service rate, find as per 11.6 section to 11.18 assume suitable missing data.

Solution:

Here arrival rate $\lambda = \frac{10}{5} = 2$ customers/minute

11.6 $\Rightarrow$ and $\mu = \frac{12}{5} = 2.4$ customers/minute

$$\rho = \frac{\lambda}{\mu} = \frac{2}{2.4} = \text{Traffic intensity}$$

$$L_S = \frac{\lambda}{\mu - \lambda} = \frac{2}{2.4 - 2} = \frac{2}{0.4} = 5 \quad \textbf{Ans.}$$

11.7 ⇒ $$L_q = \frac{\lambda^2}{\mu(\mu - \lambda)} = \frac{4}{2.4 \times 0.4} = 4.17 \quad \textbf{Ans.}$$

11.8 ⇒ $$W_S = \frac{1}{\mu - \lambda} = \frac{1}{0.4} = 2.5 \quad \textbf{Ans.}$$

11.9 ⇒ $$W_q = \frac{\lambda}{\mu(\mu - \lambda)} = \frac{2}{2.4 \times 0.4} = 2.08 \quad \textbf{Ans.}$$

11.10 ⇒ $$\rho^2 = \left(\frac{\lambda}{\mu}\right)^2 = \left(\frac{2}{2.4}\right)^2 = 0.69 \quad \textbf{Ans.}$$

11.11 ⇒ $$L_n = \frac{\mu}{\mu - \lambda} = \frac{2.4}{0.4} = 6 \quad \textbf{Ans.}$$

11.12 ⇒ $$W_n = \frac{1}{\mu - \lambda} = 2.5$$

11.13 ⇒ Let $k = 2,$

$$\rho^{k+1} = \left(\frac{\lambda}{\mu}\right)^2 = \left(\frac{2}{2.4}\right)^3 = 0.58 \quad \textbf{Ans.}$$

11.14 ⇒ $$\rho^k = \left(\frac{\lambda}{\mu}\right)^2 = 0.69 \quad \textbf{Ans.}$$

11.15 ⇒ $$\rho^k(1 - \rho) = \left(\frac{2}{2.4}\right)^2 \left(1 - \frac{2}{2.4}\right) = 0.115 \quad \textbf{Ans.}$$

11.16 ⇒ Let $t = 3$ minutes

$$W_s(t) = e^{-(\mu - \lambda)\, t} = e^{-0.4 \times 3} = 0.3 \quad \textbf{Ans.}$$

11.17 ⇒ $$1 - W_s(t) = 1 - 0.3 = 0.7 \quad \textbf{Ans.}$$

11.18 ⇒ $$W_q(t) = \rho\, e^{-(\mu - \lambda)t} = \frac{2}{2.4} \times 0.3 = 0.25 \quad \textbf{Ans.}$$

Chapter 12 *SIMULATION*

12.1 INTRODUCTION

Where mathematical model faces too complexity in solving real world situation, a numerical technique tool called 'Simulation' is needed to describe the system and yield analytical solution of the problem. It provides a trial and error method towards the optimal solution.

12.2 MONTE-CARLO SIMULATION

This technique is based on creating a series of random numbers. It yields a solution which is very close to optimal. The name 'Monte-Carlo' is derived from a resort Monte-Carlo situated in Monaco of SE France. In this resort the players gamble through betting system on the roulette table.

12.2.1 Generation of Random Numbers (RN)

A random number table (1-digit, 2-digits, 3-digits ...... etc) is available in any 'Industrial Engineering' book. Here we will use congruence method to generate *RN*.

(*i*) Mixed congruence method:

Let $$y_{i+1} = \frac{ay_i + b}{m}$$

for $a = 21$, $b = 53$ and $y_0 = 46$ (seed) and module $m = 100$

$$y_1 = \frac{21\,y_0 + 53}{100} = \frac{21 \times 46 + 53}{100} = 10 + \text{remainder } 19$$

$$y_2 = \frac{21 \times 19 + 53}{100} = 4 + \text{remainder } 52$$

$$y_3 = \frac{21 \times 52 + 53}{100} = 11 + \text{remainder } 45$$

$$y_4 = \frac{21 \times 45 + 53}{100} = 9 + \text{remainder } 98$$

$$y_5 = \frac{21 \times 98 + 53}{100} = 21 + \text{remainder } 11$$

....

So the generated *RN* is the remainders of y_1, y_2, y_3, y_4 and y_5 and so on ......

RN = 19, 52, 45, 98, 11 ......

(*ii*) Multiplicative Congruence: Put $b = 0$ in the equation

$$y_{i+1} = \frac{a\,y_i + b}{m} = \frac{a\,y_i}{m}.$$

$$y_1 = \frac{21 \times 46}{100} = 9 + \text{remainder } 66$$

$$y_2 = \frac{21 \times 66}{100} = 13 + \text{remainder } 86$$

$$y_3 = \frac{21 \times 86}{100} = 18 + \text{remainder } 6$$

$$y_4 = \frac{21 \times 6}{100} = 1 + \text{remainder } 26$$

$$y_5 = \frac{21 \times 26}{100} = 5 + \text{remainder } 46.$$

....

The *RN* = 66, 86, 6, 26, 46, ...

(*iii*) Additive congruence: Here the formula is

$$y_{i+1} = \frac{y_i + b}{m}$$

$$\therefore \quad y_1 = \frac{46 + 53}{100} = 0 + \text{remainder } 99$$

$$y_2 = \frac{99 + 53}{100} = 1 + \text{remainder } 52$$

$$y_3 = \frac{52 + 53}{100} = 1 + \text{remainder } 5$$

$$y_4 = \frac{5+53}{100} = 0 + \text{remainder } 58$$

$$y_5 = \frac{58+53}{100} = 1 + \text{remainder } 11$$

....

So, the RN = 99, 52, 5, 58, 11 ....

12.2.2 Demand Pattern Simulation

Example 1

For a 100 day period, the daily demand is shown below. Using the given data simulate a ten-day sequence of demand values and find the average daily demand.

Daily Demand	0	1	2	3	4	5	
No. of days	9	21	39	21	5	5	Total = 100

Solution:

The random numbers are used to choose the 10 days.

Daily demand	*Probability*	*Cum. Probability*	*Random No.*
0	0.09	0.09	00—09
1	0.21	0.30	10—29
2	0.39	0.69	30—69
3	0.21	0.90	70—89
4	0.05	0.95	90—95
5	0.05	1.00	96—99

Let us choose any last two digits from *RN* table. This is 67, 84, 01, 77, 90, 14, 15, 74, 44 and 77 corresponding generated demand is 2, 3, 0, 3, 4, 1, 1, 3, 2 and 3. The total generated demand is 22.

$$\therefore \quad \text{Average daily demand} = \frac{22}{10} = 2.2 \quad \textbf{Ans.}$$

12.2.3 Inspection Work Simulation

Example 2

The output of a production line is checked by a inspector for one or more of three different types of defects called A, B, and C. If defect A occurs, the item is scrapped. It defect B or C occurs, the item must be reworked. The time required to rework a defect B is 20 minutes and that of C is 35 minutes. The probabilities of A, B and C defects are 0.20, 0.25 and 0.15 respectively. For ten items coming off the assembly line determine the number of items without any defects, the number of items scrapped and the total minutes of rework time. Use the following random numbers.

RN for defect A ⇒ *48, 55, 91, 40, 93, 01, 83, 63, 47, 52*

RN for defect B ⇒ *47, 36, 57, 04, 79, 55, 10, 13, 57, 09*

RN for defect C ⇒ *82, 95, 18, 96, 20, 84, 56, 11, 52, 03*

Solution:

We assign random numbers 00—99 according to probabilities of occurrence defects *A*, *B*, *C* (0.2, 0.25 and 0.15 respectively)

Defect A	*RN*	*Defect B*	*RN*	*Defect C*	*RN*
Yes	00—19	Yes	00—24	Yes	00—14
No	20—99	No	25—99	No	15—99

Let us now simulate the 10 items produced in the assembly line according to RN given against *A*, *B* and *C*.

Item No.	*Defect A*	*Defect B*	*Defect C*	*Summary of defect*	*Remarks*
1 →	No →	No →	No		
2 →	No →	No →	No		
3 →	No →	No →	No		
4 →	No →	Yes →	No →	B →	Reworked
5 →	No →	No →	No		
6 →	Yes →	No →	No →	A →	Scrapped
7 →	No →	Yes →	No →	B →	Reworked
8 →	No →	Yes →	Yes →	B, C →	Reworked
9 →	No →	No →	No		
10 →	No →	Yes →	Yes →	B, C →	Reworked

Item Nos. reworked	*Time of Rework*	*Item No. scrapped*	*Item Ok (No defects)*
4	20 mins	6	1
7	20 mins		2
8	20 + 35 mins		3
10	20 + 35 mins		5
			9
4 Nos.	150 mins	One no	Five nos.

Chapter 13

MARKOV CHAINS

13.1 INTRODUCTION

Properties of vectors and matrices are reviewed here because of its use in this chapter.

The vector v means an n-tuple of numbers.

$$v = (v_1, v_2, ..., v_n).$$

The v_i are called the components of v. If $v_i = 0$, then v is called the zero vector. If we multiply v by a scalar real number k it becomes kv.

Thus $$kv = (kv_1, kv_2, ..., kv_n).$$

The conditions that two vectors are equal are that the corresponding components are equal *i.e.*,

If $$u = (u_1, u_2, ... u_n)$$

and $$v = (v_1, v_2, ... v_n)$$

for $u = v$, we get

$$u_1 = v_1, u_2 = v_2, ... u_n = v_n.$$

A matrix A is the rectangular array of numbers

$$A = \begin{pmatrix} a_{11} & a_{12} & \cdots & a_{1n} \\ a_{21} & a_{22} & \cdots & a_{2n} \\ \cdots & \cdots & \cdots & \cdots \\ a_{m1} & a_{m2} & \cdots & a_{mn} \end{pmatrix} \qquad ...(1)$$

The $(a_{11}, a_{12}, ..., a_{1n})$, $(a_{21}, a_{22}, ..., a_{2n})$, ..., $(a_{m1}, a_{m2}, ..., a_{mn})$ are called rows of A.

And $\begin{pmatrix} a_{11} \\ a_{21} \\ \cdots \\ a_{m1} \end{pmatrix}, \begin{pmatrix} a_{12} \\ a_{22} \\ \cdots \\ a_{m2} \end{pmatrix}, \ldots\ldots, \begin{pmatrix} a_{1n} \\ a_{2n} \\ \cdots \\ a_{mn} \end{pmatrix}$ are called columns of A.

a_{ij} is the ij-entry which appears in the ith row and the jth column. Thus $A = (a_{ij})$.

The equation (1) is $m \times n$ matrix *i.e.*, m rows by n columns. For $m = n$ the matrix is called n-square matrix. Note that a matrix having only one row may be viewed as a vector, and vice-versa. The multiplication of A and B is possible when the numbers of column of A is equal to the number of rows of B.

Thus A is an $m \times p$ matrix and B is an $p \times n$ matrix.

Their product AB is $m \times n$ matrix whose ij-entry can be obtained by multiplying the elements of the ith row of A by the corresponding elements of the jth column of B.

$$\begin{pmatrix} a_{11} & \cdots & a_{1p} \\ \cdots & \cdots & \cdots \\ a_{i1} & \cdots & a_{ip} \\ a_{m1} & \cdots & a_{mp} \end{pmatrix} \begin{pmatrix} b_{11} & \cdots & b_{1j} & \cdots & b_{1n} \\ \cdots & \cdots & \cdots & \cdots & \cdots \\ \cdots & \cdots & \cdots & \cdots & \cdots \\ b_{p1} & \cdots & b_{pj} & \cdots & b_{pn} \end{pmatrix} = \begin{pmatrix} c_{11} & \cdots & c_{1n} \\ \cdots & \cdots & \cdots \\ \cdots & c_{ij} & \cdots \\ \cdots & \cdots & \cdots \\ c_{m1} & \cdots & c_{mn} \end{pmatrix}$$

where $c_{ij} = a_{i1}\, b_{1j} + a_{i2}\, b_{2j} + \ldots\ldots + a_{ip}\, b_{pj} = \sum_{k=1}^{p} a_{ik}\, b_{kj}$

If A is an n-square matrix, then

$$A^2 = AA,\ A^3 = AA^2,\ A^4 = AA^3,\ \ldots\ldots$$

In addition, if v is a vector of n components, then the product $v\,A$ is also a vector of n components. For $v \neq 0$ is a fixed vector (or fixed point) of A, if v is "left fixed", *i.e.*, is not changed, when multiplied by A *i.e.*,

$$vA = v.$$

For scalar $k \neq 0$, we have

$$(kv)\,A = k\,(vA) = kv.$$

Example 1.

$$\begin{pmatrix} r & s \\ t & u \end{pmatrix} \begin{pmatrix} a_1 & a_2 & a_3 \\ b_1 & b_2 & b_3 \end{pmatrix} = \begin{pmatrix} ra_1 + sb_1 & ra_2 + sb_2 & ra_3 + sb_3 \\ ta_1 + ub_1 & ta_2 + ub_2 & ta_3 + ub_3 \end{pmatrix}$$

Example 2.

If $A = \begin{pmatrix} 1 & 2 \\ 3 & 4 \end{pmatrix}$, then

$$A^2 = \begin{pmatrix} 1 & 2 \\ 3 & 4 \end{pmatrix} \begin{pmatrix} 1 & 2 \\ 3 & 4 \end{pmatrix} = \begin{pmatrix} 1\times1+2\times3 & 1\times2+2\times4 \\ 3\times1+4\times3 & 3\times2+4\times4 \end{pmatrix}$$

$$= \begin{pmatrix} 1+6 & 2+8 \\ 3+12 & 6+16 \end{pmatrix} = \begin{pmatrix} 7 & 10 \\ 15 & 22 \end{pmatrix}.$$

Example 3.

$$(1, 2, 3)\begin{pmatrix}1 & 2 & 3\\ 4 & 5 & 6\\ 7 & 8 & 9\end{pmatrix} = (1 + 8 + 21, 2 + 10 + 24, 3 + 12 + 27) = (30, 36, 42).$$

Example 4.

Let $v = (2, -1)$ a fixed point of $A = \begin{pmatrix}2 & 1\\ 2 & 3\end{pmatrix}$

So $$vA = (2, -1), \begin{pmatrix}2 & 1\\ 2 & 3\end{pmatrix} = (2 \times 2 + (-1)2; 2 \times 1 + (-1)3)$$

$$= (4 - 2, 2 - 3) = (2, -1) = v$$

Thus $2v = (4, -2)$ is also a fixed point of A; because

$$(2v)A = (+4, -2)\begin{pmatrix}2 & 1\\ 2 & 3\end{pmatrix} = (4 \times 2 + (-2)2, 4 \times 1 + (-2)3)$$

$$= (8 - 4, 4 - 6) = (4, -2) = 2v.$$

13.2 PROBABILITY VECTORS, STOCHASTIC MATRICES

13.2.1 Probability Vectors

$v = (v_1, v_2, \ldots\ldots, v_n)$ is called a probability vector if v_i are non-negative and $\sum_{i=1}^{n} v_i = 1$.

Example 5.

If $$u = \left(\frac{3}{4}, 0, -\frac{1}{3}, \frac{1}{2}\right), v = \left(\frac{1}{2}, \frac{1}{4}, 0, \frac{3}{2}\right) \text{ and } w = \left(\frac{1}{8}, \frac{1}{4}, 0, \frac{5}{8}\right)$$

Then

- u is not a probability vector because third component *i.e.*, $-\frac{1}{3}$ is negative.
- v is not a probability vector because the sum of its components is greater than 1;
- w is a probability vector because $\frac{1}{8} + \frac{1}{4} + 0 + \frac{5}{8} = 1$ and all components are non-negative.

13.2.2 Stochastic Matrix

$P = (p_{ij})$ is called a stochastic matrix if

$$\sum_{\substack{i=1\\ j=1}}^{i=m,\, j=n} p_{ij} = 1 \text{ and all } p_{ij} \geq 0.$$

p_{ij} are probability vectors.

Example 6.

$$u = \begin{pmatrix} \frac{2}{3} & 0 & \frac{1}{3} \\ \frac{1}{2} & \frac{3}{4} & -\frac{1}{4} \\ \frac{1}{2} & \frac{1}{4} & \frac{1}{4} \end{pmatrix}, v = \begin{pmatrix} \frac{1}{4} & \frac{1}{4} \\ \frac{1}{3} & \frac{2}{3} \end{pmatrix} \text{ and } w = \begin{pmatrix} 0 & \frac{1}{2} & \frac{1}{2} \\ 0 & 1 & 0 \\ \frac{1}{3} & \frac{2}{3} & 0 \end{pmatrix}$$

- u is not a stochastic matrix since the entry in the second row and third column is negative.
- v is not a stochastic matrix since the sum of the entries in the first row is less than one.
- w is a stochastic matrix since each row equals to unity and all entries are non-negative.

13.2.3 Theorem of Product of Stochastic Matrices

If A and B are stochastic matrices, then the product AB is also a stochastic matrices.

Thus all powers of A *i.e.*, A^n are stochastic matrices.

13.2.4 Regular Stochastic Matrices

P is said to be regular stochastic matrices if all the entries of some power P^m are non-zero positive.

Example 7.

The stochastic matrix $A = \begin{pmatrix} 0 & 1 \\ \frac{1}{2} & \frac{1}{2} \end{pmatrix}$

Now $$A^2 = AA = \begin{pmatrix} 0 & 1 \\ \frac{1}{2} & \frac{1}{2} \end{pmatrix}\begin{pmatrix} 0 & 1 \\ \frac{1}{2} & \frac{1}{2} \end{pmatrix} = \begin{pmatrix} 0\times0+1\times\frac{1}{2} & 0\times1+1\times\frac{1}{2} \\ \frac{1}{2}\times0+\frac{1}{2}\times\frac{1}{2} & \frac{1}{2}\times1+\frac{1}{2}\times\frac{1}{2} \end{pmatrix} = \begin{pmatrix} \frac{1}{2} & \frac{1}{2} \\ \frac{1}{4} & \frac{3}{4} \end{pmatrix}$$

As power of A *i.e.*, A^2 is having all the elements as non-zero positive numbers, the matrix A is regular.

Example 8.

The stochastic matrix $A = \begin{pmatrix} 1 & 0 \\ \frac{1}{2} & \frac{1}{2} \end{pmatrix}$

Now $$A^2 = \begin{pmatrix} 1 & 0 \\ \frac{3}{4} & \frac{1}{4} \end{pmatrix}, A^3 = \begin{pmatrix} 1 & 0 \\ \frac{7}{8} & \frac{1}{8} \end{pmatrix} \text{ and } A^4 = \begin{pmatrix} 1 & 0 \\ \frac{15}{16} & \frac{1}{16} \end{pmatrix}$$

As there is a zero in the 1st row of all the powers of A, the stochastic matrix A is not regular.

13.3 FIXED POINTS AND REGULAR STOCHASTIC MATRICES

Theorem 1: *If P be a regular stochastic matrix, then*

(i) *P has a unique fixed probability vector t, and the components of t are all positive.*

(ii) *the sequence P, P^2, P^3, ... of powers of P approaches the matrix T whose rows are each the fixed point t;*

(iii) *if p is any probability vector, then the sequence of vectors pP, pP^2, pP^3, ... approaches the fixed point t;*

Thus P^n approaches T means that each entry of P^n approaches the corresponding entry of T, and pP^n approaches t means that each component of pP^n approaches the corresponding component of t.

Example 9:

The regular stochastic matrix $P = \begin{pmatrix} 0 & 1 \\ \frac{1}{2} & \frac{1}{2} \end{pmatrix}$ and the probability vector with two components of $t = (x, 1 - x)$

If $t\,P = t$, we have

$$(x, 1 - x)\begin{pmatrix} 0 & 1 \\ \frac{1}{2} & \frac{1}{2} \end{pmatrix} = (x, 1 - x)$$

or
$$\left(\frac{1}{2} - \frac{1}{2}x, \frac{1}{2} + \frac{1}{2}x\right) = (x, 1 - x)$$

Thus
$$\frac{1}{2} - \frac{1}{2}x = x \Rightarrow x = \frac{1}{3}$$

and
$$\frac{1}{2} + \frac{1}{2}x = 1 - x \Rightarrow x = \frac{1}{3}$$

Thus $t = \left(\frac{1}{3}, \frac{2}{3}\right)$ is the unique fixed probability vector of P.

By theorem under section 3, the sequence P, P^2, P^3 approaches the matrix T whose rows are each the vector t.

$$\therefore \qquad T = \begin{pmatrix} \frac{1}{3}, & \frac{2}{3} \\ \frac{1}{3} & \frac{2}{3} \end{pmatrix} = \begin{pmatrix} 0.33 & 0.67 \\ 0.33 & 0.67 \end{pmatrix}$$

and
$$P^2 = \begin{pmatrix} 0.5 & 0.5 \\ 0.25 & 0.75 \end{pmatrix}, P^3 = \begin{pmatrix} 0.25 & 0.75 \\ 0.37 & 0.63 \end{pmatrix}$$

$$P^4 = \begin{pmatrix} 0.37 & , & 0.63 \\ 0.31 & ; & 0.69 \end{pmatrix}, P^5 = \begin{pmatrix} 0.31 & 0.69 \\ 0.34 & 0.66 \end{pmatrix} \Rightarrow \text{ approaches to } T.$$

Example 10.

Find the unique fixed probability vector of the regular stochastic matrix

$$P = \begin{pmatrix} 0 & 1 & 0 \\ 0 & 0 & 1 \\ \frac{1}{2} & \frac{1}{2} & 0 \end{pmatrix}.$$

Solution:

Method 1: Let the probability vector with three components be

$$t = (x, y, 1 - x - y), \text{ such that } t\,p = t.$$

$$\therefore \quad (x, y, 1-x-y)\begin{pmatrix} 0 & 1 & 0 \\ 0 & 0 & 1 \\ \frac{1}{2} & \frac{1}{2} & 0 \end{pmatrix} = (x, y, 1-x-y)$$

$$\therefore \quad \left.\begin{array}{l} \frac{1}{2} - \frac{1}{2}x - \frac{1}{2}y = x \\ x + \frac{1}{2} - \frac{1}{2}x - \frac{1}{2}y = y \\ y = 1 - x - y \end{array}\right\} \text{ or } \begin{array}{l} 3x + y = 1 \\ x - 3y = -1 \\ x + 2y = 1 \end{array} \text{ or } \begin{array}{l} x = \frac{1}{5} \\ y = \frac{2}{5} \end{array}$$

Thus $t = \left(\frac{1}{5}, \frac{2}{5}, \frac{2}{5}\right)$ is the unique fixed probability vector of P.

Method 2: Let $v = (x, y, z)$ is the fixed probability vector

$$\therefore \quad (x, y, z)\begin{pmatrix} 0 & 1 & 0 \\ 0 & 0 & 1 \\ \frac{1}{2} & \frac{1}{2} & 0 \end{pmatrix} = (x, y, z)$$

$$\text{or} \quad \left.\begin{array}{l} \frac{1}{2}z = x \\ x + \frac{1}{2}z = \\ y = z \end{array}\right\}$$

We know that the system has a non-zero solution; hence we can arbitrarily assign a value to one of the unknowns.

Let $z = 2$, so $x = 1, y = 2$

$\therefore$ $v = (1, 2, 2)$ is a fixed point of P.

As we know any real multiply of v will also be a fixed probability vector

So $$t = \frac{v}{5} = \left(\frac{1}{5}, \frac{2}{5}, \frac{2}{5}\right).$$

13.4 MARKOV CHAINS

Let $X_1, X_2, \ldots\ldots$, be outcomes of a sequence of trials, which satisfy the following two properties:

(*i*) Each outcome belongs to a finite set of outcomes $\{a_1, a_2, \ldots\ldots, a_m\}$ called the state space of the system, if the outcome on the nth trial is a_i, then we say that the system is in state a_i at time n or at the nth step.

(*ii*) The outcome of any trial depends at most upon the outcome of the immediately preceding trial and not upon any other previous outcome; with each pair of states (a_i, a_j) there is given the probability p_{ij} that a_j occurs immediately after a_i occurs.

Such a stochastic process is called a (finite) Markov chain. The numbers p_{ij}, called the transition probabilities can be arranged in a matrix.

$$P = \begin{pmatrix} p_{11} & p_{12} & \cdots & p_{1m} \\ p_{21} & p_{22} & \cdots & p_{2m} \\ \cdots & \cdots & \cdots & \cdots \\ p_{m1} & p_{m2} & \cdots & p_{mn} \end{pmatrix}$$ called the transition matrix.

Thus for ith row $(p_{i1}, p_{i2}, \ldots\ldots p_{im})$ of transition matrix P there is each state a_i; if the system is in state a_i, then this row vector represents the probabilities of all the possible outcomes of the next trial and so it is a probability vector. Thus we have the following theorem. "The transition matrix P of a Markov chain is a stochastic matrix".

Example 11

A man either drives his car or catches a train to work each day. Suppose he never goes by train two days in a row; but if he drives to work, then the next day he is just as likely to drive again as he is to travel by train. Construct transition matrix of the Markov chain.

Solution:

Let $\{t$ (train), d (drive)$\}$ is the state space of the system. This is a stochastic process of Markov chain because the outcome on any day depends only on what happened the preceding day. The transition matrix of the Markov chain is

$$\begin{array}{c} \\ t \\ d \end{array}\begin{array}{c} \begin{matrix} t & d \end{matrix} \\ \begin{pmatrix} 0 & 1 \\ \frac{1}{2} & \frac{1}{2} \end{pmatrix} \end{array}$$

The first row corresponds to the fact that he never goes by the train two days in a row and so he definitely will drive the day after he travels by train.

The second row of the matrix corresponds to the fact that the day after he drives he will drive or go by the train with equal probability.

Example 12

Three boys A, B and C are throwing a ball to each other. A always throws the ball to B and B always throws the ball to C; but C is just as likely to throw the ball to B as to A. Construct transition matrix of the Markov chain.

Solution:

The state space of the system is {A, B, C}. This is a Markov chain since the person throwing the ball is not influenced by those who previously had the ball. The transition matrix of the Markov chain is

$$\begin{array}{c} \\ A \\ B \\ C \end{array}\begin{array}{c} \begin{array}{ccc} A & B & C \end{array} \\ \begin{pmatrix} 0 & 1 & 0 \\ 0 & 0 & 1 \\ \frac{1}{2} & \frac{1}{2} & 0 \end{pmatrix} \end{array}$$

1st row $\Rightarrow$ A always throws the ball to B *i.e.,* assign A to B as one (1) others elements of the 1st row will be 0.

2nd row $\Rightarrow$ B to $C \Rightarrow$ Assign 1 there and others zero.

3rd row $\Rightarrow$ C to A and C to B likely equal probability *i.e.,* 1/2 and 1/2 other one is 0.

13.4.1 Higher Transition Probabilities

p_{ij} means the system changes from state a_i to the state a_j in one step: $a_i \to a_j$. The question may arise that what the probability is that the system changes from state a_i to the state a_j in exactly n step *i.e.,* $p_{ij}^{(n)}$

$$a_i \to a_{k_1} \to a_{k_2} \dots\dots \to a_{k_{n-1}} \to a_j$$

The following theorem answers this question.

Theorem: *Let P be the transition matrix of a Markov chain process. Then the n-step transition matrix is equal to the nth power of P; that is,* $P^{(n)} = P^n$.

Now suppose that, at some arbitrary time, the probability that the system is in state a_i is p_i; we denote these probabilities by the probability vector $p = (p_1, p_2, \dots\dots, p_m)$ which is called the probability distribution of the system at that time. In particular, we write

$$p^{(0)} = \left(p_1^{(0)}, p_2^{(0)}, \dots\dots, p_m^{(0)}\right)$$

as the initial probability distribution, *i.e.,* the distribution when the process begins, and we write

$$p^{(n)} = \left(p_1^{(n)}, p_2^{(n)}, \dots\dots, p_m^{(n)}\right)$$

as the nth step probability distribution *i.e.,* the distribution after the first n steps and we write the following theorem.

Theorem: *Let P be the transition matrix of a Markov chain process. If* $p = (p_i)$ *is the probability distribution of the system at some arbitrary time, then pP is the probability 'distribution of the system one step later and* pP^n *is the probability distribution of the system n steps later'. In particular*

$$p^{(1)} = p^{(0)} P,$$
$$p^{(2)} = p^{(1)} P,$$
$$p^{(3)} = p^{(2)} P,$$
$$\dots\dots\dots\dots$$
$$p^{(n)} = p^{(0)} P^n.$$

Example 13.

Let
$$P = \begin{array}{c} \\ t \\ d \end{array}\begin{array}{c} \begin{array}{cc} t & d \end{array} \\ \begin{pmatrix} 0 & 1 \\ \frac{1}{2} & \frac{1}{2} \end{pmatrix} \end{array}$$

$$P^4 = P^2 \,.\, P^2 = \begin{pmatrix} \frac{1}{2} & \frac{1}{2} \\ \frac{1}{4} & \frac{3}{4} \end{pmatrix}\begin{pmatrix} \frac{1}{2} & \frac{1}{2} \\ \frac{1}{4} & \frac{3}{4} \end{pmatrix} = \begin{array}{c} t \\ d \end{array}\begin{pmatrix} \frac{3}{8} & \frac{5}{8} \\ \frac{5}{16} & \frac{11}{16} \end{pmatrix}$$

Thus the probability that the system changes from state t to state d in exactly 4 steps is $\frac{5}{8}$ *i.e.*,

$p_{td}^{(4)} = \frac{5}{8}$, similarly $p_{tt}^{(4)} = \frac{3}{8}$, $p_{dt}^{(4)} = \frac{5}{16}$ and $p_{dd}^{(4)} = \frac{11}{16}$.

Now suppose that on the first day of work (see exp. 11), the man tossed a fair die and drove to work if and only if a 6 appeared. In other words, $p^{(0)} = \left(\frac{5}{6}, \frac{1}{6}\right)$ is the initial probability distribution, then

$$p^{(4)} = p^{(0)} p^{(4)} = \left(\frac{5}{6}, \frac{1}{6}\right)\begin{pmatrix} \frac{3}{8} & \frac{5}{8} \\ \frac{5}{16} & \frac{11}{16} \end{pmatrix}$$

$$= \left(\frac{35}{96}, \frac{61}{96}\right) \text{ is the probability distribution after 4 days}$$

i.e.,
$$p_t^{(4)} = \frac{35}{96}, \; p_d^{(4)} = \frac{61}{96}.$$

13.4.2 Stationary Distribution of Regular Markov Chains

Let P is the transition matrix of a regular Markov chain. Thus the sequence of n-step transition matrices P^n approaches the matrix T whose rows are each the unique fixed probability vector t of P; hence the probability $p_{ij}^{(n)}$ that a_j occurs for sufficiently large n is independent of the original state a_i and it approaches the component t_j of t. We write the following theorem.

Theorem: *If P be the transition matrix of a regular Markov chain, then in the long run, the probability that any state a_j occurs is approximately equal to the component t_j of the unique fixed probability vector t of P.*

Example 14.

$$P = \begin{matrix} & t & d \\ t & 0 & 1 \\ d & \frac{1}{2} & \frac{1}{2} \end{matrix}$$

The unique fixed probability vector of the above matrix is $\left(\frac{1}{3}, \frac{2}{3}\right)$ (see Example 9).

Thus, in the long run, the man will take the train to work $\frac{1}{3}$ of the time, and drive to work the other $\frac{2}{3}$ of the time.

13.4.3 Absorbing States

A state a_i is absorbing if and only if the ith row of the transition matrix P has a 1 on the main diagonal and zeros everywhere else. (The main diagonal of an n-square matrix $A = (a_{ij})$ consists of the components $a_{11}, a_{22}, \ldots\ldots a_n$.

Example 15.

$$P = \begin{matrix} & a_1 & a_2 & a_3 & a_4 & a_5 \\ a_1 & \frac{1}{4} & 0 & \frac{1}{4} & \frac{1}{4} & \frac{1}{4} \\ a_2 & 0 & 1 & 0 & 0 & 0 \\ a_3 & \frac{1}{2} & 0 & \frac{1}{4} & \frac{1}{4} & 0 \\ a_4 & 0 & 1 & 0 & 0 & 0 \\ a_5 & 0 & 0 & 0 & 0 & 1 \end{matrix}$$

The states a_2 and a_5 are each absorbing, since each of the second and fifth rows has a 1 on the main diagonal.

13.4.4 Ergodic Markov Chain

If it is possible to go from one state to another in a finite number of steps, regardless of present state, then the Markov chain is called ergodic Markov chain.

Example 16.

Show that the following transition matrix is ergodic Markov chain.

Future states

$$\text{Present states} \quad \begin{matrix} & 1 & 2 & 3 & 4 \\ 1 & \frac{1}{3} & \frac{1}{3} & 0 & \frac{1}{3} \\ 2 & 0 & \frac{1}{2} & \frac{1}{4} & \frac{1}{4} \\ 3 & \frac{1}{4} & 0 & \frac{1}{2} & \frac{1}{4} \\ 4 & 0 & 0 & \frac{1}{3} & \frac{2}{3} \end{matrix}.$$

Solution:

Now from state 1, it is possible to go directly to every other states except 3.

For state 3, it is possible to go from state 1 to state 2 and from state 2 to state 3. Therefore, it is possible to go from state 1 to any other state.

Similarly, from state 2, it is possible to go to state 3 or 4, then from state 3 to state 1, or from state 4 to state 3 to state 1. Also, from state 3 it is possible to go directly to state 1. Finally, from state 4, it is possible to go to state 3, then from state 3 to state 1. Hence above transition matrix is an ergodic.

Example 17

A manufacturing company has a certain piece of equipment that is inspected at the end of each day and classified as just overhauled, good, fair or imperative. If the item is imperative it is overhauled, the procedure that takes one day. Let us denote the four classification as states 1, 2, 3 and 4 respectively. Assume that the working condition of the equipment follows a Markov process with the following transition matrix.

$$P = \text{Today}\begin{matrix} \\ 1 \\ 2 \\ 3 \\ 4 \end{matrix}\overset{\text{Tomorrow}}{\begin{matrix} 1 & 3 & 3 & 4 \\ & & & \end{matrix}}\begin{bmatrix} 0 & 3/4 & 1/4 & 0 \\ 0 & 1/2 & 1/2 & 0 \\ 0 & 0 & 1/2 & 1/2 \\ 1 & 0 & 0 & 0 \end{bmatrix}$$

If costs Rs. 125 to overhaul a machine (including lost time) on the average and Rs. 75 if production is lost if a machine is found imperative, using the steady-state probabilities, compute the expected per day cost of maintenance.

$$[p_1, p_2, p_3, p_4]\,[P] = [P_1, P_2, P_3, P_4]$$

Solving, we get

$$p_1 = p_4,\ p_2 = \frac{3}{4}p_1 + \frac{1}{2}p_2,\ p_3 = \frac{1}{4}p_1 + \frac{1}{2}p_2 + \frac{1}{2}p_3$$

$$p_4 = \frac{1}{2}p_3 \text{ also } p_1 + p_2 + p_3 + p_4 = 1.$$

Simplifying we have

$$p_1 = \frac{2}{11},\ p_2 = \frac{3}{11},\ p_3 = \frac{4}{11},\ p_4 = \frac{2}{11}$$

Hence the expected (average) cost per day of maintenance will be equal to

$$\frac{2}{11} \times 125 + \frac{2}{11} \times 75 = \text{Rs. } 36.36 \quad \textbf{Ans.}$$

Example 18.

Brand Switching models

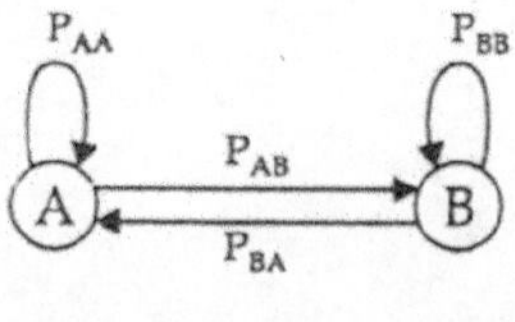

The figure shows a brand switching model whose transition matrix is as follows

$$\text{From}\begin{array}{c} \\ A \\ B \end{array}\overset{\text{To}}{\begin{array}{|cc|} \hline A & B \\ P_{AA} & P_{AB} \\ P_{BA} & P_{BB} \\ \hline \end{array}}$$

Example 19.

Suppose there are two market products A and B. Let each of the brands have exactly 50 % of the total market in the same period and the market size is fixed. The transition matrix is given below

$$\text{From}\ \begin{array}{c} \\ A \\ B \end{array}\overset{\text{To}}{\begin{array}{c} A \quad B \\ \begin{bmatrix} 0.8 & 0.2 \\ 0.5 & 0.5 \end{bmatrix} \end{array}}$$

If the initial market share break down is 50 % for each brand, then determine their market shares in the steady state.

Solution:

$$[0.5\ 0.5]\begin{bmatrix} 0.8 & 0.2 \\ 0.5 & 0.5 \end{bmatrix} = [0.4 + 0.25 \quad 0.1 + 0.25]$$

$$= [0.65 \quad 0.35]$$

Next period A brand 65 %

B brand 35 %

for equilibrium (*i.e.*, steady state)

$$\underset{\displaystyle A \quad\ B}{(\underset{\downarrow}{x}, \underset{\downarrow}{1 - x})}\begin{bmatrix} 0.8 & 0.2 \\ 0.5 & 0.5 \end{bmatrix} = (x, 1 - x)$$

solving $0.8x + 0.5\,(1 - x) = x$,

or $$x = \frac{0.5}{0.7} = \frac{5}{7}$$

$$A = \frac{5}{7}$$

$$B = 1 - A = 1 - x \quad \text{or} \quad B = \frac{2}{7} \quad \textbf{Ans.}$$

INDEX

U

V

W